Francophone Sephardic Fiction

Sephardic and Mizrahi Studies

Series Editors: Jane Gerber and Judith Roumani

Being Sephardic has meant various things to various individuals at different times and in different places. In its narrowest definition "Sephardic" has defined Jews from the Iberian Peninsula and more specifically from al-Andalus or Muslim Spain. With the expulsion of Iberian Jewry in the fifteenth century and their dispersion throughout the Mediterranean world a broader definition of Sephardic Jewry has evolved. Today Sephardic Jewry denotes a global diaspora in which indigenous Jewries from many lands have retained distinctive cultures while sharing many customs and memories or associations with medieval Iberia. The role of the scholar is to try to capture these differences. Sephardi-Mizrahi studies lack the geographical concentration, of course, of regional or national studies. Even the supposed linguistic unity of a national culture is missing, though some languages do present themselves as candidates. Thus there can be endless debates about what fits into Sephardi-Mizrahi studies and what doesn't. What may not have fitted in the past may actually fit today. As a transnational field, influenced by a number of other cultures, Sephardi-Mizrahi studies fit in well with the current emphasis on multicultural, diaspora, and post-colonial studies.
We welcome prospective proposals and abstracts for monographs, edited collections, and occasional translations of important texts.

Titles in the series

Francophone Sephardic Fiction: Writing Migration, Diaspora, and Modernity by Judith Roumani
Jewish Folktales from Morocco: Tales of Seha the Sage and Seha the Clown, by Marc Eliany with an introduction by Annette B. Fromm
Jews and Muslims in Morocco: Their Intersecting Worlds, edited by Joseph Chetrit, Jane S. Gerber, and Drora Arussy
Jews in Southern Tuscany during the Holocaust: Ambiguous Refuge, by Judith Roumani

Francophone Sephardic Fiction

Writing Migration, Diaspora, and Modernity

Judith Roumani

LEXINGTON BOOKS
Lanham • Boulder • New York • London

Published by Lexington Books
An imprint of The Rowman & Littlefield Publishing Group, Inc.
4501 Forbes Boulevard, Suite 200, Lanham, Maryland 20706
www.rowman.com

86-90 Paul Street, London EC2A 4NE

Copyright © 2022 by Judith Roumani

All rights reserved. No part of this book may be reproduced in any form or by any electronic or mechanical means, including information storage and retrieval systems, without written permission from the publisher, except by a reviewer who may quote passages in a review.

British Library Cataloguing in Publication Information Available

Library of Congress Cataloging-in-Publication Data

Names: Roumani, Judith, author.
Title: Francophone Sephardic fiction : writing migration, diaspora, and modernity / Judith Roumani.
Description: Lanham : Lexington Books, [2022] | Series: Sephardic and Mizrahi studies | Includes bibliographical references and index.
Identifiers: LCCN 2022005121 (print) | LCCN 2022005122 (ebook) | ISBN 9781793620095 (cloth) | ISBN 9781793620118 (paper) | ISBN 9781793620101 (ebook)
Subjects: LCSH: African fiction (French)--History and criticism. | African fiction (French)--Jewish authors--History and criticism. | Sephardic authors--Africa, North. | Emigration and immigration in literature. | Jewish diaspora in literature. | LCGFT: Literary criticism.
Classification: LCC PQ3984 .R68 2022 (print) | LCC PQ3984 (ebook) | DDC 843/.914098924061–dc23/eng/20220401
LC record available at https://lccn.loc.gov/2022005121
LC ebook record available at https://lccn.loc.gov/2022005122

In memory of Jacques
To David, Elisa, Mo, Ace, Jewel, and Aster
And in memory of Ralph Tarica, friend and mentor

Contents

Acknowledgments	ix
Introduction: Migratory Writing and the Novel	1
Chapter 1: From Orality to Writing: Storytelling in Sephardic Literature	27
Chapter 2: The "Portable Homeland": Ryvel and Koskas	47
Chapter 3: The End of Symbiosis: Sephardic Novelists and the Sudden Ruptures of History	65
Chapter 4: Migratory Writing by Bensoussan (Algeria/France), Bouganim (Morocco/Israel), Kayat (Tunisia/Sweden)	81
Chapter 5: Modernity and Beyond	99
Chapter 6: A Return into History	113
Conclusions	133
Bibliography	145
Index	165
About the Author	171

Acknowledgments

It is so hard to adequately thank everyone who has helped me over several decades, but I'd like to start with the Fulbright Commission and their staff, in particular the late Dr. Renée Taft and Daniel Krauskopf, the anonymous Israeli selection committee, which awarded me a senior research grant at the Ben Zvi Institute of the Hebrew University of Jerusalem, Michel Abitbol, then director of the institute, its chief librarian Robert Attal, Ruta and Moka Abir (generous hosts). To Moshe Maoz, and also the staff and librarians at the Ben Zvi Institute and the Truman Institute at the Hebrew University, as well as Harvey Goldberg, David Ruderman, Shira Wolosky, and the late Alan Mintz. Over the years, the staff at the study facilities of the Library of Congress (my second home), Sharon Horowitz and Nahid Gerstein, and the librarians at the New York Public Library too, were very helpful in pandemic times, as were those at the Library of Congress. I owe a debt to John McCormick, who set me on a path of appreciating literature in its historical context.

Above all, to my husband Jacques Roumani z'l, and my children Elisa and David, who have grown up with this project. With gratitude to my anonymous readers, and for the encouragement of Guy Dugas, Yael Halevi-Wise, of Ralph Tarica z'l, Sandra Cypess, and Regina Igel (and especially to the latter for reading my manuscript and making valuable suggestions), as well as Bernard Cooperman, who enabled me to teach a course on this topic at the University of Maryland, College Park. To Esther Bendahan for her generosity, to the late Nine Moati, and much gratitude to those who granted me interviews: Albert Memmi, Claude Kayat, Marco Koskas, Michel Abitbol, Shmuel Trigano, and Mois Benarroch. Thanks also to Chantal Assoulen, Esther Knafo, and Annette B. Fromm (especially) for essential help. Errors and omissions are solely my own. I'd also like to thank staff at Lexington Books, particularly Sara Noakes, Linda Kessler, and Judith Lakamper, the latter for her patience, her faith in the project, and for giving it the final boost to publication.

With profound thanks to the following publishers for permission to include adapted versions of my publications that appeared in: *Pe'amim*, journal of the Ben Zvi Institute, Vol. 36 (1988): "Migration in the Novels of North African Jews: Bensoussan, Bouganim, Kayat."; Indiana University Press, Prooftexts Vol. 4, No. 3, 1984: "The Portable Homeland of North African Jewish Fiction: Ryvel and Koskas."; Stanford University Press, my chapter in *Sephardism,* edited by Yael Halevi-Wise (2012): "'Le Juif Espagnol': The Idea of Sepharad in Colonial and Post-Colonial Judeo-Francophone Fiction." All translations throughout the book are by the author, unless noted otherwise.

Introduction
Migratory Writing and the Novel

Modern Sephardic writers can be viewed as nomadic writers, whose lives often epitomize the modern nomadic condition. They are occupied in "herding words through space" in the evocative phrase of Jacques Madelain.[1] In contrast to the conventional view of the novelist, planted at his or her heavy writing table, surrounded by a weighty library, integrated within a monolingual homeland or nation-state, they cross boundaries, bridge cultures, embody the nomadic, migrant condition. Modernity has challenged Sephardim in the extreme, over the twentieth century, particularly Sephardic writers. From being relatively settled traditional people, mostly inhabiting various key empires in the Middle East and around the Mediterranean at the turn of the last century, they have experienced the collapse of these empires, drastic modernization, the shock of the Holocaust, the horror of wars, decolonization and often virtual expulsion from their millennial homes. The exception to the description of "relatively settled people" is the subgroup of the Western Sephardim, those from Iberia, who were already uprooted by Spain's 1492 decree of expulsion and persecutions in Spain, and Portugal's forced conversions, in 1497, and began their search for new homes five hundred years ago. Thus, almost all Sephardim were launched, willy-nilly, on personal paths of exile where they created new lives, professions, personalities and identities in their countries of refuge.

Who are the Sephardim? The short answer to this question is "the people of Sepharad," but the answer itself raises other questions.[2] Narrowly, Sefarad has been used to apply to the Iberian Peninsula, therefore Sephardim are often narrowly defined as "the Jews from Spain" or "the Jews from Iberia." The Spanish scholar Paloma Díaz-Mas thus defines them and when referring to non-Ashkenazim in Israel distinguishes between the "true Sephardim" and other Sephardim, i.e., those who cannot trace a bloodline back to the Iberian Peninsula.[3] Other Spanish scholars generally follow this same definition, as they are usually concerned with examining a persecuted religious minority in Spain, and their descendants. Hence, "Sefarad" can be used in Spanish either as a geographical term, a synonym for Spain or the Iberian Peninsula, or as a term for the cultural universe of the specific Jewish communities that had been situated within Spain and Portugal before the expulsion from Spain in 1492 and the forced conversion in Portugal in 1497.[4] Maimonides himself did not refer to himself as a 'Sephardi,' but after his name would sometimes add "De Sefarad." North American, French, and other scholars who study the language of Ladino or Judeo-Spanish also often prefer to limit their definition of Sephardic culture to the particular linguistic group which, to its great credit, has preserved key aspects of Jewish Peninsula dialects (also known as "Ibero-Romance") down to this day.[5] The speakers did not always take pride in the Iberian connection, as we see in an essay by David Bunis,[6] where he points out the lack of prestige of Ladino/Judeo-Spanish among its speakers: some other language, such as Turkish, Hebrew, or French, was always considered more desirable by the educated. Today, Sephardim who use this language often refer to themselves as the "Judeo-Spanish." Within the definition of Sephardim, scholars have often distinguished between Eastern (or Oriental) Sephardim of the Ottoman Empire, and Western Sephardim of Europe and the New World. Moshe Lazar in 1972 wrote of "the Sephardic tradition" saying that "Sephardic in this volume refers primarily to the civilization created by the Jews living in medieval Spain and their descendants." He continued "for a brief, incisive comparison of the Sephardic and Ashkenazic (East European) communities see Professor Abraham Heschel's essay, 'The Two Great Traditions.'"[7] Thus, Lazar's definition implies that the essence of Sephardic culture was created in Spain, but when set in opposition to the Ashkenazi tradition, would embrace also Jews who did not trace their ancestry to Spain.

A term in current use that we have not yet discussed is "Mizrahim," a geographical term meaning Jews of the East. An important study by Sarah Abrevaya Stein in the field of Sephardic historiography suggests that

> Sephardi, Middle Eastern and North African Jews circulated in rich and diverse cultural worlds, developed deep and abiding relationships with non-Jews, helped shape local, regional and national cultures and politics. . . . Scholars of Sephardi and Middle Eastern Jewries must transform our understanding of certain concepts that have proven critical to the field of Jewish studies (and . . . Ottoman and Middle Eastern studies) as a whole . . . what is needed is a debunking of the stark division between Ashkenazim, Sephardim, and Mizrahim—divisions that invite monolithic readings of the Islamic world and of Europe as well. This new departure provides an opportunity to examine local contexts with a more finely tuned eye and to inhabit transregional landscapes.[8]

The term "Mizrahi" has been receiving greater academic acceptance in recent decades, beyond a somewhat derogatory use in earlier years as equivalent to "Oriental Jews."[9]

In 1999, Moshe Lazar published the Ladino source book entitled *Sefarad in My Heart*.[10] Like Heschel's 1952 essay, the title of Lazar's collection implies a more abstract definition of Sepharad: less a geographical place than perhaps a language, a worldview, a portable culture or place in the heart. In fact, this invaluable collection of source texts gives a unique impression of the enormous creativity and tenacity of the Jews of Iberia and elsewhere both under persecution within Spain from a hundred years before the actual expulsion and following it, and as they struggled to preserve their culture while scattered around the Mediterranean and further afield.

A broader definition of Sepharad, beyond Iberia, embraces exactly this portable faith or homeland of the heart. Its numerous proponents include Daniel Elazar in his 1989 book, *The Other Jews: The Sephardim Today*.[11] Another recent confirmation of this is David Wacks' paper, "Sefarad" (2021), "Sefarad has been as much an idea as a physical place."[12] Elazar, though, characterized the Sephardic world as being broader than the descendants of the Jews from Spain: Sephardim, he maintained, share a common tradition going back to Babylon of the first millennium. Elazar suggests that the intertwining of Sephardic and Middle Eastern Jewries goes back before Spain and therefore began long before the modern period.

What, specifically, is the Babylonian tradition?[13] My answer will necessarily only give a schematic answer regarding a deep and vast topic. First and foremost, it was based on the Babylonian Talmud, which has had more authority and diffusion than the Jerusalem Talmud. Then the tradition stems from the prestige of the academies of Babylonia which, under the *geonim*, prevailed for at least five hundred years, until the tenth century. Around that time, academies in such places as Kairouan on the coast of Tunisia, and Cordoba in Spain, began to gain more ascendance, but still paid their respects to Babylonia. The Jewish communities around the Mediterranean and to a lesser extent in Europe were linked, despite all the difficulties of travel and communication, by written *responsa* covering questions of religious and ritual life, emanating from Babylonia, initially, and later from the newer more western centers. Just as today, when English and French-speaking Jewish communities and their leadership have great prestige, the Arabic-speaking communities of the Middle East and Andalusia, were then vastly influential (although the *responsa* themselves were in Hebrew). Among the great Talmudic scholars and philosophers, Maimonides (1135–1204, honored with a statue in the town of his birth, Cordoba), when forced to flee Spain sometime between the ages of thirteen and twenty, because of Almohad persecution, turned to the Islamic world, arriving first in Fez (where he was once again persecuted), and later journeying on to Cairo, where he and his family settled. There, he served as a physician while writing his magisterial works in Talmud interpretation and philosophy, in Hebrew and Arabic. Maimonides may even have believed that apostasy to Islam was, for Jews, perhaps less heinous than converting to Christianity.[14] Regarding poetry, both secular and religious, in which we accord preeminence to the Jewish poets of the Golden Age of Spain who wrote in Hebrew, we should give due credit to Dunash Ben Labrat (920–990), who introduced Arabic poetic forms (learned in Babylon under Saadia Gaon), to the Iberian Peninsula, this innovation inaugurating the Golden Age of Spanish Jewish poetry, both liturgical and secular. The Spanish Castilian culture and language-in-formation, proceeding with the reconquest gradually southwards over several centuries, created instability for this cultural flourishing; the Christian Reconquista benefited from the knowledge and wisdom of Jews and Muslims, providing opportunities for the three cultures to interact, even more than it contributed to them. In this longer view, Spain (especially Christian Spain) can be viewed as an interlude rather than the origin of Sephardic culture, which was stamped out, persecuted, expelled, and forced to retreat back to south-eastern Europe, North Africa and the Middle East.[15] The Western Sephardim, who scattered to northern Europe and thence to the New World, are the exception to this. This rough simplification of Sephardic waves of migration leads us to the rabbinical debate as to whether Jews should prefer life under Edom (Christianity) or Ishmael (Islam). As Bernard Septimus suggests, the preference and nostalgia for Sefarad are hard to explain considering the expulsions of Jews and Muslims from the Iberian Peninsula and Sicily (a Spanish colony) at the end of the fifteenth century, the pre-1492 persecutions, and subsequent centuries of inquisitional activity.[16] Perhaps the pendulum swings when one considers different centuries. As Europe became more ascendant and the touchstone of civilization, persecution of Jews subsided from its more brutal forms (excluding the secret chambers of the inquisitions).

The broader Sephardic world can be seen to embrace Jewish communities of the Middle East and North Africa or the Maghreb, and would extend beyond the Ottoman Empire, both in the West (to include Morocco) and in the East. In this view, the three major elements shared by most Sephardim and differentiating them from Ashkenazim are common *minhagim* [customs], the *nusach sefarad* [order and melody of prayers], and religious law or *halakha* (religious Sephardim follow the original *Shulhan Arukh* without the *mapa* or gloss of Moshe Isserles, required for Ashkenazim—i.e., Sephardim require just the table, without the tablecloth). Even today, a Sephardic Jew from, say, Tunisia, can step into a Sephardic synagogue anywhere in the world and feel at home. Currently, in Miami, Florida, a Syrian congregation is led by a rabbi of Tunisian descent. In Maryland, a mixed congregation of Sephardim from many places, but predominantly of Moroccan origin, has as its spiritual leader a rabbi of Iraqi origin. In London, a synagogue of Jews from Greece has a rabbi of Libyan origin. These are just a few personally experienced examples. Daniel Elazar asserts that, just as the geographical term Ashkenaz did not originally apply to Germany, the term Sepharad (whose earliest known use dates back to the frustratingly short biblical Book of Ovadia) did not necessarily originally denote Spain, but came to be applied to it (or rather, Iberia) sometime between the first and the eighth century CE. Therefore, just as Ashkenazim do not need to have originated from Germany, but rather from a particular cultural world, to be Ashkenazim, so Sephardim, in this view, can be fully Sephardic without their ancestors having come from Spain. Elazar's argument has borne fruit as well as controversy in the contemporary Sephardic world (see below, note 24, on the views of Zion Zohar and Mark R. Cohen).

International and national Jewish organizations such as the World Sephardi Federation and the American Sephardi Federation have come into being in response to issues that concern all Sephardim/Mizrahim. One issue, of course, has been the perceived discrimination against Sephardim/Mizrahim in the state of Israel in recent decades, and there are other contemporary political issues in which Sephardim have a shared stake, such as the question of whether Jews who became refugees from Arab countries following the foundation of Israel might act as a counterweight to the claims of Palestinian refugees from Israel (in numbers they were roughly similar) in an eventual settlement of the Israeli-Palestinian conflict. In this sense Aviva Ben-Ur is correct in saying that the term "Sephardi" has a political connotation today.[17] Sephardic culture has been undergoing a renaissance in the United States and above all in France, where Jews originating from North Africa and the Middle East have joined together with Ladino/Judeo-Spanish speakers from Turkey, Greece, and other countries. In Spanish-speaking countries, too, and even in Spain, there are signs of a renaissance in Sephardic life. Particularly in Latin America, one has to distinguish between Sephardim and neo-Sephardim, who are likely to be Ashkenazim who speak Spanish fluently and write their literature in Spanish.[18] And then there is a subject beyond the scope of this book, the interest in returning to Jewish roots on the part of the descendants of conversos. Some scholars have expressed a certain skepticism regarding the relatively recent enthusiasm for Spanish roots among Sephardim, pointing out that this is a modern phenomenon. David Bunis writes:

> One has the impression that many Sephardim today, even those who have no interest in Judezmo, and perhaps ridicule it, often feel a deep sense of proud identification with Spain of the Golden Age and with the Spanish language. I would be the last one to find fault with this; many of today's Sephardim are

indeed the descendants of medieval Spanish Jewry. Rather, the picture I have tried to present in the present article was meant to show that, at least according to the available Judezmo sources, such sentiments were not necessarily to be found among Judezmo speakers before the modern era, when, with the help of the Haskalah historians, the Eastern Sephardim began to reclaim the glory of their long-forgotten, and perhaps imaginary, past.[19]

Other writers have viewed the Mediterranean/Middle Eastern Sephardic experience of the early Middle Ages as the core Sephardic identity, although they might use a different term. Ammiel Alcalay describes the links between Sephardic groups then and now, though he prefers to revive the old term "Levantine."[20] Even today Sephardim from North Africa, or Syria, or Iraq, sing the poetry of Moshe Ibn Ezra, Yehuda Halevi, Shlomo Ibn Gabirol, and many other poets—the *piyutim*, the *bakashot*, and the *selichot*—in their homes and synagogues in Paris, Rome, New York, Jerusalem or Netanya, originally composed in al-Andalus, Babylon, or other parts of the Islamic world a thousand years ago. The Israeli novelist Haim Sabato writes vividly (in Hebrew) of how this tradition lives on in Jerusalem today. Hillel Halkin has written of the pathways of the poet Yehuda Halevi's world, in which attachment to Spain itself was overshadowed by a religious impulse to pray in Jerusalem.[21] He translates Halevi's famous lines as "My heart is in the East but all the rest of me in the West. . . . Gladly I'd leave all the best of grand Spain" or, more literally, "My heart is in the East and I am at the end of the West. . . . It would be easy for me to leave all the goodness of Spain." Peter Cole (who translates the same lines as "My heart is in the East and I am at the edge of the West. . . . I'd gladly leave behind me all the pleasures of Spain") and others describe the origins of the Spanish Hebrew poetry of the Golden Age in ways of making poetry brought from Baghdad (as mentioned earlier).[22] The bridge between the poetic world of Spain and that of Baghdad was, as we have noted, the poet Dunash ben Labrat, who in the mid-tenth century brought about a literary revolution. This age of pre-nationalism reaches across the age of European and later Arab and other Middle Eastern nationalisms, to clasp hands with certain post-nationalist aspirations (at least in parts of Western Europe) of today.

Today terms such as "Levantine" and "Oriental" Jewry are hardly used, and the main challenge to the broad use of the term "Sephardi" comes from those who distinguish between "Sephardim" and "Mizrahim." A sensitive description of these differences through the eyes of a teenage girl in modern Mexico City is included in Rosa Nissan's novel *Novia que te vea* [May I see you a bride] (2000). Here the "real Sephardim" clearly feel superior to the "Arab Jews" (unless they are of Syrian origin).[23] The same can be said of André Aciman's *Out of Egypt* (1994), where the narrator's mother cannot shake off the stain of being from an "Arab Jewish" family, almost worse than her having a physical disability. It is undeniable that historical experience (the exile from Spain versus continuous residence in Muslim lands until the twentieth century) and language (Ladino/Judeo-Spanish versus other Judaic languages such as Judeo-Arabic) mark off the so-called core Sephardim and their culture, though after five hundred years these differences have dimmed. Distinguishing among subgroups is also always a fascinating academic activity, as it is a social one. However, the general acceptance of the broad use of the term "Sephardim" and the common historical experiences of Sephardim and Mizrahim in modern and even in more distant times,[24] in my view may make the term appropriate, in a work about twentieth-century non-Ashkenazi Mediterranean/Middle Eastern Francophone Jewish prose writers.[25] It certainly obviates the need for so many adjectives.

Perhaps the issue of "Who are the Sephardim?" should be addressed, as Johann Sadock has suggested, by looking at Sephardic cultures, literatures and identities as pluralities, linked by their overarching traditional and modern Sephardic ethos.[26] Moreover, the lesson is well taken from sociologists and anthropologists that ethnic identity is very often fluid, evolving within communities, families, and individuals over their lifetimes.[27]

This is not to say that Sephardim were unaffected by the age of nationalism, but they did not necessarily benefit by it. Just as, after 1492, the new unified Spain of Ferdinand and Isabel had no use for its Jewish or Muslim minorities (except grudgingly as New Christians, less politely called *marranos* and *moriscos*), so many new nations of the Middle East in the twentieth century could allow no space for their Jewish communities, though they had sometimes been rooted in the country for two thousand years, a long time before the advent of Islam. At the same time many Sephardim before and after 1948 embraced Jewish nationalism and moved to Israel, often in a messianic spirit.

Earlier, around the turn of the twentieth century, Sephardim were also moving, but mainly northward or westward away from the crumbling Ottoman Empire.[28] Far-reaching changes had been going on during the nineteenth century, when Western-oriented schools (French-language Alliance Israélite Universelle schools in the Maghreb, Turkey, and many other places, the English-language Shamash school in Baghdad, Italian schools in Libya) opened the minds of young Sephardim to a new self-view that was essentially Western,[29] and to perceived better opportunities in the West. Other factors such as devastating city fires, war between Turkey and Greece in the Balkans, the Arab awakening in the Middle East, the threat of military conscription in Turkey and the country's emerging definition of itself as essentially a Muslim and Turkish nation rather than a multiethnic entity, led to a sense of instability: all these causes brought Sephardim to uproot themselves. The earlier the migration, often the more successful, as families and even communities could gradually reassemble, according to their own timetable, on the other side of the globe, rather than being pushed into hasty departures as traumatized refugees deprived of practically all their means, as would happen during the Holocaust and later.

In whatever frame of mind or material circumstances the Sephardim migrated, there were successes and somewhat-less-than-successes,[30] the latter being people who would have returned to the old country if they could. The caveat to the general success story of Sephardim post-migration would be the acculturation that those who immigrated to Israel experienced, since many received a relatively poor education and have remained at the lower end of the economic and social spectrum until recently. Whether economically successful or not, behind the modern sophistication there is always a rich tradition, spurned or prized. Parts of the religious culture and of the traditional oral culture are now being recuperated and viewed as precious elements of Sephardic identity.[31]

A number of recent scholarly approaches to Sephardic life and literature bear discussion, in order to see exactly where a study like this one belongs in the field. Although this study draws on such approaches, it essentially has grown out of my years of reading Sephardic fiction published in several languages, but particularly French. Because of the close connections made between events in history, individual biographies, and the fiction, I limit myself here to works authored by (broadly defined) Sephardic Jews. I thus exclude any writing by Ashkenazim or by non-Jewish writers on Sephardic subjects. An excellent study, Yael Halevi-Wise's *Sephardism: Spanish Jewish History and Modern Literary Imagination*[32] covers those works and shows how Sephardic themes have been harnessed in the service of diverse other causes. As the present study, despite being limited to Francophone Sephardic writers, and despite focusing on writers originating from the Maghreb, is broad and comparative, some personal preferences have obviously come into play, as well as personal linguistic abilities, but I have tried to give an overview of some of what I have not covered in my detailed analysis. Poetry and other genres, such as historiography, could not be included due partly to space limitations and partly to the desire to compare prose texts with prose texts rather than bringing in other genres,[33] thereby showing how writers responding to the challenges of modernity and migration have used similar tools in perhaps similar ways. The growth of a genre also has its own internal logic, novelists and prose writers naturally being interested in reading each other's work. While there is a focus on Sephardic literature in French, this can be justified because the majority of Sephardim were exposed to a French education in the early part of our period and therefore naturally expressed their literary aspirations in French. Aron Rodrigue has pointed out how crucial was the role of the Alliance Israélite Universelle (AIU), and its dedicated teachers, in this acculturation. The role of French-language newspapers in encouraging Sephardim to use French in Turkey or Greece is also very important. French was not just a language, but a cause: the possibility of bringing an enlightened, modern, European civilization to Jews in the Balkans, the Middle East, and the Maghreb, and of freeing them from age-old shackles, whether internal or external. For Jews originating in countries like Algeria, which were part of the French colonial system, adopting French as one's mother tongue was a welcome and obvious choice.[34] An excellent educational system allowed some to contemplate writing literature in French.[35] The same was occurring in Spanish-speaking countries, with regard to Spanish schools and Spanish literary production by Sephardim, but unfortunately we have little space to follow that path in this particular book. Ladino as a literary language was already waning in this period, and writing in English and Hebrew has likewise mostly been taken up in recent years. The historical shocks that Sephardim have experienced, the dislocations and linguistic discontinuities, expulsions, uprootings, and the Holocaust, have led to long periods with little literary production in many countries.

Modern written prose fiction can express the transition from traditional (often oral) modes of literature to modern, written genres such as the novel. Thus we need to look at the traditional culture, the folktales, proverbs, ballads, etc., and see how twentieth-century writers incorporated elements from these into their modern novels. They may use characters from oral literature (e.g., the Dhoja/Joha figure, sometimes comic, sometimes wise, so common in all the Middle Eastern cultures). They may mirror the paths of traditional wisdom, whether women's tales (more imaginary) or men's tales, which usually end with a moral. They may be practical or fantastic, as they follow the forms of different types of tales, because traditional genres, presented seriously or humorously, often underlie these modern creations. References to oral storytelling, a tale-within-a-tale technique, as in the *Thousand and One Nights*, cyclical techniques, often take us back to an age of oral literature. East-West contrasts and dichotomies are a part of the oral-to-written process, and the reader will also want to be alert for these, expressed in interesting or humorous anachronisms.

Another concept relevant to literature by Sephardim is that of a cultural homeland. I talk about this in some detail in chapters which discuss mainly North African Jewish writers and how they have seen their work as reflecting or reconstituting the essence of a cultural homeland for North African Jews. For this purpose, one may draw on studies of cultural space and spatial form in literature. It has been useful to study the idea of organic nationalism (inherited by Third World literatures from European Romanticism) and how this has shaped modern novels. Although it gave rise to many paradoxes in new literatures, the idea that literature should mirror in some way the organic existence of the nation has been a potent one. Using spatial form,[36] and through techniques and images evoking a cultural space, Sephardic writers have also attempted to invoke the form of the 'old country,' the old Sephardic way of life, the tastes and smells of childhood spent in distant lands. Writerly habits, like Albert Memmi's keeping on his writing desk a few objects reminding him of his childhood, are intended to unlock the writer's imagination and memories. Techniques for evoking cultural space, even if it is what Memmi calls "Le Royaume du Dedans—The Kingdom of Within" are thus frequently used among Sephardic writers. All too soon, the cultural homeland had to become a 'portable homeland,' one that Sephardim could carry within themselves as, whether of their own free will or, more usually, due to exodus or actual expulsion from their homes in the Middle East and North Africa, they had to embark on new migrations and new forced encounters with modern life and post-modern incoherence. A return to history in some recent novels is not mere nostalgia for its own sake but a serious attempt to reconcile the past with the present.

Modern studies of identity and how it is expressed in literature obviously have great relevance for Sephardic literature. Everyone is aware of the importance of ethnic cultural identity today for modern individuals, and numbers of studies incorporate the concept. One title, for example, is Paloma Díaz-Más and María Sánchez Pérez, *Los Sefardíes ante los retos del mundo contemporáneo: identidad y mentalidades* (2010) a collection of twenty-six contributions, divided into language and cultural identity, mentalities, memory, oral tradition and identity, women's roles, westernization and transnationalism.[37] Other studies are Edna Aizenberg and Margalit Bejarano, *Contemporary Sephardic Identity in the Americas: A Collection of Interdisciplinary Studies* (2012),[38] and Monique Balbuena's 'Textual Identities of the Sephardic Diaspora,' the original title of her *Homeless Tongues*. This latter study (of poetry, therefore outside our field) examines writers from Algeria, Israel, and Argentina in terms of multilingual identity. Aviva Ben-Ur, as noted above, has studied Sephardim who immigrated to the United States in *Sephardic Jews in America: A Diasporic History*. Memory and identity depend on each other, and such studies as *La Mémoire sépharade* (2000), edited by Hélène and Shmuel Trigano, as well as other volumes that Shmuel Trigano has edited, have perhaps been not only reflective but formative of the contemporary concept of Sephardic identity.[39] The loss of identity, the search for identity, the rejection of identity, the preservation of identity, the creation of a new identity—all these aspects have preoccupied and impelled writers who come from Sephardic backgrounds, whether immediate or recent, or who have re-found one by searching in the distant past.

Sephardic studies and the study of Sephardic literature can also be viewed as a branch of diaspora studies, which today emphasize minorities as changing ethnic groups in various stages of both integrating into their host culture and maintaining ties with the homeland of origin. Paradoxically today the latter is easier than ever before because of modern travel and communications. Diaspora studies as a modern field evolved outside Jewish studies, despite the common identification of 'diaspora' with the Jewish 'galut' or exile from the land of Israel. Scholars in Jewish studies today consider that views of the home outside Israel as an unchanging, undifferentiated 'galut' are no longer helpful. Certainly, that is an important point with regard to Sephardic writers, who can be found at an almost infinite number of points along the spectrum between commitment to Sephardic identity and acculturation to their host country, and may combine both ends of the spectrum at the same time. The identification of the home country becomes moot for Sephardim whose ancestors could have been first exiled from ancient Israel, then perhaps from Spain, then from Turkey or a North African country (the former Ottoman Empire), to a new home whose language they write in but whose culture they may not fully identify with. Criticism of the idea that diaspora is 'galut' might already be a case of setting up a straw man just in order to knock it down. It can be fruitful, though, to bring to bear concepts from diaspora studies to the Sephardic Diaspora and its literature.[40] Some linkings of migration studies and Jewish studies often collide with anti-Semitism. Bryan Cheyette makes us aware of this as he argues for a comparative approach across Jewish and postcolonial literatures, focusing on well-known writers such as Primo Levi and Jean Améry, Muriel Spark and Salman Rushdie, and advocating for a "post-ethnicity."[41] The traumas have also been studied by psychologists, for example Daniel Sibony, of Moroccan origin, who wrote in *Psychopathologie de l'actuel* of exile as an illness, and also believes in laughter as a therapy.[42]

The re-evaluating of Jewish experience in the diaspora began in the mid-twentieth century, in various countries. In the Francophone world, Richard Marienstras's *Etre un peuple en diaspora* was one of the pioneering texts re-validating diaspora in the mid-1970s.[43] Pursuing the development of a critical corpus on migration and literature, the *Yale French Studies* journal in the early 1990s devoted two full numbers to "Post/Colonial Conditions: Exiles, Migrations, and Nomadisms," edited by Ronnie Scharfman and Françoise Lionnet.[44]

Jonathan Ray has written about historically porous medieval Spanish frontiers in *The Sephardic Frontier*; he has a long article defining 'Sephardi' as a sub-ethnic identity and putting Sephardic studies in the context of diaspora studies (*Jewish Social Studies*, 2008).[45] Such approaches to Jewish and Sephardic cultures, as both self-contained and porous at the same time, and moreover in flux, can be very useful when considering modern Sephardic literature. David Wacks writes about the concept of not just diaspora but 'double diaspora'—the original exile from the land of Israel and then the exile of the Sephardim either from al-Andalus to Christian Spain, or from Spain itself. His book *Double Diaspora* pinpoints how Iberian Jewish/Sephardic literature made transitions across languages (Hebrew and Romance) and across geographical boundaries to become a diaspora literature: "the forge of a new phase of Sephardic cultural identity: the fusing of Hispanic and Jewish cultural identity" (208).[46] Also quite recently, Dario Miccoli writes of "Sephardic Jewish Heritage across the Mediterranean: Migration, Memory and New Diasporas."[47] He finds that over the years there has been "a degree of reimagination of the past," so that the old homeland has become "largely an imaginative construct." (p. 499). However, "evoking and overemphasizing cosmopolitanism or Frenchness helped . . . to gain space in the respective post-migratory national arena," and states "this shows the importance of conceiving the Sephardic Mediterranean as a composite 'borderland,' where old and new memories, objects and feelings are preserved . . . what comes out of this borderland are new post-migratory diasporas, in which divergent cultural and national affiliations and half-forgotten memories . . . can be found" (p. 500).

Is Sephardic literature a minor literature? If it is, in relation to which literatures is it a minor one? Jewish literature? French literature? Spanish literature? Or even, recently, American literature? Dan Miron (in a work that does not actually relate to Sephardic literature at all) quotes Kafka's expression about Jewish writers who wrote in German: "They existed among three impossibilities, which I just happen to call linguistic impossibilities: . . . the impossibility of not writing, the impossibility of writing German, the impossibility of writing differently." This famous formulation of Kafka's has been quoted, Miron tells us, by Gilles Deleuze and Felix Guattari in an essay *Kafka: Toward a Minor Literature*.[48] Unlike Deleuze and Guattari, though, Miron considers the main motive of German Jewish literature, "despair" (as Kafka calls it), to be a perfectly adequate inspiration for literature, and the works of Heine, Kraus, Kafka, Walter Benjamin, Paul Célan to be brilliant examples of the German baby stolen out of its cradle, trained to become a gypsy dancer dancing on a tightrope.[49] Miron also suggests the idea that the further one goes from the center of the galaxy (e.g., German literature) the more a minor literature like Jewish literature can shine. Following this line of thought, perhaps if Sephardic literature can distance itself more from its various parent literatures listed above, the more it will be able to shine independently, in its own right.

The question brings us to linguistic issues, for it is almost rare for a Sephardic novel to be written cover to cover with every word in the same language. Bilingualism, trilingualism, and diglossia are often evident, pointing to the author's or the characters' multiple linguistic allegiances. It is not unusual for a Sephardic writer to be born in one country, have moved to a second, and to write in the language of a third. Many of our twentieth-century writers focus on their third diaspora—the exile from the lands in which their ancestors took refuge after they may have left Spain. Thus, Elias Canetti was born in Bulgaria, moved to Britain, and wrote in German. Albert Cohen was born in Greece, lived in France and Switzerland, and wrote in French. Naim Kattan was born and grew up in Iraq, moved to France, then Canada, and writes in French. Elia Karmona was born in Turkey, moved to Egypt and then back to Turkey, and wrote in Ladino. Andre Aciman was born in Egypt, moved to France, Italy, and the United States, and writes in an English stylistically informed with French. Victor Perera was born in Guatemala, moved to the United States, and wrote his autobiography in an English interspersed with Ladino words. And so on. Examples of bilingual poetry abound.[50] Some writers (e.g., Jane Mushabac of New York, Mois Benarroch of Jerusalem) write in two languages and have translated their work from one to another. One can, of course, trace this multi-or bilingualism back to the Golden Age of Spanish Jewry, when Maimonides wrote his *Mishnah Torah* in Hebrew and his *Guide for the Perplexed* in Arabic. Conventionally, philosophical or scientific works would be written in Arabic and poetry (whether religious *piyutim* or more secular poetry) would be written in Hebrew.[51] The *muwashshah* poems would include a couple of lines in a Romance dialect at the end of a short sonnet-like poem. Miron includes a discussion of these practices and, on a theoretical level, distinguishes between "differential diglossia" (where one language is used for one purpose, another for another purpose) and the rarer "integral diglossia" (where authors would attempt to furnish all their work in two different languages).[52] A notable phenomenon is feigned bilingualism or diglossia, where an author pretends to know another language but really doesn't. The classic case is Luis de León's archaizing Aramaic, used in his composition of the *Zohar*, allegedly written many centuries earlier by Shimon Bar Yohai. Another case is the Algerian Elissa Rhaïs's garbled version of Spanish dialogue in her novel *L'Andalouse*. Pseudoepigrapha (false authorial attribution) are also connected with this practice, a connection that we shall be examining.

In my study, the broader theme of ethnic identity is channeled into a specific consideration of the role of migration. Migration allows different ethnic groups to rub up against each other, often with tensions, giving rise to the suffering of a sense of exile, and literature tempted by nostalgia. Migration, and the tension between place and diaspora, leading to the examination of diaspora as a migrant locality, has been discussed by Dalia Kandiyoti, in *Migrant Sites: America, Place and Diaspora Literatures* (2009).[53] This study takes us full circle back to the topic of spatiality and place in literature, as it reformulates diasporic spatialities. Migration may be due to expulsion, or to various kinds of unfavorable or oppressive circumstances in the country of origin, or simply to a desire for a new start, but can often, especially among writers, lead to a sense of exile. The positive side of exile, if there is one, is that some writers do not find their voices until they are in exile and perhaps achieve better perspective than before on their culture of origin.[54] Much has been written in comparative literature studies on the writer and exile;[55] moreover, migration can be understood not only in the physical sense but also in the sense of changing times and evolving cultures, in a Proustian sense. At the very end of our period, Andre Aciman, referred to by a reviewer as "the prince of nostalgia," would probably have written in a Proustian way even if he had not been forced to leave Egypt. The passing of time and people, the perceived changes in one's environment, if one lives long enough, can be enough to trigger the writerly impulse. One must feel that something has been lost to the world in order to act on the impulse to mend it, to repair the broken vessels, by writing. Modernity and especially post-modernity are in themselves imperfect states that inspire the urge to write.

Another approach to Sephardic literature involves Sephardism, the use of Sephardic motifs, but in a cause that may or may not have to do with Sephardic identity. The impressive novel *Sefarad* (2001, translated into English as *Sepharad*, 2003) by the Spanish novelist Antonio Muñoz Molina has little to do with pre-expulsion Spain except obliquely, in the references which range from Primo Levi's Sephardic origins, to the entreating look of a possibly Sephardic Holocaust victim on a forced march when he sees a Spaniard in Nazi uniform, to the look in the eyes of a young girl in a Velázquez painting: he closes the book with the speculation that "someone is looking at that girl's face, someone who notices or recognizes in her dark eyes the melancholy of a long exile" (p. 381).[56] The book takes us deep into the suffering of not only Sephardim but also the victims of Stalinism, and the defeated Republicans of the Spanish Civil War in the 1940s, as well as the sufferings imposed on non-Sephardim such as a recurring meditation on Kafka, and the writer Jean Améry, the friend, fellow-inmate and correspondent of Primo Levi, who, like Levi, committed suicide. There are no mentions of the expulsion or the inquisition, but the idea of Sepharad as accumulated human suffering and sorrow seems to underlie everything in this brilliant and tragic novel. A novel in French with the same title, Eliette Abécassis' *Sépharade* (2011) has a more romantic bent: an elderly father announces on the eve of his son's marriage that he is going to reveal "the secret of the Sephardi"; the novel does include stories of the expulsion and the inquisition, and a traditional-style Moroccan Jewish wedding, but focuses on an ill-starred love affair between Moroccan Jews, and the power of a curse and the evil eye to keep lovers apart. The publishers bill it as "le grand roman du monde sépharade" (the great novel of the Sephardic world).⁵⁷ Another whole critical study, if there were world enough and time, might be devoted to the attitudes to Sephardic identity and culture in Spanish-language literature, but I must mention the novels of a Moroccan-Israeli novelist who writes in Spanish, Hebrew, and occasionally the Moroccan Jewish language of Haketia, Mois Benarroch. His *Bufanda Blues* (2016) and other writings such as *La trilogía tetuaní* (2021), a combination of three earlier novels, have led to his being hailed as the best Sephardic writer of Israel by the most highbrow newspaper of Israel. His most Sephardic novel is said to be the first one mentioned, a sad but humorous account of an Israeli writer's journey to Spain to participate in a writers' conference, and the story of finding and losing a comforting scarf over a period of about ten days. This rather thin plot line gives rise to meditations on the emotional state of a writer taken to Israel from Morocco as a young boy, the traumas of exile (from Spain, from Morocco); the eternally exilic condition of Jews, and the loss of a dear friend in Jerusalem, somehow melding in with the comfort and subsequent loss of the warm scarf, much appreciated during a cold Spanish winter, all in a semi-humorous and wry tone of regret, nostalgia, and search for identity, helped by his writerly vocation, but not enough to ally his pain. The "best Sephardic writer" often laments that the public does not buy his books, demonstrating that among the educated, reading public (Jewish, or in Israel) there is currently not much room for more than a token Sephardic writer. This one is determinedly non-profound, dwelling on superficial details of his adventure with the scarf, including a farcical conversation with a condemned *converso* at an *auto de fe* in Madrid, from which the victim escapes: overall the novel is something of a parody of novels of Sepharad with aspirations to historical profundity.

Yael Halevi-Wise has edited a volume encapsulating these approaches across various literatures. "This collection of essays about the history of Spain's Jews focuses on Sepharad from a distance, obliquely, as a prism through which we examine different ways in which modern authors have used the history and heritage of Spain's Jews to discuss their *own* national preoccupations at times of heightened political consciousness," she writes (p. 1). Thus, for example, in English literature the history of the Sephardim, and in particular the experience of *judeoconversos* with the Spanish Inquisition, were used historically by Protestants as a means of promoting the idea that Spain should be regarded as a hostile country full of Catholic fanatics. In French, also, negative stereotypes of the Spanish were fostered during the colonial period when France and Spain were potential rivals in North Africa, as I discuss in my own chapter in *Sephardism*.⁵⁸ The eternally ambivalent and potentially modernizing or post-modern figure of the *converso* has inspired much literature in several languages, and for a summary of this vast and profound topic the reader is referred to a book by Dalia Kandiyoti, *The Converso's Return*.[59]

Matthias Lehmann shows how the process of secularization and modernization of Sephardim inhabiting the Ottoman Empire gradually gained steam and accelerated over the nineteenth century, as does Sarah Abrevaya Stein.[60] By the latter half of the nineteenth century, a Ladino secular literature was emerging and continued into the twentieth century, while Sephardim also began to write modern prose fiction in other languages, such as Hebrew or French. Across the Ottoman Empire and the Middle East, Sephardim were being educated in the French-language schools of the Alliance Israélite Universelle, acquiring Western values, modes of thought, and tastes in literature. These aesthetic developments were interrupted by the intrusion of history, often in a brutal way. Turkish and Greek nationalism (War of 1911–1912) exacerbated the rise of antisemitism and induced or forced many to emigrate. The Holocaust cut short a vast number of Sephardic lives and disrupted the development of Sephardic culture,[61] especially in the Ladino-speaking heartland (in Greece and in the Balkans), while North Africa was not spared. Thus, secular Ladino fiction saw almost no development after its early decades and promise. Decolonization in many North African and Middle Eastern countries, and the Arab-Israeli conflict, cut short millennial Jewish histories, uprooted ancient communities, and forced Jews to flee. All these events caused long-lasting disruptions in the cultural and linguistic lives, as well as economic security, of most of the Sephardim. Very few were spared from these unfortunate setbacks. These events marked the end of symbiosis and the beginning of new migrations and uprootedness.

How have Sephardim dealt with these disruptions? Many Sephardic writers embrace modernity and post-modernity through such techniques as displacement, a major part of the philosophy of one of the founders of post-modernism, Jacques Derrida, who happened to be a Sephardic Jew from Algeria (see the discussion of Derrida in the chapter "Beyond Modernity"). Among many writers, there is a deliberately light approach, embodying modernity and post-modernity through humor, irony, and a kind of pragmatism. One form of expression in literature has been an almost nostalgic, though more often ironic, looking back, expressed in autobiography, family history, and even descriptions of imagined journeys back to the place of origin. A return to traditional religion is also occasionally expressed in literature, despite the strong secular bent of modern fiction.

Why have I chosen to discuss Sephardic writing in French? Despite the difficulties I have just pointed out, many Sephardim did enter the modern age with an important tool for dealing with its complexities: the French language. Thanks to the Alliance schools, which may have contributed to the decline of Ladino/Judeo-Spanish by promoting French, modern literary and scientific thought processes and a prestigious language which was almost a lingua franca in the Mediterranean and Middle East, enabled many Sephardim to overcome their cultural difficulties and enter modern Western societies successfully. Here is how Avraham Galante, a prominent journalist of the early twentieth century, and paradoxically one of the promoters of Ladino, described (in French) the importance of the French language for the Sephardim of Turkey:

> With the introduction of the French language in community schools and the founding of the schools of the Alliance Israélite Universelle, Jewish children possessed ... a foreign language and literature that could serve them as spiritual nourishment. What did adults and people of a certain age, whose intellectual abilities were completely pitiable, do? They only knew Judeo-Spanish. ... They were lacking the slightest elementary notions of common knowledge in life.[62]

Avraham Galante, and recent writers such as Haim-Vidal Sephiha and Marie-Christine Varol, speak of a certain synergy between Ladino or Judeo-Spanish (as it is usually called in French) and the French language. They refer to "Judéo-fragnole" the Judeo-Spanish strongly marked by French, and the distinctive French of the Levant, strongly marked by Turkish and Judeo-Spanish.[63]

Even today, even in America, one can enter many Sephardic synagogues and observe the worshipers conversing in French, acknowledging each other with kisses on both cheeks ('les trois bises')—and feel that French culture still reigns. Like other Jews, Sephardim were grateful for the opportunities for equality that France had provided them under Napoleon. In the Ottoman Empire, French was widely used from the mid-nineteenth century on and had great prestige among Sephardim who were products of Alliance schools. However, Esther Benbassa and Aron Rodrigue introduce an important nuance: "the acquisition of French proved to be the most direct and long-lasting result of the Alliance interlude in the history of Eastern Sephardi Jewry. ... The boundaries of Judeo-Spanish ethnicity shifted, and appropriated, co-opted, domesticated, and Judeo-Hispanized French. The very fact of speaking French (in a distinctive local accent common to all Eastern Sephardim) became yet another marker of Sephardi distinctiveness." Benbassa, Rodrigue, and others also point out that the Alliance's role went beyond language and education, stretching into many other spheres related to modernity, such as poverty alleviation and health.[64]

The devotion of the teachers and their sense of mission is exemplified in the life and writings of Vitalis Danon. Born in Edirne, Turkey under the Ottoman Empire in 1897, he trained as a teacher in Paris, and spent his entire working life as an instructor and later school principal in Sfax, Tunisia. The salary was minimal, but his idealism and determination allowed him to overcome his own slender means and a lack of budget for the school, to make a lasting impression on Jewish life in Sfax. His lively novel *Ninette de la rue du péché* (1938) (*Ninette of Sin Street*) dramatizes the obstacles faced by both teachers and the poor and undereducated Jews whom they sought to raise up through a thorough French education, and indeed succeeded.[65] French was also of course the prestigious language of international diplomacy, and of the social circles that revolved around it. The works of historians such as Avraham Galante and Joseph Nehama, periodicals published in French, and French linguistic elements incorporated into modern Ladino, all drew Sephardim further into a French orbit. The fact that Algerian Jews had received French citizenship in the mid-nineteenth century, and that in other countries, such as Tunisia, Sephardim felt almost accepted as equals by the French colonizers, made their adhesion to the French language and culture unshakable. The commitment was not unshakable on the Vichy French side: Algerian Jews were deprived of their French citizenship by the abrogation of the Crémieux Decree and application of the Vichy *Statut des Juifs* during the war, though they later had citizenship restored. Many wealthier and less wealthy North African Sephardim moved by choice in the 1960s to France (or Belgium, or Switzerland) in preference to Israel, while some emigrated to French-speaking Canada. The scholar Sarah Sussman points out the 'otherness' that greeted Algerian Jews, bearing their complicated identity, on their arrival in France.[66] The *renouveau juif* [Jewish revival or renaissance][67] that began from the late 1960s in France took off partly because of the large numbers of Sephardim who had immigrated a few years earlier from Tunisia, Algeria and Morocco, and had by now settled down and were experiencing nostalgia for their Sephardic origins, making French Jewry one of the most influential globally in cultural terms. There were also large numbers of originally Turkish Jews who had been moving to France since the 1920s. During the Holocaust years many who had allowed their Turkish citizenship to lapse could not renew it, and were not able to seek refuge from the Nazis in a reluctant Turkey, thus being thrown on the mercies of the French people.[68] The world of *la francophonie* is moreover alive and well today in Israel.[69] As Edmond Jabès, the Egyptian Sephardic writer, once said, expressing perhaps a similar feeling regarding French among many Sephardim, "La langue est ma patrie" [Language is my homeland].[70]

What are the boundaries of this study? It cannot be a definitive or exhaustive literary history: it is impossible to study or even mention every novel by every Francophone Sephardic writer over the course of the twentieth century. And the method that I prefer of close analysis relating literature to history requires that a certain amount of space be dedicated to the particular novel under consideration, with its circumstances. Therefore, much has depended on personal taste; the choices I have made do not mean that I could not have equally well discussed other accomplished and outstanding novels. Those I discuss are, I hope, at least representative of many others too. Some of those are either mentioned in passing as points of comparison, or referred to in the bibliography which, given the flourishing state of the field by the end of the twentieth century, and into the first quarter of this one, also should not be construed as exhaustive. My own particular focus, within the field of Sephardic francophone literature, as the reader will see, is the Maghreb (North Africa), and I have no doubt failed to do justice to writers in other geographical areas, i.e., Canada, Egypt, and even Lebanon, all of which have been or are home to Sephardic writers as well.

The multifaceted and pluralistic Sephardic ethos, a product of both the diverse countries of origin and the many and different temporary and ultimate destinations, is of necessity hard to pin down. It may involve Sephardim being quintessentially modern people, originating in traditional communities, but now far more individualistic. The rapid and traumatic transitions they have undergone lead to tensions that are channeled often in literary writing: a creativity dedicated to survival and beyond, expressed in brilliant flashes of literary production across the globe.

NOTES

1. Jacques Madelain, *L'Errance et l'itinéraire: Lecture du roman maghrébin de language française* (Paris: Sindbad, 1983).

2. I addressed this issue in an earlier article, "'Un Juif Espagnol': Sephardism and the Idea of Sepharad in Jewish Francophone Writers of Colonial and Post-Colonial Times," *International Sephardic Journal* 2:1 (Spring 2005), pp. 108–131, and developed it further in my chapter in Yael Halevi-Wise, ed., *Sephardism: Spanish Jewish History and the Modern Literary Imagination* (Stanford: Stanford Univ. Press, 2012).

3. See Paloma Díaz-Mas, *Sephardim: The Jews from Spain*, tr. George Zucker (1986; Chicago: Univ. of Chicago Press, 1992), p. 187. A similar approach is used by Maria Rosa Menocal, in her impressive book, *The Ornament of the World: How Muslims, Jews, and Christians Created a Culture of Tolerance in Medieval Spain* (Boston: Little, Brown, 2002). She identifies al-Andalus as the heart of medieval Spain, and Sefarad as well, ascribing the flourishing of Jewish culture to the extremely liberal interpretation of the *dhimma* status of minorities in Islamic Spain.

4. See e.g., Isidro Bango, *Remembering Sepharad: Jewish Culture in Medieval Spain* (Madrid: State Corporation for Spanish Cultural Action Abroad, 2004). For my review of this book, see *La Lettre Sépharade*, 17: April 2004, 8–10.

5. See Hannah Pressman, "Ladino as Sephardi Cultural Bedrock," *Hadassah Magazine*. (Nov.-Dec. 2021): 14–16.

6. David Bunis, "The Changing Faces of Sephardic Identity as Reflected in Judezmo Sources," *Neue Romania* 40 (2011), 45–75. Bunis prefers the term Judezmo as the name of the language, arguing that that is how the people who spoke it referred to it over the post-expulsion centuries.

7. Moshe Lazar, *The Sephardic Tradition* (New York: Norton, 1972). Heschel's essay was published in *The Earth is the Lord's* (New York: Henry Schumann, 1952).

8. Sarah Abrevaya Stein, "Sephardi and Middle Eastern Jewries since 1492," pp. 327–362 in Martin Goodman, Jeremy Cohen, David Sorkin, eds., *The Oxford Handbook of Jewish Studies* (Oxford: Oxford Univ. Press, 2002), p. 347.

9. E.g., there is a new book in Hebrew entitled *The Long History of the Mizrahim* (not seen). It was presented in a zoom presentation on Oct. 27, 2021, under the same title, organized by Dario Miccoli, and including many of the scholars (mostly Israeli historians, anthropologists and sociologists) who have contributed to the book. For a 2018 protest against the derogatory use of the term, see Haim Ovadia, "Sephardic or Mizrahi?" *Sephardic Horizons* 8:1–2, https://www.sephardichorizons.org/Volume8/Issue1&2/Ovadia.html.

10. Moshe Lazar, ed., *Sefarad in My Heart: A Ladino Reader* (Lancaster, CA: Labyrinthos, 1999).

11. Daniel Elazar, *The Other Jews: The Sephardim Today* (New York: Basic Books, 1989), esp. pp. 14–23.

12. David Wacks, "Sefarad," *Humanities Commons, LLC Medieval Iberian*, Oct. 18, 2021. http://dx.doi.org/1017613/zene-w672.

13. See R. I. Zwi Werblowsky and Geoffrey Wigoder, eds., *The Oxford Dictionary of the Jewish Religion* (New York, Oxford: Oxford University Press, 1997), entries "Babylonia," "Responsa."

14. An enlightening text on Maimonides' context is Sarah Stroumsa, *Maimonides in his World* (Princeton: Princeton University Press, 2009).

15. The earliest Jews in Spain were supposedly deported there from Jerusalem or Babylon by Nebuchadnezzar; then many arrived during the Roman period, after the destruction of the Second Temple, and later, and a third wave entered with the Muslim conquerors in 711–715. See also below, note 19.

16. See Bernard Septimus, "Hispano-Jewish Views of Christendom and Islam," in Bernard Cooperman et al., eds., *In Iberia and Beyond: Hispanic Jews Between Two Cultures* (College Park, Md.: University of Maryland,1991).

17. See *Sephardic Jews in America: A Diasporic History* (New York: New York University Press, 2009, 2012).

18. On the subject of Sephardim and neo-Sephardim, see the work of Edna Aizenberg and Margalit Bejarano, *Contemporary Sephardic Identity in the Americas: A Collection of Interdisciplinary Studies* (Syracuse: Syracuse Univ. Press. 2012). See also idem, the chapter "Sephardim and Neo-Sephardim in Latin American Literature," in Yael Halevi-Wise, ed., *Sephardism: Spanish Jewish History and the Modern Literary Imagination* (Stanford: Stanford Univ. Press, 2012), pp.129–42.

19. David Bunis, "The Changing Faces of Sephardic Identity as reflected in Judezmo Sources," *Neue Romania* 40 (2011), 45–75.

20. Ammiel Alcalay, *After Jews and Arabs: Remaking Levantine Culture* (Minneapolis: Univ. of Minnesota Press, 1993).

21. Hillel Halkin, *Yehuda Halevi* (New York: Nextbook/Schocken, 2010), poem quoted from pp. 115–116.

22. Peter Cole, *The Dream of the Poem: Hebrew Poetry from Muslim and Christian Spain 950–1492* (Princeton: Princeton Univ. Press, 2007), pp. 2–5, poem quoted from p. 164. See also note 23 (p. 346) which elaborates on Elazar's original point, and refers to Yosef Haim Yerushalmi and Yom Tov Assis, two other well-respected Israeli scholars who expressed similar views to Elazar's in the 1990s.

23. See Yael Halevi-Wise, in Margalit Bejarano and Edna Aizenberg, *Contemporary Sephardic Identity in the Americas* (Syracuse: Syracuse Univ. Press, 2012), "A Taste of Sepharad from the Mexican Suburbs, " pp. 184–201, esp. p. 196 describes this "nuanced ethnic awareness."

24. Mark R. Cohen, "The Origins of Sephardic Jewry in the Medieval Arab World," in Zion Zohar, ed., *Sephardic and Mizrachi Jewry from the Golden Age of Spain to Modern Times* (New York: New York University Press, 2005), pp. 23–39, presents Spanish Jewry's life under Christianity as an interlude for Sephardim, as the Reconquista progressed, until the expulsion from Spain and the return of many Sephardim to Islamic lands in the Ottoman Empire. Sephardic culture, he says, is characterized by having flourished mostly under Islam (e.g., in Babylon and al-Andalus) while Ashkenazi culture developed in Christian lands. It is not Spain as such that characterizes Sephardim, but their lives in Arab and Muslim lands. See also the introduction by Zion Zohar.

25. For example, the impulse to distinguish between Sephardim, Mizrahim, and Romaniote Jews is expressed in the book by Aviva Ben-Ur, cit. She cites examples of groups that have maintained separate identities, such as the Syrian Jews of Brooklyn, and characterizes Sephardic unity as an "umbrella" identity. The American Sephardi Federation is, she says, the main expression of it in America today (pp. 42–46). I would suggest that the many Sephardic synagogues in America and elsewhere today that embrace not only 'heartland' Sephardim but also those from Morocco to Iran who share, despite variations, similar *minhagim*, *nusach*, and *halakha*, exemplify the continuance of a tradition that goes back before Spain.

26. Email correspondence, Feb. 17–22, 2012.

27. See Luis Roniger, "The Western Sephardic Diaspora: Ancestral Birthplaces and Displacement, Diaspora Formation and Multiple Homelands," *Latin American Research Review*, 54:4 (Dec. 2019), 1031–1038. https://doi.org/10.25222/larr600.

28. See e.g., "The Taranto-Capouya-Crespin Family History: A Microcosm of Sephardic History," Leon B. Taranto, Part III. "More on the Taranto, Capouya and Crespin Families," *Sephardic Horizons*, 2:2 (Spring 2012). https://www.sephardichorizons.org/Volume2/Issue2/taranto.html.

29. See the portrayals of these processes in Matthias Lehmann, *Ladino Rabbinic Literature and Ottoman Sephardic Culture* (Bloomington: Indiana Univ. Press, 2005), and Sarah Abrevaya Stein, *Making Jews Modern: The Yiddish and Ladino Press in the Russian and Ottoman Empires* (Bloomington: Indiana Univ. Press, 2004).

30. Examples of both may be found in Devi Mays' history, *Forging Ties, Forging Passports: Migration and the Modern Sephardi Diaspora* (Stanford: Stanford University Press, 2020). See also my review in *Sephardic Horizons* 11:2 https://www.sephardichorizons.org/Volume11/Issue2-3/Roumani.html.

31. In "Sephardic Scholarly Worlds: Toward a Novel Geography of Modern Jewish History," *Jewish Quarterly Review* 100:3 (Summer 2010), pp. 349–84, Julia Philips Cohen and Sarah Abrevaya Stein point out that already from the later nineteenth century modernizing and enlightened Sephardic scholars had a sense that their cultural world would soon dissolve, and were anxious to preserve its history for posterity. For a modern expression of this same paradoxical attitude, see e.g., the Tunisian writer Annie Fitoussi, whose main character, living in modern France, declares that she detests anything that smells of the past, yet the novel is entitled *La Memoire folle de Mouchi Rabbinou*, (Paris: Mazarine,1985), evoking the memory of a miracle-working Tunisian rabbi who was more powerful than death itself.

32. See note above.

33. Monique Balbuena has discussed poetry in depth in her *Homeless Tongues: Poetry and Languages of the Sephardic Diaspora* (Stanford: Stanford University Press, 2016), which provides lengthy analyses of some Spanish and Ladino poets as well as one who writes in French.

34. See Aron Rodrigue, *Images of Sephardi and Eastern Jewries in Transition: The Teachers of the Alliance Israélite Universelle*, 1860–1939 (Seattle: Univ. of Washington Press, 1993). Other works on *francophonie* are: David Mendelson, ed., *Emergences des francophonies: Israël, La Méditerranée, le monde* (Limoges: Presses universitaires de Limoges, 2001); Jean-Benoît Nadeau and Julie Barlow, *The Story of French* (New York: St. Martin's Press, 2006), esp. pp.338–362, "La Francophonie." For Muslims in the Maghreb, the use of French has been fraught with issues due to an understandable post-independence nationalist preference for some form of Arabic, in turn brought into question by non-Arab minority languages such as Berber.

35. Leon Sciaky's book, *Farewell to Salonica* (1946; Philadelphia: Paul Dry Books, 2003) shows how important the French-language lycee was in the lives of young Jewish Salonikans in the early twentieth century. The alumni association extended the school's influence and was a vibrant focus for the modern, more intellectual elites before the Jews began to scatter. Sciaky himself does not seem to have set foot in France, but his education equipped him more than well for a career in the United States. See e.g., pp. 189–90, p. 261. Simultaneously, a French education excluded Jews from the Greek state, and opened much broader horizons. Monique Balbuena discusses the importance of French education for Sciaky in "Ladino in US Literature and Song," *Cambridge History of Jewish American Literature* (Cambridge: Cambridge Univ. Press, 2016), pp. 297–319.

36. On spatial form, see Jeffrey Smitten et al., eds., *Spatial Form in Narrative* (Ithaca: Cornell Univ. Press, 1981).

37. Madrid: Consejo Superior de Investigaciones Científicas (CSIC), p. 201, Cambridge History of Jewish American Literature (Cambridge: Cambridge University Press, 2016), 0.

38. Margalit Bejarano and Edna Aizenberg, *Sephardic Identity in the Americas: An Interdisciplinary Approach* (Syracuse: Syracuse University Press, 2012). See the review by Regina Igel, *Sephardic Horizons* 4:2 (Spring 2014), https://www.sephardichorizons.org/Volume4/Issue2/Igel.html.

39. The authors clearly opt for the broader definition of Sephardic identity, along the lines of Elazar. "Nous prenons la denomination de 'sépharades' dans son acceptation la plus globale" (We use the term 'Sephardi' in its most global accsense), p. 9 in Hélène and Shmuel Trigano, eds., *La mémoire sépharade: Entre l'oubli et l'avenir* (Paris: In Press Editions, 2000), also pp. 9–10.

40. An interesting comparative perspective emerges in Minna Rozen, ed., *Homelands and Diasporas: Greeks, Jews and their Migrations* (London: I.B. Tauris, 2008), e.g., Shmuel Refael, "Spain, Greece or Jerusalem? The Yearning for the Motherland in the Poetry of Greek Jews," pp. 211–223.

41. Bryan Cheyette, *Diasporas of the Mind: Jewish and Postcolonial writing and the Nightmares of History*, (Newhaven: Yale University Press, 2013).

42. Daniel Sibony, *Psychopathologie de l'actuel* (Paris: Seuil, 1999), part of a trilogy entitled *Événements*. He has also written a number of novels, one of which, *Marrakech, le départ* (2009), is highly relevant to our chapter on uprooting.

43. Richard Marienstras, *Etre un peuple en diaspora: essais* (Paris: Maspero, 1975); see also Philippe Lazar, "Richard Marienstras, inoubliable pionnier du 'diasporisme,'" in *Diasporiques*, NS 14 (June 2011). On studies of the Jewish diaspora see *The Jewish Diaspora as a Paradigm: Politics, Religion and Belonging*, Nergis Canefe, editor: "Perhaps it is indeed the 'Jewish talent' in constructing and cultivating longings for a symbolic, mythical homeland and establishing an intricate and multifaceted identity around this unyielding sense of loss that separates the Jews from other diasporas." This work asserts that while being paradigmatic, the Jewish diaspora is unique and different from diasporas of other nations and peoples (pp. 7–9).

44. No. 82 and No. 83, (1993). Notable is a study of the Jewish writer and traveler, Isabelle Eberhardt (1877–1904), by Hédi Abdel-Jaouad, "Isabelle Eberhardt: Portrait of the Artist as a Young Nomad," in Vol. 2, pp. 93–120. She was a young Jew exiled from Russia who sought identity in wandering the Sahara, and wrote prolifically. These two issues were also published as a book by Yale University Press.

45. Jonathan Ray, *The Sephardic Frontier: The Reconquista and the Jewish Community in Medieval Iberia* (Ithaca: Cornell University Press, 2006). "New Approaches to the Jewish Diaspora: The Sephardim as a Sub-Ethnic Group," *Jewish Social Studies* 15:1 (2008), pp. 10–30.

46. See David Wacks, *Double Diaspora in Sephardic Literature* (Bloomington: Indiana University Press, 2015). See also the review by Vanessa Paloma Elbaz, *Sephardic Horizons* (6:2), Spring 2016, https://www.sephardichorizons.org/Volume6/Issue2/Elbaz.html.

47. Dario Miccoli, "Sephardic Jewish Heritage across the Mediterranean: Migration, Memory and New Diasporas," in Simona Pinton and Lauso Zagato, eds., *Cultural Heritage Scenarios* 2015–2017 (Venice: Edizioni Ca'Foscari, 2018), pp. 485–505. Miccoli looks mainly at immigrant associations of Algerian and Egyptian Jews in France and Israel.

48. Gilles Deleuze and Felix Guattari, *Kafka: Toward a Minor Literature* trans. Dana Plan (Minneapolis: Univ of Minnesota Press, 1986). Deleuze and Guattari have also been criticized for excluding multilingualism from their concept of a minor literature. See Monique Balbuena, "A Symbolist Kinah? Laments and Modernism in the Maghreb," in Tamar Alexander et al., eds., *Iggud: Selected Essays in Jewish Studies Vol. 3, Languages, Literatures, Arts,* (Jerusalem: World Union of Jewish Studies, 2007), 67–84; see also Balbuena's dissertation, "Diasporic Sephardic Identities: A Transnational Poetics of Jewish Languages," University of California, 2003.

49. Dan Miron, *From Continuity to Contiguity: Toward a New Jewish Literary Thinking*, Stanford: Stanford Univ. Press, 2010, pp. 310–12.

50. See e.g., Ronda Angel Arkin, "Claiming Angels," in *Sephardic Horizons* 2:1 (Winter 2012) https://www.sephardichorizons.org/Volume2/Issue1/Arking.html.

51. On the use of Arabic among Jews during the Golden Age of Spain, see David Bunis, "The Changing Faces of Sephardic Identity as Reflected in Judezmo Sources," *Neue Romania* 40 (2011), pp. 45–75. He suggests that nostalgia for Iberia did not exist during the first few centuries after the expulsion, and is a recently manufactured phenomenon among Sephardim.

52. See the chapter "Jewish Diglossia—Differential and Integral," in Miron, cit., pp. 278–302.

53. Dalia Kandiyoti, *Migrant Sites: America, Place and Diaspora Literatures* (Lebanon, NH: Dartmouth College Press, 2009). See esp. the introduction, pp. 3–24.

54. The exile of Spanish Jews, as well as the vast numbers of Spanish writers and exiles, over the years, is discussed by Henry Kamen in *The Disinherited: Exile and the Making of Spanish Culture 1492–1975* (New York: Harper Collins, 2007).

55. E.g., Dalia Kandiyoti, op. cit. Also André Aciman, ed., *Letters of Transit: Reflections on Exile and Memory* (New York: New Press, 1999) and *False Papers: Essays on Exile and Memory* (New York: Picador, 2009).

56. Antonio Muñoz Molina, *Sefarad* (2001); *Sepharad* trans. Margaret Sayers Peden (New York: Harcourt, 2003).

57. Eliette Abécassis, *Sépharade* (Paris: Albin Michel, 2011). In other media, one may mention the Portuguese film *Sefarad*, directed by Luis Ismael, the story of the crypto-Jews of Belmonte and of the Portuguese army captain, Artur Carlos de Barros Basto, who attempted to help them, with disastrous personal results (see Vivienne Roumani-Denn's review of this film in *Sephardic Horizons*, 20:1, Spring 2020, https://www.sephardichorizons.org/Volume10/Issue1/Roumani-Denn.html). One may also mention Henry Green's project, 'Sephardi Voices,' an audiovisual archive, which collects interviews with Jews from threatened Muslim Eastern communities, and the book coming out of it, *Sephardi Voices: The Untold Expulsion of Jews from Arab Lands*, to be published in 2022. No doubt the title of 'Sepharad' has been used in other languages too, that I may not be aware of.

58. Halevi-Wise, ed., *Sephardism*, cit.

59. *The Converso's Return: Conversion and Sephardi History in Contemporary Literature and Culture* (Stanford: Stanford University Press, 2020). See the review in *Sephardic Horizons* by Jane Gerber, https://sephardichorizons.org/Volume11/Issue2-3/Gerber.html.

60. Sarah Abrevaya Stein, *Making Jews Modern: The Yiddish and Ladino Press in the Russian and Ottoman Empires* (Bloomington, Indiana, 2004).

61. See e.g., the harrowing book by Isaac Jack Lévy with Rosemary Lévy Zumwalt, *The Sephardim in the Holocaust: A Forgotten People* (Tuscaloosa: University of Alabama Press, 2020).

62. "Avec l'introduction de la langue française dans les écoles communales et la fondation des écoles de l'Alliance Israélite Universelle, les enfants juifs possédaient . . . une langue étrangère avec une littérature qui pouvaient leur servir de nourriture spirituelle. Que faisaient donc les adultes et les personnes d'un certain âge, dont les conditions intellectuelles étaient des plus lamentables? Ils ne connaissaient que le judéo-espagnole. . . . Ils manquaient des moindres notions élémentaires des connaissances usuelles de la vie." Avraham Galante, *Histoire des juifs de Turquie* (Istanbul: Editions Isis, 1940), Vol. 9, p. 213. This chapter, "La Presse judéo-espagnole mondiale," first published in 1935. Gloria Ascher gives a charming account of her Sephardic Turkish father's 'Frenchness' as revealed in his 1920 diary, in "Jew, Turk, Frenchman, American: Sephardic Identities in Alfred Ascher's Judeo-Spanish Diario" *Sephardic Horizons* 3:2 (Summer 2013), https://www.sephardichorizons.org/Volume3/Issue2/Diario.html

63. See e.g., Marie-Christine Varol, *Manuel de judéo-espagnol*, trans. Ralph Tarica as *Manual of Judeo-Spanish* (College Park: University Press of Maryland, 2008), pp. 15–16. "Ultimately to replace the latter, French coexisted easily with Judeo-Spanish, brought it the modern terminology that it was lacking, and provided it with euphemisms."

64. Esther Benbassa and Aron Rodrigue, *The Jews of the Balkans* (Oxford: Blackwell, 1995), p. 89. See also Jane Gerber, *The Jews of Spain: A History of the Sephardic Experience* (New York: Free Press, 1992), p. 240. Also Aron Rodrigue, *Images of Sephardi and Eastern Jewries in Transition* (Seattle: Univ. of Washington Press, 1993) which shows how the teachers served as role models of how to be a modern, French-speaking Jew.

65. Published in English translation by Jane Kuntz, trans., edited by Lia Brozgal and Sarah Abrevaya Stein (Stanford: Stanford University Press, 2017. See my review in *Sephardic Horizons*, (10:2), Spring 2020, https://www.sephardichorizons.org/Volume10/Issue2/Roumani.html.

66. Sarah Sussman, "Jews from Algeria and French Jewish Identity," pp. 217–242 in Hafid Gafaïti et al., *Transnational Spaces and Identities in the Francophone World* (Lincoln, Nebraska: Univ. of Nebraska Press, 2009).

67. See Paula E. Hyman, *The Jews of Modern France* (Berkeley: Univ.of California Press, 1998), esp. Ch. 10, "A Renewed Community," pp. 193–214, for an excellent summary covering developments up to the end of the twentieth century.

68. See the review by Albert Garih of Corrie Guttstadt et al., *Mémorial des Judéo-Espangols déportés de la France: Muestros dezaparesidos* (Paris: Éditeur Muestros Dezaparesidos, 2019) *Sephardic Horizons* (11:1) Winter 2021, n. pag. https://www.sephardichorizons.org/Volume11/Issue1/Garih.html.

69. E.g., David Mendelson, ed., *Emergence des francophonies: Israël, la Méditerranée, le monde* (Limoges: Presses universitaires de Limoges, 2001). On

Jabès, see Helena Shillony's "'La langue est ma patrie'—Edmond Jabès et le français," pp. 87–92.

70. Perhaps the first to say this was a Portuguese poet, Fernando Pessoa (1888–1935): "O idioma português é minha pátria" (with thanks to Regina Igel).

Chapter 1

From Orality to Writing
Storytelling in Sephardic Literature

Jewish storytelling embraces many centuries, going back to the beginning of Jewish time. Oral discussions were given preference in the time of the Babylonian Talmud; Haggadah and Midrash have been major tools of Jewish education. As just one example, the Haggadah of Pesach, attests.

Moshe Lazar discusses the encyclopedic Ladino *Me'am Loez* and its use of storytelling, beloved by Sephardim across the Ottoman Empire in the eighteenth, nineteenth, and even early twentieth centuries. He tells how merchants would take time off and gather to hear *Me'am Lo'ez* stories.[1] Dov Noy, at the Hebrew University, as well as numerous other scholars in the field of folklore, devoted a lifetime and many volumes to collecting Jewish folktales from around the world.[2] Anthropologists and folklorists have paid particular attention to transplanted communities and how their oral traditions of storytelling have fared under new skies and new cultures. For example, André Elbaz has followed the evolution of Sephardic oral literature in Canada for some time, and originally authored *Folktales of the Canadian Sephardim*.[3] He remarked that the younger generation in Canada is cut off from its cultural roots, and thought that magical tales would disappear as well as the tales of saints. The didactic tales of Talmudic origin would survive because of their ties to traditional religion. The humorous Joha[4] tales would survive also, he thought, due to their universal character.

The Arabian Nights are tales that were based on folktales, stories of Aladdin and Ali Baba, and the tales of Antar, shared across the Middle East.[5] They present a complicated picture however, as they are a far from unadulterated source, having been reintroduced back into the Middle East in the nineteenth century by a French writer residing in Cairo, basing himself on an eighteenth-century French translation.[6] Their continued popularity in both East and West earns them a place in both cultures. A "Special Issue on Storytelling," in *Prooftexts*, brings together folktales in Hassidic tradition, the legends of the Ari, and storytelling among the Jews of South Bronx. The Afterword by David G. Roskies discusses the crucial role of storytelling in many Jewish literary genres on the brink of modernity, embracing tradition or modernism, from Hasidism to Sholom Aleichem.[7] Albert Memmi has often employed the figure of the traditional storyteller in the souk as the archetype of the writer and intellectual. In his third novel, *Le Scorpion, ou la confession imaginaire* (1969) a storyteller buys a carpet to sit on, sets himself up in the marketplace, and then wonders what to tell his audience. He decides to tell them his life story, embroidered as necessary to make the narrative more interesting. This novel is in fact one of Memmi's more experimental writings, as it includes several different narrative personae, each telling his story in a different voice or style. In this way, Memmi indicates that the source of modern fiction is in supposedly traditional storytelling.

Elias Canetti (writing in German) admiringly described the dignified storytellers of Marrakesh, in Morocco, and called them "elder and better brothers to myself. . . . I . . . found myself here among authors I could look up to since there was not a line of theirs to be *read*" (pp. 78–79). The Israeli novelist and rabbi, Haim Sabato, has his fictional Shai Agnon, walking the streets of Jerusalem, pause before a Sephardic storyteller: "he noticed a man with a shining face in the alley near the entrance to the synagogue. The man stood encircled by a group of people who were listening to him and were rapt with attention. The writer too began to listen and his eyes lit up . . . that storyteller was Ezra Siman Tov" (see below, note on Sabato).[8] The use of all these storytelling figures indicates that modern and post-modern novelists still aspire to the position of authority enjoyed by a traditional storyteller in the public space. Since the storyteller's subject-matter is often in some way traditional, the novelists may also (but not always) draw on the values of traditional culture too.

One might attempt to trace a development within Judeo-Mediterranean literature (as one could within Jewish literature as a whole, or within various world literatures) from the oral to the written genres, and within written genres from short stories to the novel, but all this would entail a great deal of generalization. Scholars, theorists and critics have written about the importance of 'voice'—for example, in David Rosenberg's translation of the Bible there is an emphasis on voice as a quality—implying freshness, brilliance, new insights. Walter J. Ong wrote presciently in 1971 about the "literate orality of popular culture today," stating that the orality of the technological age is different from primitive orality. In primitive orality, formulary devices are important: "It includes all manner of proverbs, adages, apothegms, proverbial phrases, and the like, the 'old said saws' that weave through and support virtually all early writing, keeping even learned writing close to oral performance for centuries, from antiquity through the productions of Renaissance humanists . . . as well as the speech of residually oral folk everywhere still today."⁹ The theorist M. M. Bakhtin has emphasized the productive tensions between the speaker's creativity and society's hold on meaning, through an ear for the nuances of speech behavior. Bakhtin has passages on silence, on slips of the tongue, and on laughter.[10]

By necessity, Sephardic culture in many countries has had recourse to oral literature, due to the need to escape from danger, or forced expulsions. The most recent have been the expulsions from Middle Eastern countries from the early nineteen fifties to the sixties, when Jews were forced to leave such countries as Tunisia and Egypt with almost nothing in their hands. After a period of settling down, the new novels that came out of such communities in exile have tried to recreate a sense of orality, of freshness, spontaneity, and the rhythms of oral literature and folktales, as we shall see in the next chapter in the work of Ryvel and Koskas and will find also in Memmi's writing.

In oral storytelling there is always potential unpredictability, because traditional storytellers, who memorized their tales, would rely on repetition and formulas for memorization, mnemonic devices, but with each performance, allowed for the possibility for variation and spontaneity. Novelists producing written texts have tried to somehow recreate this sense of spontaneity. This chapter will begin by discussing several Sephardic novelists who do not write in French, but have evinced a similar ethos to the Francophone writers. The chapter will eventually focus on Albert Cohen, perhaps the father of modern Francophone Sephardic writing, and his possible influence on several Francophone writers who came after him, such as Albert Memmi and Albert Bensoussan.

Elias Canetti was an almost-Mediterranean Sephardic writer (actually, from Bulgaria) who wrote within the German cultural orbit, studied first in Switzerland, then in Vienna, lived in various other places such as Paris, and ended up settling in London after fleeing the Nazis, later winning a Nobel Prize for literature. His wife Veza (short for Venezia), of similar background and experience, also wrote brilliant and innovative novels that were mostly published years after her death. Both of them place an emphasis on orality. Elias is best known perhaps for his several volumes of autobiography. The first volume deals with his earliest memories and is entitled *The Tongue Set Free*,[11] while a late volume of his memoir is entitled *Earwitness*; a travel account is entitled *Voices of Marrakesh*.[12] Thus, several of his books place an emphasis on orality. The tongue of the title of the first book comes from a harrowing experience as a very young child when the boyfriend of his nurse threatened to cut off the little boy's tongue unless he was quiet about whatever goings-on he had seen or heard. Growing up in polyglot Ruse, Bulgaria, which Canetti calls Ruschuk, he was part of a traditional Sephardic community of families that had fled Spain in 1492 for the Ottoman Empire. The book consists of short stories about his family and about the various ethnic groups who lived in or visited the town. Everyone in town knew seven or eight languages, and many stories related to the benefits of being multilingual, such as the one about someone being able to uncover a murder plot (pp. 27–28). He particularly relished the folktales, sometimes scary to a child, that the Christian servant girls told him. Canetti's later work (all in German except his last book, which was in English) is famed for its trenchant analysis and pithy aphorisms.

Veza Canetti's writing, likewise in German, in contrast, saw publication only many years after her death. Her novel *The Tortoises* portrays the world of German Jewish refugees in Vienna, who cannot make up their minds to leave and save themselves from the Nazis or may have already lost their chance. They tell stories to each other, anecdotes of brushes with earlier benign authorities, experiences that are utterly inadequate to prepare them for confronting the cruel obstacles that the Nazis will raise. Another novel, *Yellow Street*,[13] is likewise about German Jews encountering the gathering clouds of Nazism. Her sensitivity to the human voice in these conversations is very marked.

Turning to the Spanish-speaking world, Isaac Chocrón, of Venezuela, wrote an engaging epistolary novel based[14] on a fictional return to the land of his ancestors, Morocco. A fictional Venezuelan with few links to society (his father, wife and child have all just perished in an earthquake), returns first to Spain and its North African colony Melilla to conclude some family business, then to Tangiers, falling in with its low life and eventually, willfully or not, is found drowned on the beach. The novel, presumably reflecting Isaac Chocrón's own Moroccan origins, can be read as a return to Maghrebian roots for a Latin American Sephardi. Chocrón is primarily known as a playwright; therefore, this epistolary novel is something of a departure for him but, like his plays, formally depends on alternating individual voices. The protagonist, Daniel, still in shock from the tragedy that has befallen him, at first relates that he cannot bear to hear the empty chatter of the Spanish in the Madrid restaurants, and falls easily into the habit of expressing himself in letters as he corresponds with several people back in Caracas. He maintains that he hears the sound of the writer's voice as he reads the responses, thus linking the epistolary format, one of the oldest forms of the novel, to oral storytelling.[15]

A Mexican Sephardic writer, Angelina Muñiz-Huberman, besides being a novelist, also specializes in short stories, as we may see in her collection *Huerto cerrado, huerto sellado* (1985). Probably a descendant of *conversos*, her Spanish family, established for a long time in Spain, went to Mexico in 1939, fleeing from the Spanish Civil War. Her stories tell of crypto-Jews, mainly in medieval Spain. She also writes of the defeated indigenous peoples of Central America, who were likewise forcibly converted and had to conceal any loyalty to their previous religion underground. In both cases, oral traditions were passed down in utmost secrecy from one generation to the next. Her language is often spare in the extreme, mere hints and turns of phrase sufficing to indicate the anguish of alienation from one's suppressed religious roots.[16] Some stories evoke the world of the *romances* or ballads, often fragments of epics, full of ambiguity. "The Fortunes of the Infante Arnaldos," though presented in prose form, reads almost like oral poetry or song: "Who could have hoped for such a fortune as he, the Infante Arnaldos on the high sea! A midsummer vision, a falcon's flight, on St. John's Day in the morning" (p. 57)

One should also mention the narrative poetry in Ladino/Judeo-Spanish, which has come down to us via the communities of exiles in Morocco and the Eastern Mediterranean. This tradition was alive and well in Salonika until the Nazi Holocaust, which almost put an end to this tradition. The long narrative poems of Bouena Sarfatty, originally of Salonika and later Canada, have kept the tradition alive until recently.[17]

From Central America, Guatemala to be precise, also come the stories of Eduardo Halfon, a family name of Sephardic origin. He is the author of the well-received *El Boxeador polaco* [The Polish Boxer] (2008), a collection named for one of the narratives.[18] They rely on narrators who never ask the probing questions they should be asking and lapse into silence frequently. The reader has to do some imaginative work to piece together the dramas and personal tragedies of his overly discreet narrators, as he brings us an otherwise telling portrait of contemporary Guatemala and the place of Jews within it. His stories involve sympathy for other minorities as well, such as the indigenous people of Guatemala and European Gypsies (Roma, Sinta).

Another short story writer of Spanish-sounding name (and probably origin) is Haim Sabato, whose family came from Aleppo, Syria, to settle in Jerusalem. His tales in Hebrew of the Sephardim of Aleppo and Jerusalem make fascinating reading. Sabato's *Aleppo Tales*[19] weaves a portrait of a proud community, delighting in its cantors and their hymns, and their spontaneously composed oral poetry,[20] a community which is forced to abandon its Syrian town and move to a refugee camp near Jerusalem. These stories show the traditional universe of the Aleppo Jews both before and after their uprooting and partial reconstituting in Jerusalem. The rich fabric of traditional and modern writing that informs Sabato's work has been described as reminiscent of Shai Agnon's works, and his tales bring us a taste of a contemporary Sephardic culture that values and respects oral literature.

Perhaps the most well-known Israeli Sephardic writer today is the novelist A. B. Yehoshua who, though he deals with a number of profound issues concerning Israel and Zionism, has devoted several books to a Sephardic sensibility. His *Mar Mani* [*Mr. Mani*][21] chronicles several generations of a

Sephardic family, from the Balkans to Israel. Yehoshua's Sephardic novels will be discussed in a later chapter, too, but this novel in particular constantly evokes orality. It is structured as a series of conversations between people who may only have a distant connection with the family, if at all, but are being told many intimate details about a member of the Mani dynasty. There is a vein of slight madness in the family (there is a hint of mania in their name, Mani), and the dynasty barely survives and perpetuates itself in each generation. The author only allows us to hear one side of each of these conversations, which gives the effect of overhearing one side of a telephone conversation. Thus the reader is obliged to contribute to creating this novel by making the mental effort of imagining and filling in the gaps. The Mani universe covers the Eastern Mediterranean—Salonika, Rhodes, Beirut, and Jerusalem—the universe of the Eastern Sephardim, and the descendants of the exiles from Iberia, for almost five centuries. The oldest conversation in the book deals with the late eighteenth and early nineteenth centuries. Here the characters' conversation in Hebrew is interspersed with words in Ladino or Judeo-Spanish, diglossia whose purpose is likewise to heighten the effect of orality. Yehoshua's discrete conversations, despite dealing with history, have a spatial dimension as well, since they evoke the cultural space of the Sephardim as it once was.

This chapter has taken a short excursus into Sephardic literature in other languages, but now it is time to focus on a number of French-language Mediterranean writers whose works exhibit the relationship between orality, storytelling, Sephardic culture, and the genre of the novel. Probably the intellectual and artistic father of them all, in the twentieth century, is Albert Cohen. Born in Greece in 1895, he lived later in France and Switzerland, eventually taking Swiss citizenship. Like most of our Jewish writers, he was educated in the French language, but was inwardly marginal to French identity. Through his French writing, there echo the voices of the Sephardic community of his birthplace, Corfu, the voices of extravagant and picturesque characters with a foot in the present and a foot in the past, and who had little idea of what was considered decorum in Cohen's time and French-influenced circles.

While the Alliance Israélite had several French-language schools in his native Greece, Cohen did not attend any of these but acquired French when he moved with his family at the age of five from Corfu to Marseilles. Cohen published his first novel, *Solal*, in 1930, and then several more, but fell silent for virtually thirty years as he pursued a career in Geneva as an international civil servant,[22] until the publication of his major novel, *Belle du seigneur* (the title is the same in English), in 1968. He is usually viewed as a French writer, but his name has frequently been invoked as a Sephardic writer as well,[23] since his novels oscillate between the colorful folkloric world of traditional Jewish life he experienced in the island of his birth (what he called "the

Jewish Orient"), and the alienated modern bureaucratic life in international organizations.[24] The humor, mixed with tenderness and indulgence, in his portrayal of traditional Jewish mores, contrasts with the bitter irony of his protagonist's adventures among non-Jews, two worlds that cannot possibly comprehend each other. Cohen is torn between cosmopolitanism and tradition, but his personal experiences of antisemitism lead him to present Jewish life in a comic yet sympathetic light. Like others of his generation, he found it necessary to outwardly assimilate to French culture, which at that time offered him few options for expressing cultural difference.

Born around the time of the Dreyfus affair, Cohen moved five years later with his parents at a time when Greek and Turkish nationalisms were both creating difficulties for Jews. In Marseilles, Cohen grew up as a marginal and solitary child, encouraged by letters that his absent working mother left on the breakfast table each morning. The letters were stories—animal fables with happy, moral endings—and these stories represented a way for his mother and himself to subvert the harsh discipline of her daily routine, a way to express love in a rigid environment that did not leave much room for it. Cohen loved those stories and, as a lonely child, an immigrant rejected by non-Jewish children, he would write his own thoughts in the air.[25] His life story is rife with contradictions. At the age of thirteen, probably for his bar-mitzvah, he went back to Greece for a few weeks and was impressed by his patriarchal grandfather: "The mysterious majesty of the past impressed the young boy and took over his imagination. An idealized Jewish community, rich in miracles, strange powers, customs and eccentricities, came to haunt him."[26] Later, though, Cohen evinced no desire to visit either Greece or Israel, despite being a staunch Zionist. He was first and foremost a creator, his biographer Jean Blot opines, preferring dream to reality: an exile of the imagination.

Cohen's colorful Jewish characters populate all his books, apparently confirming antisemitic stereotypes while, at the same time, endearing themselves to us. Their comic antics are usually contrasted with the cool, rational, and calculating behavior of the non-Jews they admire and envy. They are an amalgam of what Cohen regards as universal Jewish traits, combined with those of relatives and individuals he encountered in Corfu (the novels transfer the stories to Cephalonia, another of the Ionian Islands). The "Valiant Ones," a group of cousins, each with his own picturesque traits, arrive to importune and embarrass their (obviously autobiographical) Westernized nephew, a high official in the League of Nations in Geneva. Their naïveté and innocence are refreshing in this world of cold calculation, portrayed in Cohen's characteristic tone of irony and sarcasm.[27]

The Valeureux cousins, of whom the most extravagant is Mangeclous [Naileater], put great emphasis on dress, concocting absurd combinations of fashion from various cultures and centuries, as they consider appropriate for the occasion. For a visit to the Jewish homeland, they dress in Alpine costumes, Boy Scout shorts, and their customary top hats. Their eighteenth-century dress for the visit to their important nephew in Geneva amuses the doorman and bellboy. There is no doubt that these characters are aspiring to the status of comic and crafty folk heroes like the traditional character Joha.[28]

The cousins, not surprisingly in view of their high expectations of a land of milk and honey, are somewhat disillusioned by their visit to Palestine, renaming it "Pollakstein." Cohen uses every opportunity to exploit the contrasts, real or stereotypical, between North and South or East and West. Though he seldom uses the terms Sephardi or Sepharad, Cohen's "Oriental Jew" and his sunny Mediterranean environment, with his emotional effusions and petty yet endearing vices, is constantly contrasted with the cold, heartless, convention-bound, and conformist North, the breeding ground of Nazism and Hitler. Albert Cohen's heart apparently lies with Sepharad, as later Sephardic writers, including Albert Bensoussan, have noticed.[29]

Did Albert Cohen have a direct influence on Judeo-Maghrebian writers? It is hard to say, but cannot be excluded. Albert Bensoussan, originally of Algeria, for one, has written directly about Albert Cohen, but other, younger writers may not have read his work directly, so it is possible that Bensoussan is the intermediary between Albert Cohen and a younger generation of writers. There is definitely a common sensibility, though, that does not necessarily require the tracing of direct influences.

Albert Bensoussan was born in 1935 in Algiers and moved to France in 1961 at the age of twenty-six, after having been a teacher of Spanish at the Lycée Bugeaud. He is the author of over thirty books, some scholarly studies, some fiction, and many consisting of largely autobiographical essays. Bensoussan's allegiance to the idea of Sepharad is apparent even in the titles of some of his works, *Les Bagnoulis* (1965), *Isbilia* (1969), *Le Marrane ou la confession d'un traitre* (1991), *Mémoire et fidelité séfarades* (1993), *L'Echelle sépharade* (1994). Bensoussan's reviewers, critics and interviewers have remarked on it. For example, Elisabeth Schousboë writes that for Bensoussan:

> Sepharad is . . . the lost land, nostalgic, ahistorical, and mythical, reuniting today, in the context of a French language, all those who have lost their native shores and participate in a Sephardic reawakening that finds a collective project in sephardism.[30]

Bensoussan has also devoted scholarly studies to Albert Cohen in which he writes that Cohen was defending Sephardic identity through his defense of what he called the "Jewish Orient" (see note 24).

Given Bensoussan's lyrical style, in both essays and fiction, one might think that the unexpected introduction into his work of fiction *Les Anges de Sodome* (1996) of a Rabbi Cohen-Solal might have been a fictional reference to one of his favorite mentors and Cohen's first novel, *Solal*. The first-person narrator of *Les Anges de Sodome*, who happens to be a professor about to retire, describes the custom before Yom Kippur of "sacrificing" a chicken. His father had learned ritual slaughtering with Rabbi Cohen-Solal of pious memory, "avait appris avec le rabbin Cohen-Solal de pieuse mémoire l'abattage ritual." However, Robert Elbaz, in a study of Bensoussan, tells us that a real Rabbi Cohen-Solal did actually live and practice in Algiers in the 1940s and 1950s.[31] It is highly possible that this interlude is historically accurate, mooring the novel in history. But there is no doubt that Albert Bensoussan, sensitive to the similarity, will have linked the coincidence in the rabbi's name to that of Albert Cohen the novelist.

Certain scenes are repeated like incantations in Bensoussan's novels: the figure of his grandfather, Mesrod, receiving his Muslim friends, notables and fellahs, in his shop at the siesta hour, and telling and retelling the stories of Joha (reminiscent of Canetti's dignified storytellers in Marrakesh), or the scenes of preparing the Algerian pastries, *fdaouches*. His books revolve around the spoken word, remembered from Algeria, one of the few aspects of life that could be transported.[32] The influence of the oral traditions of the Algerian Jews, from Joha stories to superstitions and folk beliefs, to proverbs, to the repetitive forms of oral literature, is to be found throughout Bensoussan's *oeuvre*. Bensoussan, in the end, though, does not define himself as a *conteur*, a teller of tales, but as a scribe, one who sits in the marketplace and writes down what others dictate to him. Bensoussan, in traditional fashion in *L'Echelle séfarade*, says that he is telling the tales he has heard from others, rather than inventing them.[33]

Rafael Uzan, of Tunisian origin and now living in Israel, is an artist in the naïve style of Shalom of Safed, and a natural storyteller whose tales of life in the Tunisian provincial town of Nabeul have been recorded and transcribed by an Israeli writer and artist, Irene Awret.[34] It is not clear how much of the narrative comes directly from Uzan and how much from Awret, but we can presume, perhaps, that we are indeed hearing much of Uzan's own style of storytelling.[35] She relates how, over many cups of coffee at her kitchen table, Rafael Uzan would tell his stories of Tunisia and the family's move to Israel. He is of an earlier generation than his fellow Tunisian from Nabeul, Marco Koskas, and tells of the Nazi occupation of the town, as well as the community's exodus, some to Israel and some to France. He grew up in a poor family living in a tiny hovel, but tells of the exceedingly rich Jewish cultural life in Nabeul. Like Ryvel's tales and Memmi's novels, this book forces the reader to taste the poverty and measure the strength of traditional life. One anecdote after another fills in every aspect of traditional life in Nabeul, peopling the one-room, earthen-floored homes, the alleys, the synagogues and the beaches, with all manner of eccentric, imperious, or long-suffering characters. He tells of the belief in ghouls that kept him awake at night as a child, and the strong faith that led him to move to Israel. Just as for Albert Memmi, in Tunis, the storyteller is an important early influence, here in the shape of a blind old woman who ekes her living from telling tales, and is frequently called in by the boy's father for the evening's entertainment (see the chapter "Winter Nights' Tales," pp. 6–9). The provincial boy remains securely within the circle of tradition, however, rather than rebelling against it and adopting modern values. He carries a talisman inherited from his great-grandfather, and a fifty-eight-year-old bag full of black grains, blue beads, and a silver hand. Written in the 1980s, this collection of Uzan's tales is close to the traditional worldview of Tunisian Jews, incorporating the manner of storytelling in what appears to be an unselfconscious way.

Annie Fitoussi sees the departure from Tunisia through the lens of a traditional mentality, and sees the process of leaving itself, though tragic and painful at the time, as engendering stories that, from a distance of years, can almost be seen as amusing. For younger Tunisian Jews, the transition to a modern mentality has been swift, once they reached France, but for the older people there were many obstacles to adapting themselves. In her 1985 novel *La Mémoire folle de Mouchi Rabbinou*[36] [The crazy memory of Mouchi Rabbinou], Fitoussi pits those who want to turn the page, and not remember anything about Tunisia, against those who value remembering. Whether they desire it or not, their memories (like that of the rabbi of the title) keep surging back, transformed now into stories that are told and retold. Albert Moché Touitou left Tunisia at the time of the Bizerte crisis (1961), which did not involve Jews, but swept many Tunisian Jews along on the ebb tide of French colonialism. Albert is not a man for stories, and does not want to remember, or even hear mentioned, the family's past. The stories begin, however, as the Jews are leaving:

> That summer, Tunis was bursting with stories, each one more incredible and fantastical than the next. False fractures and real casts provided hiding places, wheat sacks stuffed with dollars, unscrupulous smugglers who vanished into thin air, without forgetting the tale of that sheep with five legs, that was trying to get through unnoticed on the back of its master.[37]

Ommi M'Charda, Albert's mother, decides to stay behind in Tunis, because her estranged daughter who had eloped with a Christian and was never heard from again might return one day and, if the mother had left, would not know where to find her. Ommi M'Charda cannot remember how many children she has and almost an entire page details how she counts on her fingers, adds up her pregnancies that came to term, children who were not born alive, those who died in childhood, for whom she pauses to say some prayers, then begins the count again, the only one she is sure of being her son Albert, but as for her daughter, she has no idea whether she is alive or not. These children are the stories of her life, certainly tragic stories, eliciting from the others not sympathy but impatience. The youngish protagonist, Simone, whose emotional life seems to have come to a stalemate, finds her memory jogged and emotions rushing back after phantom encounters with the rabbi of the title, who takes the form of a homeless person hauled before the judge in the French court where Simone is a defense lawyer. The rabbi's performance could have come straight out of a novel by Albert Cohen:

> Date of birth! Spare us your unnecessary comments, or we'll put
> you in the clink (the word had come right out already)!
> Born in 1732, died in Paris in 1807, said the individual, the
> intrusion of reality into his ancient dream had scared him so.
> The public in the courtroom burst out laughing. . . .
> A foreigner, there's no shame in that, why didn't you say so before?
> An Arab?
> Arab and Jewish at the same time!
> You are abusing the court's time.
> Then Jewish and Arab, if you prefer.
> All right, you've asked for it. The court, declared presiding judge
> Raymon, orders a psychiatric examination of the accused. . . .
> (p. 202)

"Who are you?" asks Simone the lawyer, who is later examining the accused. The rabbi is a sort of catalyst of memory for the recent generations of those Jews who left North Africa at a young age and have suppressed these memories which are nevertheless part of themselves.[38] The rabbi's final words define his role "Je suis, acheva le rabbin, le plus pauvre du ghetto le plus misérable de Tunis, je suis la mémoire folle du Livre" (p. 205) (I am, the rabbi ended, the poorest inhabitant of the most miserable ghetto of Tunis, I am the crazy memory of the Book). Storytelling, we understand, has a very important place in the unleashing of memories, as one story evokes and invokes another, in a continuous chain.

Orality and the oral tradition have played a very important part in the work of Edmond Amran El Maleh (1917–2010), a Moroccan writer in French. The sounds of voices echo through and inform his writing. El Maleh's third novel *Mille ans, un jour* (1986) promises by its title's reference to *Mille et une nuits* a context of Oriental tales, but delivers something very different: a disconcerting and disturbing account of how the millennial community of Moroccan

Jews left Morocco between 1948 and 1956. Thus, a thousand years could be cancelled in one day.[39] El Maleh was a Communist who spent considerable time in hiding in Morocco, then many years in exile in France, before returning to Morocco and literary acclaim at the end of his life. Whether one agrees with his politics or not, his writing is a compelling, lyrical stream of consciousness in which voices and other sounds predominate.[40] They are first-person narratives by a Moroccan who carries around a red notebook and seems to write in it. The notebooks contain all the sense impressions of daily life in Tangiers, conversations participated in and overheard, and recurring obsessive memories of a time of violence, referring to popular demonstrations in 1965 and their bloody repression. Frequent repetitions, and backtracking, just as in a conversation or oral storytelling, reinforce the impression of orality created in El Maleh's writing. In his previous (second) novel, *Aïlen ou la nuit du récit* (1983) Elias Canetti is even addressed directly by the narrator.[41]

> The voices of Marrakesh, the close and intimate voice of Elias Canetti, *dikr*, *dikr*, what was he looking for there, wandering along the Book unfolding in streets, towns, countries, journeys, knotted stories . . . the muezzin, the call to prayer, echoed back and forth like a questioning, a stone thrown into the depths, the call moved him, he the unbeliever who had come from another religion, why?[42]

It seems that El Maleh's Moroccan *alter ego* narrator, addressing Elias Canetti, is a Muslim rather than a Jew, an unusual strategy for a Jewish writer to take. Obviously, El Maleh's identity as a Moroccan rivals his Jewish identity,[43] but his main problem with Canetti seems to be that the latter has a desire to understand, to analyze, that El Maleh rejects in favor of simple sentient experience. All begins and ends with the voices, both inside and outside his head, and which sometimes take on the figure of the storyteller, to tell a folktale about the larger than life character Charjoumaje, that veers into an apocalyptic ending as the city is flooded by the sea:

> Charjoumaje, when he looked with the black pupil of his eye, his entire kingdom and his people were covered in a thick, dense black color, and they shone bright purple on a day when the prince's cheeks turned purple from one of his impressive efforts! Charjoumaje the fabulous legend, heavenly music, honeyed tongue that bathes in light and calms the hearts; may a curse strike my ancestors, may my liver explode and be thrown to the dogs, if I am lying to you. . . .[44]

Here the author is clearly setting himself up as the storyteller in the public square, with multiple assurances that he is telling the truth, as many Sephardic writers have done.[45]

What are the specific characteristics of oral literature that carry over into modern fiction? Haya Bar-Itzhak and Aliza Shenhar suggest some in a study on Jewish Moroccan folktales. These are folktales told in the 1990s in northern Israel (a small town called Shlomi) in Judeo-Arabic, by elderly informants. They divide the narratives into tales told by men and those told by women. Men will tell didactic religious tales, such as stories of Jewish saints, which they call "legends," and "novellas of subtlety and deceit" often exhibiting intelligence and humor. Women would tell these two types, and in addition "fairy tales" or tales of fantasy, which do not have a didactic purpose.[46]

These Moroccan-Jewish folktales are paralleled in Tunisia by a type of tale called *khurafa*. They are purely oral tales, never written nor collected until modern times. Anthropologists claim that the stories express most closely the collective, popular Tunisian mind, and they have always fascinated children. Two types exist, corresponding to the deepest division in Tunisian life: tales told by men and those told by women:

> The tales of masculine and respectable men always include a moral, and a good moral. As for women, . . . let's say that their tales shamelessly mock morality and conformism and can sometimes be quite racy.[47]

Of the rich veins of women's tales and men's, it appears that those of the latter group have had the more obvious repercussions in Jewish written literature, and specifically in Albert Memmi's novel *Le Désert* [The Desert].[48] Generally, the women's tales deal with flesh-eating ogres, and other fantastic themes, easily psychoanalyzed into sexual symbolism. The humor of women's tales has shown itself in the work of several other authors, such as Annie Fitoussi, Claude Kayat, and Marco Koskas. The men's *khurafa*, in contrast, whose influence is evident in Memmi, draw morals to be applied in community and public life or consist of worldly and practical wisdom. Younous, the mentor of El-Mammi, the main protagonist, often echoes them: self-sufficiency, loyalty to one's employer, and the maximum use of one's powers of practical intellect are some of the lessons of survival which El-Mammi gradually learns. In this sense his anecdotes echo the Tunisian men's *khurafa*.

One of the names in the novel, though not the character which bears it, is reminiscent of a stock figure in the women's *khurafa*. It is the brigand El-Ghoul, in the traditional tales an ogre who seduces and marries young maidens only to dine off them later. In the novel, however, he is a primitive, simple-hearted brigand with whom El-Mammi for a while throws in his lot. Besides content, Memmi's incidents differ in form from the oral tales. They lack the repeated adages and rhymes which seem to be the focal points of *khurafa*.[49] Overall, though, Memmi has kept the moralizing impulse of Tunisian men's *khurafa*.

The tales of Joha, or Nasrudin, are also probably evoked in *The Desert*. El-Mammi shares a few of this ambiguous character's traits: he is somewhat crafty, wise in a practical way, socially marginal, and more often than he likes ends up looking ridiculous. Though El-Mammi always maintains the highest moral principles, he sometimes finds his calculations are turned against him, and becomes ridiculous in his own eyes. The humor in the novel is subtle and introspective, never slapstick, and El-Mammi's royal origins make him far different from Joha, who is often a small shopkeeper or an illiterate peasant.[50] *The Desert* echoes the more didactic purposes of the Arabic and specifically Tunisian anecdotal literature. The novel's values of skeptical wisdom, self-control and political acumen reflect the civilization of North African medieval courts. Memmi has also remembered the first duty of the storyteller: to amaze and amuse.

From the three Alberts, Albert Cohen, Albert Memmi and Albert Bensoussan, to other writers, the motif of the novelist as storyteller, with the attendant use of folktales from the tradition, of characters such as Joha, of techniques such as the use of repetition and formulae used by oral storytellers, has been paramount. Whether they employ it to give an impression of more down-to-earth sincerity, as Albert Memmi does, or whether they embark on fantastic flights of the imagination (Annie Fitoussi's "Mouton à cinq pattes" (five-legged sheep) and the wonder-working potential of her rabbi, or Elmaleh's legendary Charjoumaje) Sephardic novelists, reliable or unreliable raconteurs, intend to draw us into the world of the Jewish Maghreb or the traditional life of Corfu, Salonika or Aleppo, sometimes with humor, sometimes with a sense of mourning for what has been lost. Memory and imagination are mixed in equal measure as they weave their engaging tales.

NOTES

1. Moshe Lazar, "*Me'am Lo'ez*: The Crown-Jewel of Sephardic Culture in the Ottoman Empire," *Echoes of Sepharad* 2:2 (June 1991), 12–13, 38. For actual excerpts, see Moshe Lazar, ed., *Sefarad in My Heart: A Ladino Reader* (Lancaster, CA: Labyrintos, 1999), pp. 460–499; The *Me'am Lo'ez* contains, Lazar tells us in his introduction, "a rich mine of popular legends articulated in the fascinating style of oral storytellers" (p. 459). The listening, however, was often by the eighteenth or early nineteenth centuries in a group called a 'meldado,' which emphasizes that the story enactment was a reading, not an improvisation or performance. See Matthias Lehmann, *Ladino Rabbinic Literature and Ottoman Sephardic Culture*, Bloomington: Indiana Univ. Press, 2005.

2. See for example, Howard Schwartz, ed., *Elijah's Violin and other Jewish Folktales selected and retold,* 1983 (Harmondsworth: Penguin Books, 1987). Schwartz is primarily a poet, and chose as the title story of this collection a tale

from Egypt of the magical violin of Elijah. The late folklorist Dov Noy used to hold Shabbat evening get-togethers in his house in Jerusalem, at which each guest would tell his or her own story (they were always from many countries). Schwartz in his introduction states that in Jewish folktales divine intervention often replaced the magical aspects in tales from non-Jewish cultures. Various scholars, such as Tzvetan Todorov, have created typologies of folktales, but the subject is too vast to be dealt with here. Among numerous recent treatments, Yael Halevi-Wise has published a study of the role of storytelling within the novel, *Interactive Fictions: Scenes of Storytelling within the Novel* (2003). She discusses in particular A. B. Yehoshua's use of storytelling in *Mar Mani* (1990). While the whole novel consists of storytelling, this critic particularly focuses on the "storytelling relationship" between daughter and mother in the first chapter. Recently, Marc Eliany and Annette B. Fromm have produced a book entitled *Jewish Folktales from Morocco: Tales of Seha the Sage and Seha the Clown* (Lanham, Md: Lexington, 2021), which includes tales heard from Eliany's grandparents in Morocco, and enriches our knowledge of the facets of the Joha figure. Another name for him is Hodja.

3. He wrote in this work, "I noted several cases of changing from one language to another, which always enables an immigrant to get a quick laugh . . . a process called . . . 'code-switching.'" (p. 29). André E. Elbaz, *Folktales of the Canadian Sephardim* (Toronto: FitzHenry and Whiteside, 1982).

4. As will emerge later, this character's name (he is also known as Nasrudin) may be spelled as Joha, Djoha, Jeha, and even Seha, depending on differences in pronunciation and the languages of the storyteller. In Ashkenazi folk traditions he is known as Hershele. There is a whole bibliography on this character. Some examples: Jean Déjeux, *Djoh'a, Héros de la tradition orale arabo-berbère hier et aujourd'hui* (Sherbrook: Naaman, 1978); a lecture by Albert Memmi, "La Personnalité de Jeha dans la littérature orale des arabes et des juifs," delivered at Conference of Jewish Communities in Muslim Lands, Ben Zvi Institute, Jerusalem, Dec. 3, 1973; Guy Dugas, *La Littérature judéo-maghrébine d'expression française: Entre Jéha et Cayagous* (Paris: L'Harmattan, 1990); Marc Eliany and Annette B. Fromm, *Jewish Folktales from Morocco: Tales of Seha the Sage and Seha the Clown* (Lanham: Lexington, 2021); and a recent posting (Aug. 31, 2021) to https://www.ladinokomunita of tales of Djoha by Yehuda Hatzvi.

5. On the *One Thousand and One Nights* see endnote 9 to Chapter 2. Albert Memmi mentioned the tales of Antar as a source for his novelistic imagination, in an interview in Paris, Dec. 4, 1977 (conducted by Jacques Roumani, transcribed by Chantal Assoulin, *Sephardic Horizons*, forthcoming 12:1, Winter–Spring 2022) and has also mentioned this elsewhere. The old prints included in *Le Désert* are obviously reproductions from collections of folktales printed in Tunisia a hundred years ago, perhaps in Judeo-Arabic. One of the illustrations in the book of sketches by the talented Tunisian artist Zoubeir Turki, *Tunis, naguère et aujourd'hui* (Tunis: Maison Tunisienne de l'Edition, 1967), shows an itinerant storyteller with his staff, telling tales in a café, surrounded by intent listeners, and behind him on the wall prints of famous heroes and exploits from the stories, one of them being very similar to those that Memmi reproduced.

6. Joseph Sadun, "L'Orient pittoresque et Aladin retrouvé," pp. 169–184 in David Mendelson, ed., *Emergences des Francophonies: Israël, la Méditerranée, le monde* (Limoges: PULIM, 2001), gives a fascinating account of the itinerary of the collection *Les Mille et une nuits*, from the Middle East, to France, and back to the Middle East via a translation from French done in Cairo. The basis, though, is undoubtedly an oral tradition dating back to early medieval times.

7. David G. Roskies, "The Story's the Thing: Afterword," *Prooftexts* 5:1 (Jan. 1985), pp. 67–74.

8. Ladino/Judeo-Spanish storytellers have many traditional storytelling genres to draw on, from the fragments of medieval Spanish epics (*romances*) to short pithy moral tales ending with a proverb (*konsejas*). For a modern Sephardic storyteller, see the work (both published and in performance) of Matilda Koen-Sarano of Jerusalem. Koen-Sarano has published a collection of family tales from the Holocaust period, Matilda Koen-Sarano, *Por el plaser de kontar: Kuentos de mi vida* [The pleasure of storytelling: tales of my life] (Jerusalem: Nur Afakot, 2006) in which several stories do end with a moral being drawn, in traditional fashion.

9. Walter J. Ong, *Rhetoric, Romance and Technology: Studies in the Interaction of Expression and Culture* (Cornell: Cornell Univ. Press, 1971), p. 287.

10. Susan Stewart, review of M. M. Bahktin, *Speech Genres and Other Late Essays* in *New York Times Book Review*, Mar. 22, 1987, p. 31.

11. *Die gerette Zunge: Geschichte einer Jugend* (Vienna, Carl Hansen, 1977) trans. Joachim Neugroschel (New York: Continuum, 1979).

12. Elias Canetti, *The Voices of Marrakesh: A Record of a Visit* (1967), trans. J.A. Underwood (London: Marion Boyars, 1978). See especially the chapters "The Cries of the Blind" (pp. 23–26) and "Storytellers and Scribes" (pp. 77–80).

13. Veza Canetti, *Schildkröten* (1999), *The Tortoises*, trans. Ian Mitchell (New York: New Directions, 2001); *Gelbe Strasse* (1990) *Yellow Street*, trans. Ian Mitchell (1991). Also *Gedulde bringt Rosen* (1992), *Viennese Short Stories* trans. Julian Preece (Riverside, CA: Ariadne Press, 2006).

14. Isaac Chocrón, *Rómpase en caso de incendio* [Break in Case of Fire] (Caracas: Monte Avila, 1975). The first twenty-five pages can be found in English translation (trans. by Marilyn Rae and David Pritchard) in Roberta Kalechofsky, *Echad: An Anthology of Latin American Jewish Writings* (Marblehead, Mass.: Micah Publications, 1984), pp. 216–227.

15. The 'lost in Morocco' theme is found elsewhere in Western literature: consider, for example, Paul Bowles' novel, *Under the Sheltering Sky*. The difference here is that Chocrón and his character Daniel are not outsiders but originally from Morocco and enacting a return to roots.

16. Angelina Muñiz-Huberman, *Huerto cerrado, huerto sellado* (Mexico City: Oasis, 1985); trans. as *Enclosed Garden* by Lois Parkinson Zamora (Pittsburgh: Latin American Literary Review, 1988).

17. See Renee Levine Melammed, *An Ode to Salonika: The Ladino Verses of Bouena Sarfatty* (Bloomington: Indiana University Press, 2013); it contains many epic poems (*colas*) with stories about life in Salonika and under the Nazis.

18. Eduardo Halfon, *El Boxeador polaco* (Valencia: Editorial Pre-Textos, 2008) trans. Daniel Hahn et al., *The Polish Boxer* (New York: Bellevue Literary Press, 2012). Halfon has won several literary prizes and has published nine books of fiction in Spanish.

19. Haim Sabato, *Sipure Aleppo* (2005) *Aleppo Tales* (New Milford: Toby Press, 2004); and *Bo'i ha-ruach;* trans. Yaacob Dweck, *From the Four Winds* (New Milford: Toby Press, 2010). For analysis, see Bezalel Stern, "Beyond Agnon," http://www.jbooks.com/fiction/index/FI_Stern_Sabato.htm; also Daniel Bouskila, "A Sephardic S. Y. Agnon," *Jewish Journal (*April 18, 2013). www.jewishjournal.com/yom_haatzmaut/article/a_sephardic_s.y._agnon/ Though Sabato has often been compared to Agnon, Bouskila also underlines their differences: "The greatest difference between Agnon and Sabato is not only their ethnic backgrounds, but also their strikingly different outlook on life. Agnon's novels are filled with cynicism and bitterness. Sabato's novels are—in his own words—'filled with sparks of light, and instead of the bitter drop of fate [in Agnon's stories], a hopeful dose of faith.'"

20. Their oral poetic *tours de force* are exceeded only by the Spanish Golden Age poets. See, on this, the spontaneous poetic exploits of Yehuda Halevi and his cohorts, as described in Hillel Halkin's *Yehuda Halevi* (New York: Schocken/Nextbook, 2010), esp. pp. 3–18 (reproduced also in *Sephardic Horizons* 3:1 (Spring 2013), www.sephardichorizons.org/Volume3/Issue1/halkin.html).

21. A. B. Yehoshua, *Mar Mani* (1990); trans. Hillel Halkin as *Mr. Mani* (New York: Doubleday, 1992). See above note 2 on the views of Yael Halevi-Wise, who also tells us that the novel had great success with readers: seven reprintings during the first year of its publication, it has been widely translated, adapted to the theater, and turned into a multilingual five-part TV production (p. 140).

22. At the end of the war, he played a major part in creating an international travel document, a sort of passport for stateless persons, which he called "my best book." David Coward, "Albert Cohen and *Belle du seigneur,"* intro. to Albert Cohen, *Belle du seigneur* (London: Viking, 1995), p. xi.

23. See also my chapter, "'Le juif Espagnol': the Idea of Sepharad among Colonial and Post-Colonial Francophone Jewish Writers," in Yael Halevi-Wise, ed., *Sephardism: Spanish Jewish History and the Modern Literary Imagination* (Stanford: Stanford Univ. Press, 2012), pp. 213–234, to which the present exposition is indebted.

24. "Inevitably, in the work of Cohen there is a defense of Sephardic identity, as we would call it now, which he simply called the Jewish Orient," Albert Bensoussan writes in "Aude, Adrienne, Rebecca, Rachel: L'Image de la femme dans l'oeuvre d'Albert Cohen," *Nouveaux cahiers* 91 (Winter, 1987–88), p. 58. Bensoussan also devotes four essays to Cohen, in his *Echelle sépharade* (Paris: L'Harmattan, 1993).

25. Albert Cohen, *Carnets 1978* (Paris: Gallimard, 1979), pp. 17–18, 29.

26. Jean Blot, *Albert Cohen* (Paris: Ballard, 1986), p. 24.

27. See Albert Cohen, *Belle du seigneur* (1968; Paris: Gallimard, 1986) trans. David Coward as *Belle du Seigneur* (New York: Viking Press, 1995), esp. Chapters 12 and 13. See also Cohen's *Les Valeureux* (Paris: Gallimard, 1969). E.g., Saltiel recounts to his nephew Solal the cousins' visit to the British House of Commons, one of the exploits organized by Mangeclous: "I almost forgot to tell you that, thanks to a

subterfuge that would take too long to explain on the part of that devilish Mangeclous, we attended a session of the House of Commons, wearing long raincoats, and accompanied by the Sephardic beadle, who knows English well, and translated the debates for us, partly in French and partly in Spanish and Hebrew, which he pronounces quite correctly" (p. 291).

28. Joha is still such a popular character that there is an annual Djoha festival held in Paris in the Fall. There is a great deal of Joha literature: just a few examples that analyze the topic are: Albert Memmi, "Joha . . . " cited above; Guy Dugas, *La Littérature judéo-maghrébine d'expression française: Entre Djéha et Cagayous* (Paris: L'Harmattan, 1991), which has a portion of a chapter devoted to "Entre écrit et orale" (pp. 207–222) and another, "Un Comique séfarade," pp. 235–258.

29. For further discussion of Cohen's inherent sephardism, see Clara Lévy, "L'identité sépharade d'Albert Cohen," in *Les Sépharades en littérature; Un parcours millénaire*, ed. Esther Benbassa (Paris: Presses de l'Université Paris-Sorbonne, 2005), pp. 139–157, and Véronique Maiser, "Sépharades et ashkenazes dans l'oeuvre romanesque d'Albert Cohen," *LittéRealité* 16:1 (2004), pp. 23–30.

30. Elisabeth Schousboë, *Albert Bensoussan* (Paris: L'Harmattan, 1991), pp. 34–39 (Yael Halevi-Wise's translation).

31. Robert Elbaz, "L'Ecriture de la mémoire chez Albert Bensoussan," *International Journal of Francophone Studies* 7: 1–2 (2004), pp. 35–49, quote from p. 39. The novel is *Les Anges de Sodome* (Paris: Maurice Nadeau, 1996).

32. Elbaz makes these two points and quotes from *L'Echelle de Mesrod*, p. 9: "Il y a des couleurs, des parfums, des images obsédantes, c'est le souk, c'est la synagogue, la fièvre portuaire. . . . Mais la sagesse, les bons mots, les vocables indigènes, les grivoiseries souveraines, cela peut voyager sans bruit. Tout y est sincère et tout est fabriqué. C'est un récit, c'est un roman, une fable, un tissue de phrase. Ou peut-être un film en noir et blanc avec des sous-titres en couleurs." (There are colors, perfumes, obsessive imagery, it's the souk, it's the synagogue, the teeming of the port. . . . But wisdom, good words, indigenous terms, glorious obscenities, all that can travel soundlessly. Everything is sincere and everything is made up. It's a story, it's a novel, a fable, the substance of a phrase. Or perhaps a film in black and white, with subtitles in color.) Note the spatial aspects of his recreation of the memory of Jewish life in Algeria.

33. See Elbaz, p. 46, and *L'Echelle séfarade*, p. 114.

34. Irene Awret, *Days of Honey: The Tunisian Boyhood of Rafael Uzan* (New York: Schocken, 1985).

35. This possible source of confusion was also pointed out by a reviewer. See Lawrence Meyer, "Memories and Struggle," *Washington Post Book World*, Jan. 18, 1985, p. C6. See also my "Storytelling in Tunisian Jewish Literature," *CELFAN Review* 4:2 (Feb. 1985), pp. 17–19.

36. The full title is *La Mémoire folle de Mouchi Rabbinou, le rabbin le plus pauvre du ghetto le plus misérable de Tunis, plus fort que Mussolini, bien plus fort encore que la mort* [The Crazy Memory of Mouchi Rabbinou, the poorest rabbi from the poorest ghetto in Tunis, stronger than Mussolini, stronger even than death itself] (Paris: Mazarine, 1985). There was, in fact a historical Tunisian rabbi, Rabbi Hai Taieb, who

is believed in popular culture to have performed many miracles, and is sometimes called Rabbi Hai Taieb lo-Met.

37. Tunis, cet été-là, regorgait d'histoires les une plus invraisemblables et abracadabrantes que les autres. Fausses fractures et vrais plâtres servaient de caches, sacs de blé bourrés de dollars, passeurs peu scrupuleux qui faisaient la belle, sans oublier la fable de ce mouton à cinq pattes, qui espérait passer inaperçu sur le dos de son maître.... (p. 10).

38. Nina Lichtenstein compares this novel with "Annie Cohen's ... autofiction *Le marabout de Blida* ... written as testament to the liberating forces coming to terms with, accepting, and embracing the chaotic memory of her Algerian heritage, its devastating uprooting and North African identity.... The presence of the *marabout* and the rabbi in these texts becomes a way for the young female main characters to reconnect with their pasts. They act as a conscience speaking to the emigrated Sephardim, encouraging them to keep their memories alive by refusing to repress the vestiges of their past...." See Nina Lichtenstein, "Silent Exodus and Forgotten Voices: Sephardic Women Writers in Postcolonial Discourse," *Sephardic Horizons* 2:1 (Winter 2012), http://www.sephardichorizons.org/Volume2/Issue1/Lichtenstein.html. Lichtenstein continues, "Emissaries from the forgotten past, the *marabout* and rabbi, become catalysts for change, showing the protagonists how to move forward in a life enriched by the ineffable values bestowed by an acknowledged, remembered, and incorporated North African Jewish heritage."

39. See the article by Ronnie Scharfman, "The Other's Other: The Moroccan-Jewish Trajectory of Edmond Amran El Maleh," *Yale French Studies* 82:1 (1993), pp. 135–145, which, despite its scholarly value, tends to follow El Maleh himself, the lyrical novelist, in playing with the idea of equating Israeli operatives who organized the exodus of Moroccan Jews with Nazis who organized round-ups of Jews to be sent to the death camps. Edmond Amran El Maleh, *Mille ans, un jour* (Paris; La Pensée Sauvage, 1986).

40. Zakaria Fatih tells us that El Maleh has sometimes been anointed the James Joyce or the Proust of Morocco. Zakaria Fatih, "The Aesthetics of Fragmentation, or a Way to Read El Maleh," *Expressions maghrébines* 13:2 (Winter 2014), pp. 125–137, esp. pp. 126, 128.

41. Edmond Amran El Maleh, *Aïlen ou la nuit du récit* (Paris: Maspero, 1983), p. 55.

42. Les voix de Marrakech, la voix proche intime d'Elias Canetti, *dikr, dikr,* que cherchait-il en lui, errant le long du Livre déployé en rues, en villes, en pays, en voyages, en récits noués ... le muezzin, l'appel à la prière retentissait d'écho en écho comme une interrogation, une pierre jetée dans l'abîme, l'appel l'émouvait lui le non-croyant, venue d'une autre religion pourquoi?

43. However, in an essay, "La Mère-Méditerrannée," *Peuples méditerranéens* 30 (January–March 1985) El Maleh also established his credentials as a Mediterranean writer and as a Sephardic writer discussing roots in Spain.

44. Charjoumaje, quand de sa prunelle noire il lançait un regard, tout le royaume et son people s'enveloppaient d'une ample et dense couleur noire, ou encore s'embrassaient de rouge pourpre le jour où les joues du prince s'empourprèrent à la suite d'un de ses augustes efforts! Charjoumaje fabuleuse légende, céleste musique,

langue de miel qui emplie de lumière et apaise les coeurs; que la malédiction frappe mes ancêtres, que mon foie éclate et soit jeté aux chiens si je vous mens. . . . (p. 20).

45. Some insights may be found in the following: Ronnie Scharfman, "The Other's Other," (cit.); Bou Azza Ben 'Achir, *Edmond Amran El Maleh: Cheminements d'une écriture* (Paris: L'Harmattan, 1997) (see chapter "L'Éleveur de Mots," pp. 37–47); and the dubious comparison with Albert Memmi in Carinne Bourget, *The Star, the Cross and the Crescent: Religions and Conflicts in Francophone Literature from the Arab World* (Lanham, MD: Rowman & Littlefield, Lexington Books, 2010), pp. 43–50, from which Memmi emerges somewhat bruised.

46. See Haya Bar-Itzhak and Aliza Shenhar, *Jewish Moroccan Folk Narratives from Israel* (Detroit: Wayne State Univ. Press, 1993), pp. 16–22. The narrators also describe their three genres as, respectively, "*Ma'asseh, Hadith* and *Kassiah*"—Hebrew, Arabic, and Hebrew terms, respectively.

47. "Les contes d'hommes viriles ou respectables comportent toujours une morale et une bonne morale. Quant aux femmes . . . disons que leurs contes se moquent éperdument de la morale, du conformisme et peuvent à l'occasion être fort grivois." Abdelwahab Bouhdiba, *L'Imaginaire maghrébin: Etudes de dix contes pour enfants* (Tunis: Maison tunisienne del'Edition, 1977), p. 17.

48. Memmi (in Jacques Roumani's interview) ascribed his technique to Jewish and Arab influences, including *khurafa*, which he absorbed as a child: "Cette manière de raconteur est une manière que j'ai sucée avec le lait de ma mère. . . . Ma mère m'a raconté des centaines d'histoires. L'une des sources de ces contes était le magasin de mon père. Chaque fois que mon père s'en allait faire des commissions, l'ouvrier me racontait des histoires. . . . Des héros de la tradition, des comportements magiques, des chevauchées formidables, des crimes affreux, des transformations de l'héros—j'ai écouté tout ça depuis ma grande enfance. C'est une habitude, ce n'est pas que j'ai choisi cette méthode de travailler en quittant la tradition occidentale. . . . Par exemple, une histoire dans une histoire, ça j'ai entendue des milliers de fois." He mentions a didactic use: " . . . l'habitude, au lieu de donner une explication, de raconteur une histoire à la place: 'Tu vas comprendre mieux, je vais te raconteur une histoire. . . . '" See further discussion of this novel in Chapter 6.

49. E.g., Bouhdiba, pp. 17–18. In the same way, a Ladino/Judeo-Spanish *conseja* is a story illustrating a proverb or moral teaching, which is also the punch line.

50. Jean Déjeux, *Djoh'a, Héros de la tradition orale arabo-berbère hier et aujourd'hui* (Sherbrook: Naaman, 1978), p. 21 writes that this discussion of Joha's characteristics (pp. 21–26) is inspired by a lecture of Memmi's entitled "La Personnalité de Jeha dans la littérature orale des Arabes et des Juifs." Memmi also mentioned in the interview that the traditional stories of Joha partially inspired *The Desert*.

Chapter 2

The "Portable Homeland"
Ryvel and Koskas

The term "portable homeland"—"petite patrie portative"—originated with Albert Memmi (1920–2020), the best known Tunisian Jewish novelist, who captures in his fiction the alienation and anguish of exile and their consequences. Ryvel (pseudonym of Raphaël Lévy, 1898–1972) and Marco Koskas (1951-) represent an earlier and a later generation of Tunisian Jewish novelists respectively. Thus, three generations of twentieth century Judeo-Tunisian writers have responded to similar issues and impulses and, like Memmi, have tried to embody a portable homeland in their fiction. Ryvel's fiction is tied to a Naturalist and Realist aesthetic, while Koskas' writing is post-modern and humorous. The 'portable homeland' of the chapter title might also be rendered as 'cultural space' or 'spatial form' in fiction.[1]

The impetus behind much of Memmi's writing has been an attempt to reconcile three contrasting civilizations—Jewish, Arab, and French. Identifying with all three, Memmi's work has expressed the philosophical attitudes of modern rationalism, Existentialism, and universalism., while returning to his roots in the Judeo-Arab culture of Tunisia. Thus, homely maxims are juxtaposed with broad philosophical intimations, pictures of the texture of traditional Tunisian life with searing examinations of conscience. Whichever issues his novels have dealt with, they have always sprung from a particular place, Memmi's childhood surroundings of the old Jewish quarter or *hara* of Tunis, which was mostly demolished in the 1950s. Evoking this setting and community through fiction has been the means by which the novelist has reconstituted both his own and a collective identity, from his new home in France. Few Western readers of Memmi have realized, until fairly recently, that he has not been alone among modern North African Sephardic Jews in seeking to bring together a fragmented cultural personality through fiction. Among Tunisian writers who precede and follow Memmi, two of the most interesting are Ryvel and Koskas.

Secular Tunisian Jewish literature originated before the French Protectorate (1881–1956), in the mid-nineteenth century, and had its own language of expression, Judeo-Arabic. The written literature began with Daniel Hagège and two other Judeo-Arabic authors and was also partly due to a café-owner, Hai Sarfati, who in the 1860s, translated into Judeo-Arabic and circulated in manuscript the stories he had heard from mainly Arab storytellers.[2] Reviews, novels, stories and poetry, some translated and some original, were published over the next eighty years, at first in Livorno and later in Tunis. However, general literacy in French undermined the demand for Judeo-Arabic by the mid-twentieth century. Ryvel, writing in the 1920s and 30s, together with a few others such as Jean Vehel and Vitalis Danon, laid the basis for more contemporary Francophone novelists such as Memmi and Koskas.[3]

The *hara* with its Judeo-Arab traditions was the source of inspiration for most of these Francophone writers, as Claude Sitbon points out.[4] Due to the successful efforts of the Alliance Israélite Universelle to bring French culture to the Jews, the *hara* became relatively open to the outside world. Several Alliance teachers (Ryvel and Danon) and pupils (Memmi) were writers drawing their inspiration from Jewish life in the *hara*. Paradoxically, as elsewhere, French education brought the self-awareness necessary for original literature to come into being, at the same time as it began undermining the foundations of traditional values. Cultural change through education was thus an important issue for Ryvel, the director of the Alliance schools.[5] These schools were a major and effective instrument for spreading the French language and outlook throughout the Jewish communities of the Mediterranean and the Middle East. Ryvel obviously hoped that French education would reinforce Jewish culture, and that writing literature portraying *hara* tradition would be an effective means of preserving it. Ryvel, one of the earliest Tunisian Jews writing in French, attempts to consolidate a homeland to carry forth into colonial society in the face of impending change, while the contemporary novelist, Marco Koskas, rescues a legacy to carry across the sea to the Jews' new home in France. Ryvel's early novel, *L'Enfant de l'Oukala* (1931) and Marco Koskas' first novel, *Balace Bounel* (1979), try to evoke a cultural space through fiction, to give a literary existence to the cultural ethos of North African, or perhaps Tunisian, Jewry.[6]

Memories of the time—during the colonial period and just after—to which such literature refers are fast fading. The older Ryvel was still close to the world he described; the younger, third and fourth generations, in contrast, must try to capture this existence through the reminiscences of their elders. Representing the beginning and end of the colonial period and what it meant for Jews, each writer addresses a public removed from his subject matter: in the case of Ryvel, in culture, as he seems to be addressing a French-educated audience, both North African and French and, in the case of Koskas, in time and geography, as he addresses a French-speaking audience now mostly living in France.

The novels express an indigenous Tunisian culture evolving under the impact of colonialism. The cultural universe of North African Jewry has, for better or worse, undergone vast upheavals over the last generation, described as "the generation of metamorphosis, of the eruption of the West, of the compulsory 'crossing over' to its civilization and culture which suddenly came and interrupted the course of an existence slumbering in the folds of a medieval destiny which still held sway here in the *medinas* and *mellahs*."[7] It is therefore almost surprising that any relationship survives with the past. These two texts show that some elements of oral storytelling, a central feature of traditional Maghrebian culture, may provide not only the form of modern Jewish writing but also the key to integrating the now distant and almost exotic past into contemporary life.

Both books fall within the tradition of loosely organized written collections of stories. Probably consciously, Ryvel and Koskas have allowed this flexible form to mold their imaginations. One characteristic of Eastern, particularly Arabic, collections of tales is the frame story (such as the basic situation of Shehrazad's telling stories to Shahriyar in order to beguile his imagination and forestall her death). Other features commonly found are the mixture of levels and purposes (from the humorous to the didactic and moralizing), and an open-ended, apparently inconsistent structure emphasizing the parts over the whole.[8]

Ryvel and Koskas have each chosen to emphasize certain aspects of this tradition and reject others. A different, less literary form of storytelling to which the two novelists refer in differing degrees is the Maghrebian oral tradition of *khurafa*. These are traditional stories which children hear—the men's stories having a moral and educational purpose, and the women's stories being more humorous and fantastic, involving monsters (ghouls) which disguise themselves as humans, marry and devour their spouses.[9] The stories are equally familiar to Muslims and Jews in Tunisia and were, in one way or another, still part of the upbringing of all indigenous Jewish families in the colonial period.[10] The books also reflect a written genre of Arabic short stories and sketches, called in French *nouvelles,* frequently published in Tunisian newspapers, and based on contemporary life and social mores.[11] While all these types of short fiction could be called preparations for the full-fledged novel, they might also be doing something that the traditional novel would not do as well, i.e., providing glimpses of a society in its various aspects, so that readers become aware of a particular social microcosm as a cultural space. The changing viewpoint of the author or series of narrators adds breadth, more important in this case than forward momentum. Ryvel's collection set within the *hara* of Tunis has no constant narrative thread linking the short stories, and characters only rarely reappear from one story to another. The reader is thus continually returned nearly to the point of departure, exploring the terrain little by little as in a new city. Unlike the *One Thousand and One Nights*, Ryvel's *L'Enfant* does not have frame stories,[12] but rather a disconnected structure of separate tales linked only by their common setting, the *hara*. Ryvel's book is in the tradition of realist vignettes (exemplified in French literature by Alphonse Daudet's *Lettres de mon moulin*), which patiently reconstruct the *moeurs,* the habits, of a provincial world. However, the ideological framework implicit in the novel draws it away from the anecdotal quality of such vignettes. The thrust of the argument is that the difficult physical conditions of life in the ghetto (as Ryvel eurocentrically called it) of Tunis will block further progress for the Jews unless they become open to Western influences and education. This thesis grows throughout the book, using the stories of deprivation and tragedy as its proof.

L'Enfant de l'Oukala lays considerable emphasis on an accurate description of the physical setting in which the individual dramas take place. Ryvel's collection is set entirely in the *hara* of Tunis, with its maze of narrow passageways and dead-end alleys leading to old houses [*oukalas*], each sheltering many families. The large families in these dilapidated mansions would occupy one or two rooms and share with others a central courtyard for cooking and a rooftop for drying clothes. Sunshine and fresh air would hardly enter the streets of this quarter, which shocked Europeans visiting North Africa on behalf of the Alliance Israélite or other organizations aimed at bringing education, enlightenment and Westernization into the *hara*. Numerous accounts by travelers blame the disease, poverty and superstition they saw on the restricted and unhealthy environment.[13] Ryvel describes in the following passage, with language reminiscent of these travelers' descriptions, the interior of an *oukala* just as the Sabbath is beginning. The scientific description of the environment and customs hints at the lives of insecurity and drama led within these closed spaces:

> The oukalas—in case you are not aware—are the mansions of the old Hara. Piles of small windowless cubes enclosing a broad patio onto which they open. A whole family, often consisting of more than eight people, lives in each cube. The Lord blesses Jewish families with abundance. The patio dispenses to all glaring light, muddy water, and air heavy with the odor of piled up garbage.
>
> It is night-time, a lovely night in early autumn. The dark patio has broad streaks of light. With their door open and curtain pulled back, each room is pouring forth its splash of yellowish light. They form a sort of imaginary carpet on which, in a little while, "Eli the Nabi will set his feet." They are hands reaching out to wish each other a brotherly "Shalom."[14]

Ryvel is initially attempting to portray a *hara* life unadulterated by modern influences; a certain distancing is, therefore, evident in the stories. Some didacticism, visible in the author's zeal to include as many customs and traditions as he can, betrays his sense that his readers have to be informed.[15] Readers cannot, apparently, enter the world of the *hara* unless armed with the necessary anthropological knowledge (and a glossary). While the gap that Ryvel hopes to bridge is, for the contemporary reader at least, made deeper by his "scientific" approach, the predicaments and dangers in which his protagonists struggle for survival, or at least to understand why they suffer, make up in dramatic force for the occasionally didactic tone.

A Naturalist aesthetic viewpoint shapes Ryvel's stories. Behind the nightmarishly claustrophobic spaces in which his characters' dramas take place (in a sort of tank in which Zaïra's rabid father is imprisoned; in the cube-like rooms; in a graveyard) lies an echo of Émile Zola and such scenes as the struggle for survival in the flooded mine of *Germinal*. The tales thus reflect less a humdrum 'slice of life' than moments of heightened drama and even melodrama, an integral part of the Naturalist aesthetic.

A short tale from the middle of the book deals with childbirth, and is one of the few stories which do not end on a note of tragedy. Entitled "L'Oeillet de Jérusalem" [The Jerusalem Carnation], the story is about the family of a tailor, Pinhas. The first sentence, introducing arbitrarily shocking Naturalist imagery, has the perhaps unlooked-for effect of distancing the reader and revealing the author's assumption that his audience is a foreign, European one: "Pinhas the tailor's dwelling has the appearance of the dried scab on a wound" (p. 107). The house is crowded with neighbors as Mayha, Pinhas' wife, is about to give birth. Pinhas is praying in the corridor outside, as the women inside proffer traditional advice and remedies. The scene is a living tableau of Maghrebian customs and superstitions associated with childbirth, particularly the flower, the *oeillet de Jérusalem,* which should open in water and cause the child to be born safely. All eyes watch the flower, except those of Pinhas, who is reading the story of Jonah. Another drama, though, is going on in Mayha's mind. Her life passes before her eyes, and her attention grasps a sin she has committed:

> As the strip on which her pure life is inscribed unfolds, a black stain captures her attention. The stain enlarges, spreads and engulfs the horizon of her vision. She has sinned and this is the punishment, she is going to die.[16]

As the flower refuses to open, Mayha calls out, "Pinhas, I have sinned. Give me your pardon if you want God to have pity on your wife . . . " Pinhas is thinking that it is not up to him to judge his wife, when suddenly, "A long searing cry sweeps away his anguish." To everyone's joy, a boy has been born, Mayha is smiling and the *oeillet* has opened. Pinhas murmurs, "The Eternal One has pardoned."

A closed and traditional society, limiting people's possibilities for choosing their own future, and the harsh facts of existence in an environment with much disease and little medical care, create the drama and suspense in this story. The religious beliefs of the actors are part of the décor (like the flower) rather than a genuine part of the drama. Behind the respect and affection for tradition, there is an implicit distancing, as if the author does not expect the reader to hold the same beliefs. Despite the author's masking of his own point of view behind a faithful portrayal of traditional Jewish beliefs and customs, and despite the introduction's praise of his writing for bringing the reader the "ghetto vu du dedans" (p. 25), Ryvel does not really bring the *hara* to life on its own terms, but rather on those of an enlightened, Westernized Jew.

The last story in the novel, "La Tombe d'Eliézer" [Eliezer's Tomb] introduces a more recent period into ghetto life and relates it to the wider world. More of a vignette than a story, it describes the excitement at the news that an emissary has arrived from Russia to speak about the rebuilding of a Jewish homeland. He is to speak in French, so that a majority will understand him. This fact scandalizes the old people, for whom any language other than Hebrew would be sacrilege (Judeo-Arabic is apparently not used on official occasions). Eliézer's friends in the *souk* remind him that times have changed and that "Nowadays, our children take pleasure in reading secular books. And their lips have unlearned our prayers."[17] This hint of cultural decline under the influence of French control of Tunisia is one of the few in the book, but was probably an important issue for Ryvel.[18] Eliézer obviously expects the *shaliach* to be a religious leader, is initially shocked by his shaven face, and seems to have no conception of what a secular Zionist movement might imply. His way of thinking is entirely religious and messianic. Thus the reaction of Eliézer (the prototype of Jewish *hara* tradition) to the *shaliach*'s speech is most significant.

Eliézer enters the hall with his grandson Soussou, who will translate for him. Soussou, probably an Alliance pupil, is fluent in both French and Hebrew. Ryvel merely hints at the emissary's subject matter, but it is obviously a Zionist message: basing himself on the past history of the Jewish people, he draws a lesson from it and founds a belief on it. Despite having understood hardly a word, Eliézer "added his emotional rejoicing to that of the other" (p. 177). As a skilled Talmudist, "he had at least taken pleasure in the clash of ideas, the sensed controversy, the resonance of the sonorous sentences" (ibid.). On the way home, Soussou explains what the emissary's words meant, and Eliézer amends his dream of being buried in the holy land to one of going "in the company of his grandson, who would go and build his future in his rediscovered homeland." The book ends on this note of pious hope, an ideological opening toward the future made possible by French education, which gave the Jews of the *hara* access to the world of ideas. Soussou, the link between traditional Judaism and the modern world, will make this leap toward the outside, and the sense of immense possibility in this sketch is reinforced by its economy of words.[19]

On the philosophical level, the stories progress from absolute determinism to a more optimistic note, thus from a closed to a more open structure. The first and longest story, "L'Enfant de l'Oukala," the story of Zaïra and her drunken father who is bitten by a rabid dog, and the community's terrible decision to drown both of them in a water tank, is the most shocking and Naturalistic. The society is harsh and pitiless when the survival of the group is threatened. "L'Oeillet de Jérusalem" [Jerusalem Carnation] and "Conte de Pâques" [Passover story] (the latter based on a traditional story about a character who prospers by his wits, here transformed into a Jew and set on the day before Passover) both end on a happy note. "L'Aveugle" [The Blind Girl], a very short story about a girl blind from birth, implies that this misfortune is due to the sin of her father, a rabbi whose intellectual curiosity leads him too far into Kabbala and astronomy. The next story, "Mort ne veut troquer" [Death Takes No Substitutes], sounds from the title like one of the traditional *khurafa* stories explaining the origin of a proverb. Set "in a humble cottage bereft of sunlight and joy, in the heart of the *hara,*" (p. 143) it tells of a mother's disappointed hope that death will take away the grandmother instead of her own ill child. The next and second to last story strikes a note of hope for lives seemingly destined for waste. The illegitimate David, who has survived all his life by crime, prevents and conceals another Jew's profanation of a tomb—all this in the dream of Rebbi Gagou. Thus, from the closed tank of the first story to the vast auditorium of "La Tombe d'Eliézer," from the instinctive cruelty needed for group survival to the opportunities opened by the French language and Zionism, the thematic organization of the book opens into implied possibilities for new life. It is evident that Ryvel wished his stories to embody the cultural space of Tunisian Jewish life. One can deduce this from the variety of situations and characters evoked, often merely for the pleasure of describing them. Despite the characters' dire straits, one has a sense of the teeming life going on inside and outside the tiny rooms. The dramatic tension is not sustained for very long, as most of the stories are short. Perhaps Ryvel decided to leave his book in this fragmentary form, reminiscent of oral and written collections of tales, in an effort to limit the influence of determinism. It does not seem anachronistic to view his collection in the context of critical ideas developed long after Ryvel's time: the republication half a century later of *L'Enfant* asks that it be taken seriously as a work of fiction capable of speaking to a more modern audience. In 1930, it responded fully to the ideological demands made of literature, and more recently it also meets a modern readership's less specific preference for spatial form.

Marco Koskas' *Balace Bounel* [Bounel's Balace] (1979) is, to a much greater extent, a modern spatial narrative giving fictional existence to a specific Jewish community. Like Ryvel, Koskas writes a novel of his time, recreating Jewish life of an earlier period (the colonial phase and after, ending in the 1950s and early 1960s).[20] Despite its covering a precise historical period, and the occasional importance of historical events in the lives of the characters, *Balace Bounel* gives an impression of space rather than temporal extension. The tellers of the stories are anonymous (though there is a list of names at the end with the author's acknowledgments) and the accounts merge into each other, overlap, and contradict one another.[21] The doubling back, and recital of accounts from new viewpoints, fill out the structure, giving it a spatial dimension. Unlike *L'Enfant*, *Balace Bounel* does not give the impression that an author's hand is shaping the material into the aesthetic form suitable for fiction. The author does not (apparently) exhibit an urge to control and classify the memories and stories according to scientific and literary criteria, as Ryvel did. Freed from this obvious authorial mediation, the novel gives the illusion of being a "slice of life" to a much greater extent nowadays than does Ryvel's Naturalism.

The contrast with Ryvel's writing emerges clearly in passages in *Balace Bounel* dealing with similar scenes of traditional Jewish life in Tunisia, set in the provincial town of Nabeul (now famous for its ceramics) rather than among the poorest Jews of Tunis. The novel concentrates on the Bonan family (whose name is distorted to Bounel), The "balace" of the title is their home—a Judeo-Arabic pronunciation of "palace," for it is a rambling mansion. The Bonan family is flourishing in all respects except one: Bonan has seven daughters and no male heir to take over his import business. His young assistant, Victor, a key figure in the novel, is unknowingly destined by Bonan to be his heir and marry one of the daughters, if no male heir ensues in the meantime. The novel's first words are an invocation of memory, a formula often repeated in the text to bring the jumbled memories flooding back: "Whoever remembers Victor with the red hair who used to run about spreading the news" (Qui se souvient de Victor qui avait les cheveux rouges et répandait les nouvelles à pas de course) (p. 13).[22] Rachel, Bonan's wife, is about to give birth again and Victor is enthusiastically preparing to spread the news about the town:

> As long as it's a boy—how's it going Auntie Rachel?—it's starting Sonny—I'm off then Auntie—Off you go Sonny. Already in the street already Place de France already in the souk and already at the beach Auntie Rachel's having her pains Auntie Rachel's having her pains like greased lightening, a shooting star,

Mach 2 as they'd say much later but not about him, because whoever remembers Victor he must be a hundred if he's a day. (p. 15)[23]

This passage transitions (almost without punctuation) from interior monologue at the beginning, to dialogue, to a picture of Victor running around spreading the news, to an authorial musing about the term 'Mach 2,' to a conversation (obviously much later, in France) among family or community members reminiscing about their old life. The tone is one of simultaneously mocking amusement and open nostalgia, for a past distant in time, place and culture. Jewish life in this provincial town is remembered far differently from that of Ryvel's Tunis. Koskas' Nabeul is a lost paradise in which the Jews live indifferent to religious strictures, yet enjoying the security of a homogeneous community.[24] They have not yet mastered all the intricacies of French civilization but have seized the opportunities offered to their spirit of enterprise and ingenuity.[25] The humorous tone prevails despite momentous events in the Bonan household: as the book opens, in one room professional mourners bewail the recent death of Bonan's brother-in-law, while in the other room women of the community encourage Rachel in her labor. The women pass back and forth between one room and the other, occasionally in the confusion forgetting their roles and wailing in the wrong room. Snatches of their conversation with Victor foreshadow the conversations of forty years later, recreating the past but confusing chronology:

> So many events that Victor interlaced so much that he had to ask the mourners one of whom thought the electric light came before the streets were named while another contradicted her, saying she was sure the electric light came later because he son Haïm fell in the well the day the streets were named—no, Fortunée, Haïm fell in the well before they built the road to Tunis—and the mourners had left off mourning. (pp. 18–19)[26]

As the mourners pass from one room to the other they are obliged to climb the stairs, creating a great deal of confusion and fear in the heart of the architect of the first two-story house in Nabeul. We find

> The matrons piled one on top of another, between the first and third steps on the staircase, which had been repaired right after Rachel's brother-in-law fell down them by the architect himself, who was clutching his head as he watched the obese women breathing so heavily. . . .
> "Hold on to the banister, Sarah, I've got no strength left"
> "then stand still and give me your hand so I can reach that pesky banister"
> "no, don't give her your hand or I'll fall on top of Marie"

"if you fall on top of me, I'll die and leave seven children in indigence and destitution. (p. 23)[27]

The house itself, built by Bonan's grandfather, is a testament to the family's eccentricity in all senses, since it was the first outside the old town. Bonan has enlarged the *balace* with an elaborate veranda and the unreliable marble staircase leading to the second floor. The rambling, ramshackle house and the town of Nabeul, with the sea close by, form the contours of the novel. These spaces, and the people who inhabit them, interact freely and confidently with the outside world. The *balace*'s open and eccentric structures are the opposite of the closed conformism of the cubes in Ryvel's *hara*.

Balace Bounel's three sections deal respectively but loosely with the house of Bonan at its zenith, Bonan's decline and death, and the gradual departure for France of almost the whole community. Numerous family crises (Victor's flight, Habiba's elopement with an Arab, Rachel's suicide, etc.) intervene, as well as historical events (French pillage of the town, German occupation, the 1961 Bizerte crisis between France and Tunisia). No event is told in its entirety at one time. The narrative is like a conversation between somewhat distracted people with imperfect memories and little preconception of what is important to recall from the past—a collective stream of consciousness. There are disconcerting connections between distant events, as one narrator interrupts another. These separate voices are never differentiated; one can follow only a collective memory which weaves back and forth, filling in the fabric of the world that surrounded the Bonan family. The general voice prefers to dwell on details such as the exact proportions of the figures in the painting which Bonan commissioned, rather than on historical factors such as how he acquired the wealth and taste to enable his home to possess an original painting. As an original motif throughout the book, the painting is an important indication of the family's fortunes and ambitions. It speaks of the naivete of the family's pretensions to culture and originality. Such motifs arise and are dropped constantly throughout the novel. Character modification in response to historical forces is almost entirely absent. The collective consciousness does not aspire to change, but is content merely to fill in the features of the cultural space. The structure of the novel is devoted to reflecting the consciousness of the family and the wider Jewish community rooted in the town.

History gradually obliges the Jews of this self-sufficient world to react to events. With independence, some Jews—such as Clément, Bonan's son-in-law—join the ruling Néo-Destour Party, but are disappointed at not being accepted as Tunisian patriots. The Jews of Nabeul seem to have no use for Zionism. The Hebrew language is meaningless to them and they send to Israel only the unhealthy people that the community wants to be rid of.[28] Clément himself had earlier sabotaged an operation (called "La Grande

Nuit") organized by the American Joint Distribution Committee to take the community en masse to Israel overnight. Clément makes a fortune from his role in the American Joint operation (he charges salvage fees and sells for scrap the vehicles which he himself had disabled), and invests it in a gold bracelet.

Finally, despite his earlier vehement but ambiguous declaration that "I'd rather become an Arab than leave this country" (je préfère devenir arabe que quitter ce pays) (p. 165), his turn comes to leave Tunisia for France. His wife, Monette, is entrusted with smuggling the bracelet (stuffed inside a roast chicken) past the customs officials. As a diversionary tactic, their children are to wave flags and sing the national anthem. Monette loses her nerve and flings the chicken to some stray dogs, then bursts into laughter. One official tells his superior, "Sir, this woman is in order but she is obviously laughing at us," to which the other replies, "He who laughs last laughs best" (p. 229)[29]—perhaps an indirect comment on the humorous purpose of *Balace Bounel* (see also Chapter 5 hereafter). Leaving with empty hands, the Jews of Nabeul owe no debts and the break with the past seems absolute.[30]

Only Victor remains in the town, talking to the dead in the cemetery, keeping the keys and maintaining the houses. As years go by, he predictably begins to lose his struggle against decay, and eventually is obliged to wall up all the windows of all the houses. The narrative comes to an end with the list of absentee owners and description of Victor's walling up of their houses all on one day:

> The first house for walling up, belonging to Mardoché Haddad, a tailor, sixty-eight by now if he's still alive, father of nine children, brick and cement, . . . Gabrial Chiche brick cement brick cement brick brick, André Serrer brick cement, Gaston Temmam brick cement. (p. 234—end of the novel)[31]

The definiteness and closed nature of this ending is attenuated only by the comma which follows the last word. It suggests that the structure may not be closed, that some form of relationship between "us" and "you," the present and the past, the emigrants and the Tunisians left at home, might still exist. Granted, this is a lot to read into a comma. If true, it would be expressed through novels such as *Balace Bounel*, which work toward what Jacques Berque called a "réintégration de soi-même"[32]—a reintegration of self, which is both individual and collective.

Balace Bounel is a fully successful modern novel embodying through its structure the cultural space of Jewish life in Nabeul. Characters do not develop over time in response to circumstances, but rather appear and disappear in the complicated interweaving of stories. The multiple viewpoints do not analyze in depth, but create a many-sided view—superficial, but comprehensive in scope—of a whole culture or society. There is little room for historical change. The Jews are happy to take advantage of the new benefits offered by emancipation and the colonial regime, but rebuff the idea of interacting further with a changing society. History does not really intrude on their lives until well after the Bizerte crisis in 1961, as a result of which they are forced to leave. One might say that they are finally forced out of space and into time.

L'Enfant de l'Oukala and *Balace Bounel* both rely to a large extent on the resources of the human voice. In a traditional culture where the written word was mainly reserved for sacred texts, memorization and oral communication predominated. Voices echo from room to room in Ryvel's *hara*, ready with a witty answer or raised in anger, lamentation or prayer. The written prose conventions of Ryvel's time somewhat restrain the authentic voices by imposing a literary French. Koskas' anonymous voices can speak almost directly as they would in real life, since the familiar terms and slang are now at home in fiction and accessible to a large audience in France. One reason that such language may have become part of the literary mainstream may be the highly innovative corpus of literature produced since the mid-1950s by Maghrebian Francophone novelists. The homely French interspersed with occasional Arabic or Judeo-Arabic words is a close approximation of how people actually talk.

As with other novelists writing in various languages around the world, Ryvel and Koskas mobilize the resources of traditional culture, particularly the techniques of oral storytelling, to create a contemporary fiction. Most would agree that an important technique of oral storytelling is suspense. The traditional Middle Eastern storyteller in the marketplace would soon starve without it. Naturalist novelists in France were still in touch with the nineteenth century tradition of providing a good yarn, thus with the simplest forms of storytelling. Ryvel keeps us in suspense as to whether Mayha will survive the birth, but Koskas merely alludes to the expectation that Rachel should produce a boy, and the suspense is eventually dissipated. Both texts do share with storytelling its discontinuity, the arrest of narrative development generally associated with the novel. *Balace Bounel*'s intricate interweaving of motifs and stories (like lost household objects that turn up in odd places, suddenly reminding us of the past) resembles the open frame story arrangement of well-known collections of tales. Viewed in their relation to Tunisian *khurafa* stories, Ryvel uses the men's tradition of tales with a moral and educational purpose, while Koskas draws on the women's tradition of humorous tales purely for entertainment.

Ryvel's work is both tied to Naturalism, and an attempt to embody a living picture of *hara* life at the turn of the previous century. Koskas, with many novelists' experiments in form behind him, was able to create a highly successful first novel which spatially encompasses a whole community, and also records its demise as a result of outside events. *Balace Bounel*'s collective voice takes all narrative drama out of descriptions of important historical changes. Ryvel in contrast tends to invest a literary type of melodrama into an apparently more stable historical situation than *Balace Bounel*'s, though he is also impelled to describe and record the *hara* for its own sake. Though their techniques are different, both writers evoke quite convincingly a cultural space. They show ways of life that appeared eternal to those living them, but in fact were doomed by history to disappear within a short time. In these novels historical change is lapping away at and eroding the edges of Jewish life. As Albert Memmi has written, since the colonial period traditional Jewish life had been condemned to disappear. The colonial situation brought the Jewish communities of North Africa security, prosperity and hope; at the same time, it led to their destruction through their adoption of French civilization and together with new nationalisms, made the continuity of their life more and more difficult.

The contemporary novel and the republished one are outstanding examples of the trend from the 1970s on among Jewish writers in French to search for and celebrate their roots. It was a moot question, though, whether novelists could use what remained of the cultural space of Maghrebian Jewry to constitute the literary "portable homeland" of which Memmi spoke, and in particular whether they could sustain a new genre of Maghrebian Sephardic novels.

NOTES

1. This chapter is partially based on an article that appeared in *Prooftexts* 4 (1984), pp. 253–267. I am grateful to the late Alan Mintz for his suggestions for the original article. At that time the idea of 'cultural space' in literature was only just beginning to be accepted, but over the last few years it has taken wing. For example, Guy Dugas noted the phenomenon among Jewish Maghrebian writers in his "Ecrivains séfarades d'expression française," p. 176 in *Mémoire et fidelité séfarades 1492–1992*, ed. Albert Bensoussan et al. (Rennes: Presses Universitaires de Rennes, 1993). In 2009, Charlotte Elisheva Fonrobert discussed "The New Spatial Turn in Jewish Studies," AJS *Review* 33:1 (2009), 155–164. The March 2012 issue of *PMLA*, 127:2, devotes a whole section, consisting of six articles, to the "Practices of the Ethnic Archive." Robert Watson published an article on Algerian Jewish Writing which deals precisely with this concept, "Memories (Out) of Place: Franco-Judeo-Algerian Autobiographical Writing, 1995–2010," *The Journal of North African Studies* 17:1 (Jan. 2012), pp. 1–22. I see a direct antecedent of Watson's thought in Isaac Yetiv's 1973 analysis of Albert Memmi's two earliest novels in terms of the protagonist's successive encounters with continually more alien social realms in colonial Tunisia, expressed as a series of concentric circles. See Isaac Yetiv, "L'Aliénation dans le

roman maghrébin contemporain," in *Colloque sur les littératures d'expression française: Ecrivains du Maghreb*, 2nd ed., Paris: Editions de la Francité, 1973. See also my paper, "A Plurality of Bridges: The Sephardic Scholar as Literary Archeologist" in *Sephardic Horizons* 3:2 (Summer 2013). A fruitful application of the ideas of ethnic space and place in Israeli fiction is Yohai Oppenheimer, "Representations of Space in Mizrahi Fiction," *Hebrew Studies* 53 (2012), pp. 335–364.

2. See Chen Malule, "The Story of Daniel Hagège: Judeo-Arabic Author and Documenter of Tunisian Jewry," *The Librarians Newsletter*, 7/9/2020. www.Blog.nli.org.il/en/lbh_hagege. See also note 17 below.

3. Two collections in English have included essays discussing Jewish culture in Tunisia. Michael Menachem Laskier et al., *The Jews of the Middle East and North Africa in Modern Times* (New York: Columbia Univ. Press, 2003) has a historical essay by Haim Saadoun, pp. 444–457. Emily Benichou Gottreich et al., *Jewish Culture and Society in North Africa* (Bloomington: Indiana Univ. Press, 2011), has several essays by both Muslim and Jewish scholars relating to Tunisia. On Tunisian Jewish literature, see the special issue "Juifs de Tunisie/ Jews of Tunisia," *Revue du Centre d'Etudes des littératures et des arts d'Afrique du Nord* 7:1 (Spring 2009). The literary text by Ryvel discussed in this chapter is Ryvel, *L'Enfant de l'Oukala, roman* [The Child of the Oukala, A Novel] (Tunis: La Kahéna, 1931) (this edition not seen); *L'Enfant de l'Oukala et autres contes de la Hara* [The Child of the Oukala and Other Tales of the Hara], pref. Serge Moscovici (Paris: J. C. Lattès, 1980). The book won the Grand Prix Littéraire de la Tunisie, Prix de Carthage, in 1931. Ryvel also published four collections of stories with La Kahéna. One of them (not seen) is entitled *L'Oeillet de Jérusalem, nouvelles* (1930). It probably includes at least one of the stories republished in the 1980 edition. His collection, *Les Lumières de la Hara (nouvelles)* (Tunis: La Kahéna, 1935) also consists of similar stories, each connected with one of the Jewish holidays, such as "Tseddaka," "Le Muré," and "Selihoth rouges."

4. See Claude Sitbon, "La Littérature juive tunisienne d'expression française," in Robert Attal et al., in *Regards sur les Juifs de Tunisie* (Paris: Albin Michel, 1979), pp. 211–217.

5. Ryvel not only wrote prose but was an accomplished poet, writing in a slightly dated, Symbolist style. His extraordinary collection of Holocaust poetry, *Le Nebel du Galouth* [The Lyre of the Galut], movingly laments the destruction of European Jewry (Tunis: La Cité des livres, 1946), and is one of the earliest literary works by Sephardim on the Holocaust. See Gary Mole, "The Representation of the Holocaust in French-Language Jewish Poetry," *Covenant* 2:1 (May 2008), www.covenant.idc.ac.il, and my essay, "Sephardic Literary Responses to the Holocaust," in Alan Rosen, ed., *Holocaust Literature: A Critical Introduction* (Cambridge: Cambridge Univ. Press, 2013), pp. 326–346.

6. They are not the only two Tunisian Jewish writers to try to do this. The interior space of the home, where family members spoke Judeo-Arabic and family dramas took place, such as the mother taking to her bed and becoming a permanent imaginary invalid, after her daughter elopes, are beautifully evoked in Annie Fitoussi's *La mémoire folle de Mouchi Rabbinou,* Paris: Mazarine, 1985 (see pp. 9–27). Claude Kayat's novel *La Synagogue de Sfax* (Paris: Punctum, 2006) reduces the cultural

space of Tunisian Jewry to one building, the synagogue. The process of exclusion and uprooting is wrenching, as family by family the Jews of Sfax emigrate, leaving one person behind as caretaker. The synagogue, in its heyday, had included all the members of the community on Yom Kippur, even the character Mohammed Cohen who had been the hero of Kayat's earlier novel. Speaking Judeo-Arabic, easy relations with their Arab neighbors, loyalty to their own Tunisian *minhag*, had defined the cultural space of Tunisian Jewry.

7. Haim Zafrani, review of Edmond Elmaleh's *Parcours immobile* (the autobiography of a Westernized Moroccan Jew) *Revue des études juives* 141:1–2 (January–June 1982), p. 278.

8. For detailed description of these features, their literary origins and implications for European literature such as the *Decameron* and the *Canterbury Tales*, see Katherine Slater Gittes, "The *Canterbury Tales* and the Arabic Frame Tradition," *PMLA* (March, 1983), pp. 237–251. The structural elements might also be traced back to Apuleius' second century novel, *The Golden Ass*. David Mickelson, in Jeffrey Smitten et al., *Spatial Form in Narrative* (Ithaca: Cornell Univ. Press, 1981), pp. 74–76, "Types of Spatial Structure in Narrative," shows how Apuleius goes to great lengths to avoid a forward momentum, undermining it through interpolated tales, and thereby creating a spatial structure. See also Laurence Williams, "Reframing the Oriental Tale." *The Cambridge Quarterly* 38.2 (2009): 183–187, and Malcom C. Lyons and Robert Irwin. *Tales from 1,001 Nights* (Penguin Classics, 2012). Also Yael Halevi-Wise, *Interactive fictions: scenes of storytelling in the novel*. Vol. 123. Praeger Publishers, 2003.

9. For an anthology of traditional tales of Algerian Berbers, see Marguerite Taos Amrouche, *Le Grain magique: contes, poems et proverbes berbères de Kabylie* (Paris: Maspero, 1966). For detailed examination of Tunisian tales as evidence of collective psychology, see Abdelwahab Boudhiba, *L'Imaginaire maghrébin* (Tunis: Maison tunisienne de l'édition, 1977). Serafín Fanjul García, *Literatura popular árabe* (Madrid: Editora nacional, 1977), defines various sub-genres of popular tales (pp. 173–74). The *khurafa* stories are stories told by a member of the Udr tribe. He had supposedly been kidnapped by demons and related his adventures which no-one believed, on his return. *Ustura* (perhaps from the Latin *historia*) refers, according to the Tunisian al-Marzuqi, to all types of popular tales. The anthology by Attal et al. also has several folktales.

10. Albert Memmi, for example, has often described the formative influence for him which these tales had. See "Le Personnage de Jeha dans la littérature orale des arabes et des juifs," (Jerusalem: Ben Zvi Institute, 1973), p. 1.

11. See Fhérid Ghazi, *Le Roman et la nouvelle en Tunisie* (Tunis: Maison tunisienne de l'édition, 1970), and R. C. Ostle, "Mahmud al'Mas'adi and Tunisia's 'Lost Generation,'" *Journal of Arabic Literature* 8 (1977), pp. 153–54.

12. Two stories would be exceptions: Rebbi Gagou's dream of David's adventure in "Le Miracle," and the traditional tale embedded in "Conte de Pâques" and attributed to the character Kiki.

13. Such accounts can be found in Attal et al., esp. Lucie-Paul Marguerite, "Le Quartier juif à Tunis," pp. 67–75, and Pierre Hubac, "Voyage au fonds de la Hara,"

pp. 116–121. Albert Memmi has continued the tradition for Tunis in "Le Royaume des pauvres, " *Juifs et arabes*, 1974; *Jews and Arabs* tr. Eleanor Levieux (Chicago: O'Hara, 1975). See also André Chouraqui, *Histoire des Juifs d'Afrique du Nord* (Monaco: Du Rocher, 1998); *Between East and West: A History of the Jews of North Africa* tr. Michael Bernet (Philadelphia: JPS, 1968), pp. 235–242.

14. "Les oukalas-si vous l'ignorez-sont les palais de la vieille *Hara*. Amas de petits cubes sans fenêtres encadrant un vaste patio sur quoi ils prennent jour. Chacun est occupé par une famille, souvent de plus de huit personnes. Dieu béni avec largesse les mariages juifs. A tous, le patio dispense lumière crue, eau fangeuse, air alourdi de l'odeur des détritus amoncelés. Il fait nuit, une belle nuit de commencement d'automne. Le patio obscure a de larges taches claires. Portes ouvertes, rideau tiré, chaque chambre verse sa traînée jaunâtre. Elles font comme un tapis de rêve où, tout a l'heure, 'Elie le *Nabi* posera les pieds.' Elles sont des mains qui se joignent pour se souhaiter un fraternal *chalom*." Ryvel, p. 33. The reference to Elijah's arrival at the beginning of the Sabbath seems to imply his role in solving difficulties, but more particularly in providing for and defending poor people. In areas influenced by Islam, his name is inscribed on amulets, and folk beliefs and practical Kabbalah would describe how to bring about a meeting with him in dreams.

15. In fact, a later anthropological study, Paul Sebag, *La Hara de Tunis: L'Évolution d'un ghetto nord-africain* (Paris: Presses universitaires de France, 1959), e.g., p. 76, 81, 82, cited superstitions and customs from Ryvel, the writer of fiction.

16. "Dans le déroulement de la bande où s'inscrit sa vie pure, une tache noire capte son regard. La tache grandit, s'étend, absorbe l'horizon de sa vue: elle a péché et voici le châtiment, elle va mourir." (p. 111). Note the cinematic image for the imagination. The cinema is considered a spatial medium par excellence. Here it is used to show time standing still. The possibilities of the cinema must have captured Ryvel's imagination as a relatively recent introduction in Tunisia. Pinhas' reading aloud of the Book of Jonah punctuates his wife's pain and emphasizes the theme of mother and child passing through peril to safety. "L'Eternel a pardonné." (p. 113).

17. Ryvel, p. 174. The secular books they refer to may be French literature, or the popular literature in Judeo-Arabic. See on the latter Eusèbe Vassel, "La Littérature populaire des israélites tunisiens," *Revue Tunisienne* 11 (1904), 273–288, 371–390, 495–507.

18. As the director of Alliance schools in Tunisia, he integrated them into the state system, but at the same time increased the study of Hebrew.

19. In Ryvel's later *Les Lumières* (cit.) a Zionist orientation is much clearer. Each tale corresponds to a holiday. In the story for Passover (pp. 53–60) a grandfather tells of his desire to go to Palestine, where he is sure the elderly can make a contribution. This story and the one for Rosh Hashanah, describing a nightmare of massacre—"Selihoth rouges" (pp. 69–73)—show a belief that the situation of Jews in an Arab land, despite French rule, was still basically insecure. The stories hint at the ideological debates which must have been going on within Maghrebian Jewish communities in the 1930s. See e.g., Chouraqui, 1968, pp. 258–259.

20. Marco Koskas *Balace Bounel* (Paris; Ramsay, 1979). *Balace Bounel* received reviews uniformly full of praise on its publication and won the *Prix du Premier*

Roman. See "La Presse en parle," *Livres hebdo* No. 7, Oct. 16, 1979, p. 79; Bertrand Poirot-Delpech, "Parias," [Pariahs] *Le Monde des livres,* Sept. 21, 1979, p. 22. Koskas has authored some twenty books and has also followed a career as a private detective, some of his books being crime novels. His most recent book is *Sentimental oxymore* (San Bernadino: Createspace/Galligrassud, 2021), originally published in forty-three episodes on Facebook.

21. Poirot-Delpech describes the technique: "Inverted commas having been abolished, speech and narrative mix together. A collective being incarnates the mingled biographies. The orderly French garden of syntax conceived under our skies is becoming a sort of oriental maze. We no longer know who is speaking, or about what."

22. The phrase "Qui se souvient de . . . " recalls the title of one of the best Maghrebin novels, Mohammed Dib's *Qui se souvient de la mer* (Paris: Seuil, 1962). Dib's novel is likewise a spatial novel, enacting the collapse of the colonial structure and birth of a new collective entity, the Algerian nation.

23. "Pourvu que ce soit un fils—Où ça en est tata Rachel?—ça commence mon fils—j'y vais tata Rachel—vas-y mon fils. et déjà dans la rue et déjà place de France et deja au souk et deja à la plage, tata Rachel a ses douleurs, tata Rachel a ses douleurs, le feu follet, l'étoile filante, Mach 2 comme on dira longtemps après sans parler de lui, car qui se souvient de Victor qui a peut-être cent ans aujourd'hui."

24. Victor would "hide under a blanket to eat and smoke on Yom Kippur, God couldn't see him, specially as he made sure to close the shutters and block up all the chinks of light" (p. 16). The book is preceded by a quotation from Camus' essay "L'Été à Alger" [Summer in Algiers] in *Noces* [Nuptials], a series of vignettes which represent life in a North African town as a kind of pagan paradise or classical idyll. Camus describes the population of Algiers with a certain admiration: "This race is indifferent to the spirit. It has a cult of and admiration for the body. . . . Everything that people do here shows a distaste for stability and an unconcern for the future. People are in a hurry to get on with living." *Noces: Les Essais XXXIX* 1938 (Paris: Gallimard, 1950), pp. 64–65.

25. E.g., Bonan imports shoes made in France, ingeniously selling them in threes so that customers will have a spare shoe: "Clutching on to the ramshackle cart, the children asked please Bonan what's it mean this madin-france that you throw at us with everything—idiot it's the brand—oh, the brand how's it written?—it's two words, ignoramus, they're two people in business together, Madin and France, they started from nothing, just like me, he thought. . . . " "Agrippés à la carriole, les enfants questionnaient s'il-te-plait Bonan qu'est-ce-que ça veut dire ce madin-france que tu nous sors pour chaque article—ah, c'est la marque, et ça s'écrit comment?—en deux mots, ignorant, ceux sont deux associés, Madin-France, ils sont partis de rien, comme moi, il pensait" (p. 16).

26. "Autant d'événements que Victor enchevêtrait de telle sorte qu'il du sollicter les pleureuses dont l'une pensait que l'électricité était arrivée avant le baptême des rues, contredite par une autre qui était sûre que l'électricité était arrivé après puisque son fils Haïm était tombé dans le puits le jour du baptême des rues—mais non, Fortunée, Haïm est tombé dans le puits avant qu'ils ne tracent la route pour aller à Tunis—et les pleureuses ne pleuraient plus. . . . " (pp. 18–19).

27. "les matrons au rez-de-chaussée, empêtrées les unes dans les autres, entre la première et la troisième marche de l'escalier, reparé juste après la chute du beau-frère par l'architecte lui-même qui se tenait la tête entre les mains en regardant monter les femmes obèses au souffle si puissant que la voix de Victor–laissez-moi passer–était à peine perceptible, noyée dans les râles et les conseils qu'elles se prodigaient—retient-toi à la rampe, Sarah, car je n'ai plus de force—alors arrête-toi et donne-moi la main, que je l'atteigne cette peste de rampe—non, ne lui donne pas la main ou je tombe sur Marie—si tu tombes sur moi, je meurs et je laisse sept enfants dans la nudité et le besoin" (p. 23).

28. A different situation emerges in Attal et al., *Regards*. Isaac Mamou, a well-known personality of Nabeul, founded a Zionist organization there, translated Hebrew novels into Judeo-Arabic, and wrote about the Nazi occupation and Allied liberation of the town (pp. 190–193). The difference may be due to *Balace Bounel*'s family centered universe.

29. "Cette femme est en ordre mais elle se moque de nous . . . rira bien qui rira le dernier."

30. An insurmountable barrier separates the future (which has become the present) from the past: "un dernier rempart entre eux, entre nous, entre vous" (p. 167).

31. "La première maison à murer, celle de Mardochée Haddad, tailleur, soixante-huit ans à ce jour si il est encore en vie, père de neuf enfants, brique ciment, . . . Gabriel Chiche brique ciment brique ciment brique brique, André Serror brique ciment, Gaston Temmam brique ciment," (p. 235). Note the comma that ends this quotation.

32. Jacques Berque et al., *De l'impérialisme à la decolonization* [From Imperialism to Decolonization] (Paris: Minuit, 1965).

Chapter 3

The End of Symbiosis

Sephardic Novelists and the Sudden Ruptures of History

The Golden Age of Muslim Spain, the influence Sephardim held in Spanish Christian courts, the heartfelt patriotism of Italian Jews before Fascism and the Holocaust, the age-long rootedness of Jews in Middle Eastern countries before their expulsion from Muslim lands ... we know the end of these stories now, and what awaited the Sephardim whose assumptions of symbiosis[1] or *convivencia*[2] were each time abruptly and violently shattered as they scattered into exile. The sixteenth century Hebrew narrative *Emeq Habaka* [Vale of Tears][3] by Yosef Ha-Kohen, lamenting the sufferings of the Jews through the centuries, details one expulsion after another, down to his own days, and unfortunately not only catalogued history but also foreshadowed even more forced migrations, up to modern times. This chapter views, through the lens of novelists, the historical expulsion from Spain as a prefiguring of the modern persecution and expulsion during the Holocaust period (as it affected Italian Jews and the Maghrebian Jews), of Arab nationalism as it affected the Jews of North Africa (here, Tunisia) and the Middle East (here, specifically, Iraq). The historian Jane Gerber has brought into focus the immensity of the suffering that Jews endured during and following the expulsion from Spain. The Jewish refugees who left in 1492 and succeeded in avoiding death at sea and depredations by pirates, arrived in Morocco only to be excluded from the cities, setting up shanty towns subject to fire, disease, starvation, and attack. It took several generations for them to be integrated. Their conditions were probably worse than those of the most abject refugees of today. Even the local Jewish communities opposed their entry in both Fez and Rome because they feared the growth of antisemitism. In more recent times, the post-war expulsion of Jews from Muslim lands has been little noticed but generated both financial and emotional suffering, sometimes physical suffering too. As just one example, the last Jews left Libya in 1967, airlifted to Rome after some outright murders and threats to the lives of many Jews, traumatized, carrying the smallest of personal effects, their real estate and other possessions expropriated, many of them stateless. The end of Jewish life in Libya came after over two thousand years. Even Jewish cemeteries have been destroyed, and there is an effort now to create 'virtual cemeteries' with lists of the names of the dead who were buried in Libya and whose graves cannot be visited, among other reasons because they no longer exist. I do not intend to examine this vast historical tragedy across the Middle East in an analytical way myself, but rather review novelistic reactions and approaches to history, and see whether and how far modern Sephardic novelists themselves draw parallels with past events.

Didier Nebot, now of France, but of Algerian origin, brings us a novel, *Le Chemin de l'exil* [The Road to Exile], describing several generations of a Spanish Jewish family from Toledo, their sufferings in Spain due to persecution, forced conversion and the inquisition, and the last surviving Jewish descendant's flight to Algeria. It tells of two families, one of which converts to Christianity and attempts to lead a new life in Spain, and the other family, faithful to Judaism, whose story is continued in the surviving protagonist's harrowing journey to North Africa. This prize-winning novel was published in 1992, the year when the Quincentenary of the expulsion from Spain was widely commemorated. The author and his own family experienced, thirty years before, in 1962, another semi-forced migration from the land of his forebears, Algeria, to France.[4] Nebot is the author of nine novels, mostly relating to the North African Jewish heritage, and the director of a cultural organization, MORIAL, which preserves on the internet memories of Jewish life in Algeria.

To turn briefly to Italy, the land that provided an insecure refuge for Yosef Ha-Kohen, our medieval author, we read in Giorgio Bassani's *Il Giardino dei Finzi-Contini* (1962) [*The Garden of the Finzi-Continis*], of a self-contained garden haven provided by the estate of the wealthiest Jewish family for the young Jews of Ferrara. Though they would happily have played tennis there forever, preoccupied by their own relationships with each other, the Fascists and Nazis had other plans for them and ultimately this aristocratic family was annihilated in the Holocaust, together with many of their fellow Jews, no matter how Italian they felt themselves to be. This brilliantly realized novel dwells in the moment of its doomed protagonists, without the historical references of a Didier Nebot, author of *Le Chemin de l'exil* referred to above. I include Bassani's novel in deference to its quality as an accomplished and influential novel, even though it is in Italian. Bassani put much store in communicating his message to other Europeans, and it is well-known in the Francophone world as well.[5]

Turning now to the Middle East, Naim Kattan of Iraq, in *Adieu Babylone* [*Farewell Babylon*], chronicles the breakdown of traditional Iraqi Jewish life in the oldest diaspora, the Babylonian center from which Spanish Jewry had drawn its spiritual sustenance a millennium ago. Iraq had achieved its independence in 1932, and a few years after the 1941 *farhud* (Iraqi pogrom) the Jews of Iraq scattered, mostly moving to Israel, Iran, or Britain. Others, who had had a French education, emigrated to Paris or, in Kattan's case, Canada. Though it constituted one of the most ancient, largest and well integrated Jewish communities in the Middle East, some members even working for Iraqi independence, Iraqi Jews were evicted from their ancestral home with notorious hangings and suffering along the way. Naim Kattan, in a poignant autobiographical narrative, captures the time just preceding this moment.

Similarly, Jewish intellectuals in Tunisia, such as Albert Memmi, worked for independence for their native country. Memmi's novel, *La Statue de sel* [*Pillar of Salt*] (1953) captured a young Jewish intellectual's discovery that there would be no room for him in an independent, officially Muslim state of Tunisia. By 1956, Memmi himself had moved to France. The much younger Marco Koskas, who left Tunisia with the mass exodus in the early 1960s, shows us in *Balace Bounel* [*Bounel's Balace*] an entire community packing up its tents, or rather boarding up its houses, the pain of departure rose-tinted and blurred through his humorous lens (as we saw also in Chapter 2).

Finally, in a poetic and Proustian personal memoir, André Aciman (*Out of Egypt*, 1994) evokes the original exodus from Egypt, as his family reluctantly prepares for their own flight out of Egypt to Paris, under the pressures of Nasser's Arab nationalism. This highly literary memoir evokes not only the personal memories of a fifteen-year-old, but also the thoughts and motives of his grandparents, parents, aunts and uncles, so that we have a sense of a whole tribe uprooted and in motion.

If "to depart is to die a little," the characters in these fictions and memoirs, not to mention their authors, all left a piece of themselves behind in these involuntary departures. Forced out by modern history and politics, they evoke other expulsions, those of their ancestors, in earlier centuries.

Another refuge for the Jews of Iberia after their expulsion had been the Italian principalities and states.[6] Our medieval doctor, Yosef Ha-Kohen (whose parents had left Spain in 1492 just before his birth), was born in Avignon and spent much of his life in the region of Genoa. As permission was alternately granted and rescinded for Jews to reside there, Ha-Kohen led a migratory life.

One of the most flourishing Jewish communities of Italy was the north-eastern dukedom of Ferrara, which provided, under hospitable rulers, the dukes of Este, a more stable refuge for Jews than the Republic of Genoa.

Over the century following 1492, many *conversos* managed to leave Iberia and make their way, often via Holland, to Italy. There some managed to revert to Judaism or proceed further to the Ottoman Empire, particularly Salonika and Istanbul. Ferrara was the home of eminent Jews such as the descendants of Don Isaac Abravanel, and the temporary home of Doña Gracia Mendes, *la señora,* who rescued many other secret Jews and enabled their migration eastwards. In the early sixteenth century, Ferrara must have represented liberty for Jews, and it is thus one irony among many that Bassani's text, perhaps the most well-known Italian novel of the Holocaust, is set in Ferrara.[7]

Until the 1930s, Ferrara's Jews were a well-rooted and comfortable community. As in the rest of Italy, Jews had fought alongside other Italians for Italian unity and independence, and in the First World War, many Italian Jews had made great sacrifices for their country. The characters in this novel, based loosely on an actual family of a different but similar name, had no doubt that they were Italian and had no other national allegiance. Through Bassani's discreet and restrained way of writing, we read the dramas of young people's love affairs and passions in the forefront of their minds, while we also perceive the grinding forces of history of which they themselves are hardly aware, or to which they are perhaps indifferent. The first person narrator focuses on his love for Micòl, the daughter of Professor Ermanno Finzi-Contini, and is seemingly divided from her by class differences and family ideologies. Micòl, however, rejects him not because of class but because they are, if anything, too alike, more like brother and sister, and thus feels no passion for him. They are more than fellow Jews, they are fellow Sephardim: "That we were Jews, nevertheless, . . . counted fairly little in our case . . . the existence of that further intimacy . . . derived from the fact that our two families, not through choice, but thanks to a tradition older than any possible memory, belonged to the same religious rite, or rather to the same 'school' [Italian *scola,* i.e., the Levantine synagogue]" (p. 22). Micòl, though, may be attracted to a non-Jewish suitor, as the narrator hypothesizes at the end of the novel. The different classes of Jews are thrown together by being expelled from the local tennis club after the 1938 racial laws, and so play tennis together (and with occasional non-Jewish friends) on the private tennis court behind the high walls of the Finzi-Contini garden, which is actually a small private park. The professor, maintaining the illusion that the Finzi-Contini household is largely self-sufficient, independent of the outside world, is proud of rising to the occasion by resurfacing his private tennis court during this emergency brought about by the racial laws, but cannot imagine the much greater cataclysm awaiting Italian Jewry in 1943. As things turn out, the non-Jewish friend is sent to the Russian Front in 1941, whence he never returns, and the entire Finzi-Contini family is arrested by the Fascists in 1943 and shipped to Nazi death camps. The narrator alone is left to analyze and mourn, with the moral ambiguity of the survivor. We are given no hint in the novel as to how the narrator and possibly his family survive the later period of persecution from 1943 to 1945. Many Italian Jews left the towns where they were known to be Jews and moved to the anonymity of large cities such as Rome, changing their names and living as non-Jews.[8] This archetypal Sephardic novel of trauma and disruption sets a high standard against which to measure other novels.

Naïm Kattan, of Iraq, also represents imaginatively a drastic and unlooked-for rupture, not on the scale of the destruction of one-fifth of Italian Jewry in the Holocaust, but searing in other ways. The history of Iraqi or Babylonian Jewry reaches far back beyond Spain itself: the Golden Age of Jewish literature in Spain could not have taken place without the connections through rabbinic *responsae* and the emigration of among others a key poet, Dunash ben Labrat, connecting Spain with the scholarly, literary, religious and philosophical sources of Jewish thought as the Caliphate of Baghdad gradually ceded supremacy to the Caliphate of Cordoba. Daniel Elazar, as we have seen in the Introduction, identifies the roots of Sephardic culture in Babylon rather than in Iberia. A thousand years later, Sephardic cultures around the Mediterranean and the Middle East still recognized the inspiration of the Babylonian period. Thus in Iraq/Babylon it took a combination of a pro-German government during the war, a *farhud* or pogrom in 1941 in the interregnum before British administration, the rise of Arab nationalism and establishment of a fully independent Arab state, and the pull of Zionism and western countries, to begin dismantling this ancient, prestigious Jewish community. Even today, after nearly a century of Arab rule and hostility toward Israel, vestiges remain of Jewish life in Iraq, though the last Jews have left.[9]

Through his autobiographical novel, *Adieu Babylone* (1975) [Farewell, Babylon][10] Kattan captures the moment when Iraqi Jews became aware that they had no future in Iraq. His protagonist is a young student active in Jewish-Muslim intellectual circles in the mid-1940s, after the *farhud* but before Israel's independence. Like many Iraqi Jewish intellectuals, he speaks Arabic and is active in Arabic literary circles.[11] He is aware that his spoken Arabic identifies him as Jewish, and the main character and his Jewish friends even emphasize their accent. He tries to maintain friendships with Iraqi Arabs and brings his Arab friends home. But there is a feeling of change in the air: his Jewish friends are planning to go to university overseas, while the Muslim friends are going overseas temporarily to study, in order to come back as the future cadres of their country. An Assyrian consular official, a sympathizer and supporter, makes this clear:

> France wants to retain its influence in the Middle East. She has to train allies to defend her in the future. You're a Jew. You're going to study in France. You'll be successful and you won't come back. A Muslim, the son of a minister or a senior official, wouldn't have that choice. He would have to come home. He would spend most of his time in Paris in cafés or chasing girls, but when he came home he would have influence in his own milieu. Out of gratitude, he would use that influence to defend the interests of France. (p. 212)[12]

The protagonist and his Arab friends nevertheless make sincere plans to meet up once they arrive in London or Paris.

The implication is that, much as the Jews regret it, the national destinies of the Iraqi Arabs and Iraqi Jews are about to tear them apart. In fact, they were never to meet again, as the decades of Ba'athist ideology and the Arab-Israeli conflict would intervene.[13] Surely the *farhud* had already delivered a brutal message to the Jews: that they were not welcome in the new Iraq. But no doubt the message was slow to be accepted given the Jewish community's ancient rootedness in the country: there may have been incurable optimists who considered the *farhud* the last gasp of the old *dhimmi* order giving way to a newer, better society, rather than a harbinger of the new one that would exclude Jews. The protagonist loves the Arabic language, spends a summer learning by heart the writings of the pre-Islamic Arab poets, contributes to Iraqi Arabic journals and newspapers, and tells us several times that Jews know Arabic better than the Iraqi Arabs themselves. When as a high school student (at an Alliance school), his class visits the ruins of Babylon, he is uninterested in the history teacher's presentation but deeply affected by his English teacher's speech:

> Only the Jews can feel the upheaval of a living past under these piles of stones, he told us. Nothing ties the Arabs to Babylon. When they conquered it, we were already there. We are the true natives. We came here as captives, the slaves of Nebuchadnezzar. But we triumphed over defeat. On this ground we wrote the Talmud. The descendants of captives, the sons of slaves were great scholars, great philosophers. Are we worthy of our ancestors? he exclaimed. (p. 79)[14]

The implication is that there should always be a Jewish presence in Iraq, in honor of the glorious achievements of Jewish scholarship there. A group of idealistic young Jews, including the protagonist, are thus determined to work, together with their Arab friends, for the future of the new independent state of Iraq. But the roles reserved for them seem to be very few. They discover that the only school at the university that will allow Jews to attend is the faculty of law. The protagonist discusses his closest Jewish friend's gradual change of heart, writing that "despite Nessim's declarations about our responsibility for building a new and independent Iraq, it was obvious that he only half believed it" (p. 122). On the other hand, "he did not dare believe in the reality of the foreign countries that were calling to him" (p. 123).[15] The narrator/protagonist speaks of "le vin de l'Occident" (p. 132) ("the wine of the West," p. 124), and his own encounter with a charismatic French school examiner who suggests that he might apply for a scholarship. The liberty that women have in the West to talk freely with men is a recurring motif. The protagonist does apply for a scholarship from the French government to study in France and actually wins it. As his bus pulls out of Baghdad, bound for Beirut where he will take a ferry boat, barking dogs follow the bus, but cannot inspire fear. Tears stream down his face, and Iraq will always have a place in his heart, but he has just told Nissim not to wait too long before he leaves too. The description of the harmless (previously threatening) dogs underlines perhaps the most basic of all the reasons why a Jew would leave an Arab country: to leave behind the relationship of dhimmitude and all the emotions and behaviors it entailed: inferiority, dissembling, and above all fear.[16]

The many and complex emotions of the Jews forced to leave Iraq, the toll it took in so many areas of their lives, still have repercussions today for their descendants.[17]

Two Jewish novelists from Tunisia, Albert Memmi and Marco Koskas, also deal with the slow but agonizing process of uprooting. Memmi, whose work we have previously encountered, saw his first novel, *La Statue de sel* [Pillar of Salt] (1953),[18] received with acclaim as one of the first by a new generation of North African writers (as distinguished from French writers discussing North Africa). In several respects it was a revolutionary novel. First, as one of the earliest successful literary statements in French by an indigenous North African, it was a psychological trailblazer; second, it was a confessional novel, dealing with aspects of life which traditional circles would have preferred to be kept within the community; third, it showed the evolution of colonized society toward political independence. Poised on the threshold of a new era full of possibilities, how did Memmi's novel portray the chance for survival or transformation of the old Jewish-Arab symbiosis in a new age of political independence? In this novel, Memmi was developing his favored technique of positing an idea, then examining its consequences in a situation of genuine conflict. The idea was that a Tunisian Jew could join the nationalist movement and feel completely at home in it, accepted by the others as fully one of them. He puts the idea to a hypothetical test, and the results are not encouraging. He first describes his autobiographical main character, Mordechai,[19] participating in an incipient nationalist movement:

> There were not many of us at these secret meetings, and we felt strongly even if we had no very definite ideology. But I always left this Arab house filled with warmth and a feeling of generosity. . . . I smiled at the little street vendors and

was amiable to the ticket collector in the streetcar; when two women began to argue, I sided with the Moslem one. But the vendors did not understand my smiles, the ticket collector hardly returned my politeness, and the Moslem women formed such a solid bloc in their opposition to the Jewess that I ended up feeling sorry for her as the victim. . . . Our success depended on our work and patience and on time.

After the pogrom, however, as soon as it was again possible to move around, Ben Smaan came to see me. We went for a long walk all around the old ramparts, with me slowing my impatient gait to keep pace with his small unsteady steps. He talked a lot, perhaps to hide his own embarrassment and emotion. . . . He had worried about my personal safety but even more, he admitted, about what I might think. . . . He was sure that I had realized that it had all been cooked up. . . . It was more than ever necessary to be united. (pp. 267–69)[20]

Mordechai answers automatically, but he is thinking of his friend's death and Ben Smaan's lack of genuine sympathy:

Bissor was dead . . . no amount of research into responsibilities would ever bring him back to life. Ben Smaan was right: one had to educate the mob [showing it that it was being manipulated]. . . . But I was tired and the results were too far off. (p. 268)

The narrator then describes how he began to be drawn to the Jewish national movement, just as the war began.

Though this scene is somewhat melodramatic, Memmi in this autobiographical novel is pushing to their conclusions the logical possibilities of the situation in which he found himself. It is interesting that a pogrom did not actually take place during Memmi's youth in Tunis, though the 1930s saw rioting against Jews in some provincial towns.[21] Thus this imaginary event and scene reflect traditional insecurities and an ultimately pessimistic view of the possibilities for Jews and Arabs to live together in the new age, despite apparent goodwill on the part of some on both sides. The text quoted above, though, implies embarrassment rather than genuine sympathy on the part of the Muslim activist. Memmi himself lived in Tunisia for several post-war years. In Tunis he worked as a teacher, opened an institute of psychology, and continued to be caught up in the fervor of the Tunisian nationalist movement, helping to found a weekly magazine dedicated to the "national struggle." Memmi gives only hints about his reasons for leaving in 1956, which may be more personal and private rather than ideological, and he has maintained good relations with Tunisia.[22] In 1984 he was awarded the honor of membership in the Order of the Tunisian Republic and, earlier (1953), the prestigious literary *Prix de Carthage*.[23] In his essay *Jews and Arabs* (1974) he describes himself as an 'Arab Jew' in culture, referring to the unique emotional appeal of music, scents, foods and textures from his childhood.[24] It must not be forgotten that Memmi was the equal of the Martiniquan writer and philosopher Frantz Fanon (1925–1961) in awareness of the necessity of converting colonized man into independent man. His books *The Colonizer and the Colonized* (1957) and *Dominated Man* (1968)[25] describe the psychological process of the individual's liberation from colonial bondage. Memmi portrays Jews as having one foot in each situation, that of the colonizer and that of the colonized.

Memmi's personal relations with the Muslim majority of his country of origin are unusual. As mentioned earlier, most North African Jews assumed that independence meant that they too had to make a radical break with the past. Marco Koskas' lyrical novel, *Balace Bounel*[26] (which we discussed in depth in Chapter 2) hints at the sadness implicit in the end of an ancient provincial Jewish community. The parochial universe of Koskas' characters is as shaky as the house which his enthusiastic but over-ambitious architect built (the 'balace' of the title represents the Arabic-influenced pronunciation of the word 'palace' or villa).

Filtered through memory, the events of a generation earlier are evoked through a collective and also highly subjective memory. The distance—in terms of time, mentality, degree of traditionalism, language and geography—between then and now is what gives rise to Koskas' humor, and that makes *Balace Bounel* an entertaining book, albeit with an underlying sadness. Minor details of private, family history loom large, while what have been considered 'important' historical events are taken for granted, left in the background, perhaps understood only partially. In the departure scene at the port, an insurmountable barrier separates the future (which is becoming the present) from the past, a barrier between "those who are staying there behind the gray bars separating those who are leaving from those who are staying like one last rampart between them, between us, between you" (p. 167). In this way, this play with pronouns, Koskas portrays the tearing apart of communities—the Jewish community and within it Jewish families, and the tearing apart of the larger interfaith community of all Tunisians, Jews and Muslims.

When one considers these two Tunisian novels together, it is apparent that Memmi's novel achieves its effect through realism, while Koskas' novel uses lyrical techniques. The phrase "Qui se souvient de . . . " [Who remembers . . .] opening many of the reminiscences of Koskas' novel, evokes the title of the Algerian Mohammed Dib's novel, *Qui se souvient de la mer* [Who remembers the sea] (1962) dealing with the Algerian Revolution.[27] It also reminds us of a novel by a brother of Albert Memmi, Georges Memmi's *Qui se souvient du Café Rubens?* [Who remembers the Rubens Café?]. The Jewish novels evoke the classical *Ubi Sunt?* elegiac tone of nostalgia, while the Muslim writer Mohammed Dib portrays a society torn apart by violence and trying to remake itself in a new way. Whether realistic or lyrical, the Jewish novelists and their semi-fictional characters largely underwent an absolute rupture with their ancient and recent past.

The same can be said, with qualifications, about the fictionalized autobiography of exodus, André Aciman's *Out of Egypt*.[28] This work is only formally a memoir: the author's imagination recreates, 'remembers' family events far before his time, such as how his two grandmothers met each other, leading eventually to the first meeting of his parents, leading eventually to the birth of André, leading to what are, perhaps, his earliest memories of Jewish life in Alexandria, Egypt. Thus the text is more like an elaborately layered Proustian novel than a personal memoir. Aciman is, in fact, a professor of comparative literature with a strong interest in Proust, as evinced by his anthology, *The Proust Project*.[29] We may thus justify this inclusion, even though Aciman writes in English. Perhaps "hearing French in one's mind" might be an expanded definition of "francophone." Having left Alexandria for good as a teenager, the author visits some of his relatives who are now living in England and Venice, among other places, and finds them, though older, just as he remembers them, but more so. These colorful characters did not originate in Egypt but had moved there maybe a generation earlier from Italy, Turkey or Syria. Great Uncle Vili continues his posturing in the English countryside and has no patience for nostalgia. His professions have been "Soldier, Salesman, Swindler, Spy" and he is a "Turco-Italian-Anglophile-gentrified-Fascist Jew who had started his professional life peddling Turkish fezzes in Vienna and Berlin, and was to end it as the sole auctioneer of deposed King Farouk's property" (p. 7). His favorite phrase, delivered as an enigmatic challenge, is *"Siamo o non siamo?"* (Are we or aren't we?) The visiting great-nephew's agenda is to "speak to him of Alexandria, of time lost and lost worlds, of the end when the end came" (p. 3), and this indeed is the subject of Aciman's book. All that remains is this memoir, the old world having been as totally lost as Aunt Flora's silver cutlery, which was all she had managed to salvage when they were expelled, for over the subsequent years she spent living alone in Venice, she gradually mislaid the cutlery, piece by piece. One can imagine it coming to rest, slowly but surely, at the bottom of an odiferous Venetian canal.

From Morocco, to Egypt, to Iraq, Sephardim over the second half of the twentieth century were forced to flee their ancestral homes in Muslim lands, often taking with them little more than a suitcase and hardly any money, to start new lives on other continents, in totally different climes and cultures. That they successfully restarted their lives, from Israel to Europe to North and South America, without the aid of the United Nations or any refugee agency, except sometimes the Hebrew Immigrant Aid Society or equivalent organizations, is a tribute to them. Making comparisons would be beyond the scope of this book. My goal has simply been to describe how Sephardic writers themselves have portrayed the end of *convivencia* or symbiosis in aesthetic ways.

From Didier Nebot's imagining of the expulsion from Spain, perhaps an archetype for more recent expulsions, to Giorgio Bassani's portrayal of what must have seemed like the end of Jewish life in Italy during the Shoah, to Naim Kattan's farewell to Iraq, Albert Memmi's and Marco Koskas' departure from Tunisia, and André Aciman's reluctant leave-taking from Egypt, deep emotional pain is often masked under humor, but always present.

NOTES

1. The phrase "Jewish-Arab symbiosis" originated with S. D. Goitein, in *Jews and Arabs: Their Contacts through the Ages* (New York: Schocken, 1955), where he discusses their literary and linguistic contacts, and the fact that the two peoples underwent cultural renaissance at the same time. For contributions to this debate on the Middle East, see e.g., Bernard Lewis, "Muslims, Christians and Jews: The Dream of Coexistence," *New York Review of Books* 34:6 (March 26, 1992), pp. 48–52, and other works by Bernard Lewis, esp. *The Jews of Islam* 1984; rev. ed. (Princeton: Princeton University Press, 2014). Most works on the history of Jews in the Middle East include some reference to the issue. For a basic starting bibliography, see Daniel Elazar, *The Other Jews: The Sephardim Today* (New York: Basic Books, 1989), pp. 221–22. Jonathan Decter for example uses the term regarding the eleventh century: "Jewish migration out of Al-Andalus instigated a process of establishing Islamic Iberia as a place of memory that could be recalled as an unrecoverable ideal, as a social and cultural template to be recreated elsewhere, or as an experiment in Jewish-Islamic symbiosis that had failed." *Iberian Jewish Literature: Between al-Andalus and Christian Europe* (Bloomington: Indiana Univ. Press, 2007), p. 3.

2. There has been a long-standing debate among scholars of Spanish history as to whether the concept of *convivencia* among Christians, Jews, and Muslims in medieval Spain corresponded to any reality. After centuries of suppressing the contribution of Jews and Muslims to Spanish culture, the historians and philosophers of the Generation of 1898 began to revise that view. The modern historian Américo Castro coined the term *convivencia* in part to recognize the contributions of non-Christians to national culture, only to have it questioned by later scholars. As Benjamin Gampel states, "Recently there has been some reticence to utilize the concept of *convivencia* but there is no doubt that the term still occasions much resonance and is the point of departure for many of the reflections on medieval Iberian culture and society." See Benjamin Gampel, "Does Medieval Navarrese Jewry Salvage our Notion of Convivencia?" Paper presented at Univ. of Maryland conference, May 1991. For a continuing defense of the notion of *convivencia,* see e.g., Isidro Bango, *Remembering Sepharad: Jewish Culture in Medieval Spain* (Madrid: State Corporation for Spanish

Cultural Action Abroad, 2004); and my review of this book in *La Lettre Sépharade,* Eng. ed., 17 (April, 2004), pp. 8–10. See also María Rosa Menocal, *The Ornament of the World: How Muslims, Jews and Christians Created a Culture of Tolerance in Medieval Spain* (New York: Little, Brown, 2002).

3. *Emeq Habaka (*1560) was widely read and was circulated in Ladino translation. Yosef Ha-Kohen's life in itself was a series of tragedies and wanderings as a result of forced migrations in France and Italy. See Moshe Lazar, *Sefarad in My Heart: A Ladino Reader* (Lancaster, CA: Labyrinthos, 1999), pp. 525–538.

4. Life for Algerian Jews became extremely dangerous as they were accused by both sides, the French and the Algerians, of collaborating with the other side. This novel receives much fuller treatment in Chapter 6.

5. See Rosy Cupo, "Giorgio Bassani in Other Languages," n.d., https://www.newitalianbooks.it/giorgio-bassani-in-different-languages/. *Il Giardino* appeared in French as *Le Jardin des Finzi-Contini* with Gallimard in 1975. On the relation of the fictional Finzi-Contini family to real persons and events, see Marco Ansaldo, "La vera storia dei Finzi Contini," *La Repubblica,* June 13, 2008, http:ricercar.repubblica.it/repubblica/archivio/repubblica/2008/06/13/r2-la-vera-storia-dei-finzi-contini; Guido Fink, "Growing up Jewish in Ferrara: The Fiction of Giorgio Bassani, a Personal Recollection," *Judaism* (Summer-Fall: 2004); and my "In Search of the Garden of the Finzi-Continis, Finding the Courtyard of the Finzi-Magrinis," *Sephardic Horizons* 1:2 (Winter 2011). https://www.sephardichorizons.org/Volume1/Issue2/Articles_V1I2/TravelogueZ.html

6. On the modern history of the Jews of Italy, see e.g., Bernard Cooperman et al., ed., *The Jews of Italy Memory and Identity* (Bethesda, MD: University Press of Maryland, 2000), esp. contributions by Anna Bravo, Fabio Levi, Michele Sarfatti, and Liliana Picciotto Fargion; and David Myers et al., *Acculturation and its Discontents: The Italian Jewish Experience between Exclusion and Integration* (Toronto: Univ. of Toronto Press, 2008).

7. *Il Giardino dei Finzi-Contini* (Einaudi: 1962); tr. William Weaver *The Garden of the Finzi-Continis* 1977 (New York: MJF, 1983). The question often arises of whether the Italian Jews are Sephardim. Many, especially the Jews of Rome, trace their ancestry to the exiles brought from Palestine after the destruction of the Second Temple by the Romans, therefore co-dating the settlement of Jews in Spain. This is true, but the influence of exiles from Spain after 1492, and the large numbers who came over to Italy over the next century or so, had a great influence on Italian Jewry. If one takes the broader view of Sephardic identity as based on *nusach, halakha, minhag* (following Daniel Elazar), there is much in common. Other recent waves of Jewish immigrants to Italy have since complicated the issue (Ashkenazim, Persians, North Africans) even more. In Bassani's novel, though, the subject is two families of explicitly Sephardic origin, yet also very Italian, thus justifying its inclusion in our present study.

8. Bassani himself had joined the Resistance, was arrested then released, and moved to Rome under an assumed identity, to continue working with the Resistance. Others were protected by monks or nuns. In both cases, there was a risk of losing one's Jewish identity as the price of survival. See my interview with Marcella

Servi Siegal, "Interview with an Italian Jewish Holocaust Survivor," referred to in my *Jews in Southern Tuscany during the Holocaust: Ambiguous Refuge* (Lanham, MD: Lexington Books, 2021). Other writings by Bassani hint at more sinister reasons why some survivors were able to come back from the death camps: one of his stories in *Cinque storie di Ferrara*; *Five Stories of Ferrara* (New York, Harcourt Brace Jovanovich, 1971) "Una lapide in via Mazzini" describes a Jewish character who made his way back to Ferrara after the Holocaust, but instead of being emaciated like most victims, is immensely fat, suggesting some form of collaboration with the Nazis. He finds his name already engraved on the plaque commemorating those presumed dead and, despite his efforts to resettle, meets with rejection and eventually disappears again.

9. Scattered signs of a Jewish presence have been discovered by foreigners visiting Iraq. A Jewish archive stored in the basement of Saddam Hussein's intelligence service, Jewish books and Torah scrolls strewn around, or a rediscovered former synagogue, now turned into a mosque, were the subjects of media reports in 2003, when they were discovered, and 2013, when part of the Iraqi Jewish Archive went on display at the National Archives, Washington DC. There is a project to photograph such sites before they are totally obliterated. See e.g., Hershel Shanks, "Saddam's Jewish Archives," *Moment* 28:5 (Oct. 2003), pp. 44–49. This Jewish archive is supposedly still to be returned to Iraq.

10. Originally published as *Adieu, Babylone* (Montreal: Éditions La Presse, 1975); trans. Sheila Fischman, 2005; (London: Souvenir Press, 2007). I have used the French edition, Ottowa: Editions Lemeac, 1986.

11. Another, purely autobiographical work is Sasson Somekh's *Baghdad Yesterday: The Making of an Arab Jew* (Jerusalem: Ibis, 2008). Somekh was inspired by Arab poets in Baghdad before his departure, and in Israel became the *doyen* of Arabic literature studies. Another Iraqi Jewish writer of similar interests is professor of Arabic Shmuel Moreh. Thus, it was not unusual that Kattan was fluent in Arabic but rather typical of his circle and generation.

12. "La France veut conserver son influence dans le Moyen-Orient. Elle a besoin de former de futurs alliés qui la défenderaient. Toi, tu est Juif. Tu feras tes études en France.Tu réussiras et tu ne rentreras pas. Tu t'installeras en France ou tu iras ailleurs. Un Musulman, fils de ministre ou de haut fonctionnaire, n'aura pas le choix. Il devra rebrousser chemin. A Paris, il passera le plus clair de son temps dans les cafés, à courir les filles, mais en rentrant il jouira d'une grande influence dans son milieu. Par reconnaissance, il mettra cette influence au profit de la France bienfaitrice" (p. 230).

13. A poignant nonfiction work on the efforts of Iraqi Jews to support Iraqi nationalism, and their ultimate expulsion, is J. Daniel Khazoom et al., *No Way Back: The Journey of a Jew from Baghdad* (Sacramento: KOH Library, 2010); Sasson Somekh has a second volume, *Life after Baghdad: Memoirs of an Arab-Jew in Israel, 1950–2000* (Eastbourne: Sussex Academic Press. 2012).

14. "Les Juifs sont les seuls à pouvoir ressentir le surgissement d'un passé vivant sous ces amas de pierres," nous dit-il. "Rien ne relie les Arabes à Babylone. Quand ils en ont fait la conquête, nous y étions déjà installés. Les véritables indigènes, c'est nous. Nous sommes venus ici captifs, les esclaves de Nabuchodonosor. Mais

nous avons vaincu malgré notre défaite. Sur ce sol, nous avons rédigé le Talmud. Les descendants des captifs, les fils des esclaves furent de grands savants, de grands philosophes."—Sommes-nous dignes de nos ancêtres? s'écria-t-il (p. 78).

15. "Malgré ses affirmations sur notre responsabilité dans la construction d'un Irak nouveau et indépendant, il était désormais évident que Nessim n'y croyait qu'à moitié" (p. 130). On the other hand "il n'osait pas croire à la réalité des contrées étrangères donc il recevait l'appel" (p. 131).

16. In a more recent book, Kattan sheds more light on the substance of his first novel, *Adieu Babylone*. He writes that "Il fallait que je décrive non pas tant ce que je quittais que ce que je portais en me déplaçant. . . . Faisant le récit de mon enfance, je rendais compte des dernières années de la communauté juive de Bagdad. J'y expliquais comment mes ancêtres, prisonniers de Nabuchadnetsar, avaient résisté à leur manière à l'exil forcé, l'avaient vaincu en emportant le Livre. . . . Dans l'essai et le roman, j'ai peut-être suivi, inconsciemment et humblement, la voie tracée par mes ancêtres. Je me suis mis à la lecture du texte" (I had to describe not what I was leaving behind but what I was taking with me as I left. . . . In telling the story of my youth, I was rendering an account of the last years of the Jewish community of Baghdad. I was explaining how my ancestors, the prisoners of Nebuchadnezar, had in their way resisted forced exile, had overcome it by taking with them the Book. . . . In essay and novel, I have perhaps unconsciously and humbly followed the path laid out by my ancestors. I began to read the text.) Naim Kattan, *Ecrire le réel* (Montreal: Hurtubise, 2008), pp. 19–20.

17. These issues are effectively kept in the public eye today by organizations such as London-based Harif or U.S.-based JIMENA or SHINDC, which cast a spotlight on the sufferings of Middle Eastern Jews from other countries as well. See www.harif.org or www.jimena.org.

18. Albert Memmi, *La Statue de sel* 1953; rev.ed., pref. Albert Camus (Paris: Gallimard, 1966); trans. Edouard Roditi (New York, 1955; Boston: Beacon, 1992).

19. The Mordechai of the *Book of Esther* is a member of a threatened religious minority in the far-flung empire of Persia. This figure has much more in common with Memmi's cultural situation than any earlier biblical figure.

20. "Nous n'étions pas nombreux dans ces réunions clandestines et nos idées étaient fort vagues si nos sentiments étaient violents. Mais je sortais de cette maison arabe, plein de générosité, débordant de chaleur de cœur. La communion réalisée à dix personnes préfigurait la communion de la ville. Je souriais aux marchands de quatre saisons, faisais des politesses aux receveurs des tramways et dans les querelles entre femmes témoignais en faveur de la musulmane. Les marchands ne comprenaient pas mon sourire, le receveur répondait à peine à mes politesses, les musulmanes, négligeant mon secours, formaient un tel bloc contre la juive que je me sentais décourage, prenais en pitie la femme houspillé, . . . Le succès dépendait de notre travail, du temps, de notre patience. . . . Après le pogrome, aussitôt qu'il fut possible de circuler en ville, Ben Smaan est venu me voir. Nous avons fait un large tour le long des remparts, moi modérant mon impatience pour m'accorder à ses petits pas alourdis et cahotants. Il fut bavard, peut-être pour masquer son émotion et sa gêne et je fus presqu'muet, parce que je ne savais quoi dire. Il avait été inquiet au sujet de

ma personne, mais plus encore, m'avoua-t-il, au sujet de ce que j'aurais pu penser. Il s'excusait de ce doute. J'avais compris, il en était certain, qu'il s'agissait d'une provocation. Oui, je l'avais compris. Plus que jamais il fallait s'unir. . . . Bissor est mort; et j'ai sur les bras le mort de Bissor, dont je ne sais que faire. . . . La recherche de responsabilités ne ressuscitera pas Bissor. Ben Smaan avait raison: il fallait éduquer la foule, lui dévoiler les mystifications. . . . Mais je suis las et le résultat est si lointain" (pp. 216–217).

21. Pogroms occurred in Algeria in 1805, 1884, and 1897–98. In Tunisia there were anti-Jewish riots in 1917, 1932, and 1934. Probably Memmi had heard news of the 1941 events in Iraq, and murderous riots that occurred in Libya in 1945 and were again attempted in 1948 (*Encyc. Jud.*). For a general introduction to the situation in North Africa, see André Chouraqui, *Between East and West: A History of the Jews of North Africa* trans. Michael Bernet (Philadelphia: Jewish Publication Society, 1968; 1973).

22. These were possible in the case of Tunisia, but would not have been possible in the case of Iraq for Naim Kattan. In a short essay on Kattan, Memmi himself pointed out the different circumstances in which Jews left Tunisia and Iraq: "on leur a retiré leur passeport pour les empêcher même d'y revenir pour des vacances. Ils ont connu la peur physique, celle de la mort possible; nous, à peine . . . cependant . . . notre destinée historique fut objectivement la même. (They took away their passports so that they could not even return for vacations. They experienced physical fear, fear of possible death; we hardly did . . . nevertheless . . . our historical destiny was objectively the same.) Albert Memmi, "Naïm Kattan, mon semblable, mon frère," in Jacques Allard, ed., *Naïm Kattan: L'Ecrivain du passage* (Montreal: Hurtubise, 2002), pp. 91–94.

23. Other Tunisian Jews have specified why they themselves or their families left Tunisia. See e.g., Danielle David, "Identité perdue, identité retrouvée, identité," *CELAAN* 7: 1&2 (Spring 2009), pp. 122–134, esp. 127–29, detailing the disappointment of Jewish government employees, Tunisian nationals born in Tunisia yet consistently passed over in favor of Muslims when it came to promotions, and their sense of alienation and of being excluded from the new nation-state. Memmi was well aware of the many facets of alienation and the gradual or sudden realization of exclusion. Memmi seems to have stayed on in Tunisia for about two years after independence. In *La Terre intérieure: Entretiens avec Victor Malka* (Paris: Gallimard, 1976) he gave an external reason and a purely personal one for leaving Tunisia: "What I felt so strongly . . . simultaneously that the cause of Tunisia was a just one, and that all non-Muslim minorities would no longer have a place there. I was also working on *The Coloniser and the Colonised* and what I had seen intuitively became clearer and more coherent: a young nation was being born, was affirming itself, and for a certain time was going to expel from its life everything that wasn't precisely itself. . . . Why wouldn't I turn the page? It was even necessary for me to turn the page, in order to go forward. The proof is that I made a book out of it; that is a constant proof for me, a book ends, summarizes, and closes something. Thus I finished *The Colonizer and the Colonized* in Paris" ("Ce que je sentais si fortement . . . à la fois que la cause de la Tunisie était juste et que tous les minoritaires non musulmans

n'y auraient plus leur place. Je travaillais d'ailleurs sur le *Portrait du colonisé* et ce que j'avais vu intuitivement devenait plus clair, plus cohérent: une jeune nation naissait, s'affirmait et pour un temps allait expulser de sa vie tout ce qui n'était pas exactement elle-même. . . . Pourquoi n'aurais-je pas tourné la page? Il m'était même nécessaire de la tourner, pour avancer. La preuve en est que j'en ai fait un livre; c'est une preuve constante chez moi; un livre termine, résume et clôt quelque chose. C'est ainsi que j'achevai à Paris le *Portrait du colonisé suivi du Portrait du colonisateur.*") (pp. 135–36, 140). One study of his work, by Guy Dugas, is entitled *Albert Memmi: Ecrivain de la déchirure* (Sherbrooke: Naaman, 1984). The bibliography on Memmi's extensive work is voluminous: for bibliography prior to the mid-1980s, see my *Albert Memmi* (Philadelphia: CELFAN Edition Monographs, 1987); for 1985–2000, see Guy Dugas, *Albert Memmi: Du Malheur d'être juif au bonheur sépharade* (Paris: Alliance Israélite Universelle, 2001). For later publications, see Jonathan Judaken et al., *An Albert Memmi Reader* (Lincoln: University of Nebraska Press, 2021).

24. *Juifs et arabes* (Paris: Gallimard, 1974); *Jews and Arabs* trans. Eleanor Levieux (Chicago, J.P. O'Hara, 1975), esp. pp. 19–29.

25. *Portrait du colonisé précède du Portrait du colonisateur,* pref. Jean-Paul Sartre (Paris: Payot, 1973) trans. Howard Greenfield, *The Colonizer and the Colonized* 1965 (Boston: Beacon Press, 1967); *L'Homme dominé* (1968; Paris: Payot, 1973); trans. Eleanor Levieux, *Dominated Man: Notes Towards a Portrait* (New York: Orion, 1968).

26. Marco Koskas, *Balace Bounel* (Paris, Ramses, 1979). The novel won the *Prix du premier roman* in France, in 1979. I interviewed Koskas in Paris in November 1987 and he described how the novel achieved some notoriety in the Tunisian Jewish community due to its "washing our dirty linen in public," an understandable reaction from a traditional community. Koskas has subsequently followed a career as a private detective as well as a writer. The two careers came together after an unfortunate episode in Paris in which he was unjustly arrested, imprisoned, and kept in solitary confinement following 9/11. He describes this experience in his memoir *Avous d'abord* (Paris: Table Ronde, 2007).

27. For a comparison, see my article "Responses to North African Independence in the Novels of Dib, Memmi and Koskas: The End of Muslim-Jewish Symbiosis?" *Middle East Review* 20:2 (Winter 1988), pp. 33–40.

28. André Aciman, *Out of Egypt: A Memoir* (New York: Farrar, Straus/Picador, 1994).

29. André Aciman, ed., *The Proust Project* (New York: Strauss and Giroux, 2004), in which twenty-eight writers are invited to discuss what Proust means to them, and Aciman adds his own essay.

Chapter 4

Migratory Writing by Bensoussan (Algeria/France), Bouganim (Morocco/Israel), Kayat (Tunisia/Sweden)

For the Sephardim of the Maghreb, or North Africa, whose ancient communities were dispersed during the 1950s and 1960s to Israel, Europe and North America, the experience of migration took place under prosaic and difficult conditions, and at the time their odyssey went unsung.[1] Some succeeded in reintegrating communities based on their old geographical ties, while others did not. However, after a quasi-silence of some twenty-five years, young writers began to assess the cultural and psychological impact of the mass emigration of these communities. Though the "magic carpet" may be a useful device for Oriental storytellers, in real life transitions are never painless, and problems of displacement due to the experience of migration cannot be draped over by literary imagery. The uprooting of North African Jewry has since the 1980s been producing an imaginative literature which reflects the cultural contradictions of migration. How drastic these have been, how painful in so many ways for the immigrants, is discussed in this and other chapters. Memories painful and sweet merge with despair and hope, while confidence in the mastery of the French language meets a sudden realization that language is not enough:[2] to truly belong, to become French, was something Middle Eastern and North African Sephardic Jews might never achieve, nor perhaps would they necessarily want to. We discuss in this chapter Albert Bensoussan, a writer from Algeria who moved to France, Claude Kayat, a novelist from Tunisia who emigrated to Sweden, and Ami Bouganim from Morocco who settled in Israel.

The impetus for the newer writing by Francophone Sephardic Jews may be allied with two cultural phenomena: first, the renaissance of Jewish culture, religion, and literature which has been going on in France for several decades and, second, the flourishing francophone literature produced particularly by Maghrebian (mainly Arab and Berber) writers from the 1950s onwards, in countries which France once colonized. In fact, one of the first novels unleashing the creativity of Francophone writers was the first by a Jewish novelist, the Tunisian Albert Memmi (*La Statue de sel—The Pillar of Salt*, 1953); the impetus has thus been reciprocal. Though uprooted and exiled from their homes, North African Jews and other Sephardim have had a powerful cultural apparatus, consisting of their mastery of the French language, and their being at home within it, with which to express their feelings of uprootedness. This obviously led North African Jewish writers initially to appear to integrate more easily into French non-Jewish and Jewish literary circles and has encouraged their creativity, unlike American Sephardim, whose much smaller numbers and initial relative unfamiliarity with either English or Yiddish discouraged them from literary production.[3]

Migration may be viewed first as a historical and physical event—in the case of the Jews of North Africa, their departure for countries where they expected to find better conditions such as greater safety, stable prosperity or spiritual fulfillment. Next, it may be viewed as a psychological process, consisting of adjustment to a new culture, dealing with a degree of disappointment in the new home, and nostalgia for the former. Third, and this is the emphasis here, migration may be reflected in the literature produced by the émigrés as a deliberate attempt to use aesthetic forms to capture the socio-cultural dynamics of migration and its psychological stresses, ambivalences, and new freedoms.

The large Maghrebian Jewish communities which survived the Holocaust period and Second World War scattered, as the dates for independence of the North African countries approached.[4] The psychological and cultural costs of the uprooting of these ancient communities, pre-dating Islam, and the departure of large numbers of Jews—many of whom had had no intention of leaving—at very short notice, can hardly be measured. In almost all cases the North African Jews left for countries of very different civilizations from their original home. Conventionally, the generation that migrates is considered "the generation of the desert," the lost generation, the one of transition, the one that has to devote its energies to the material side of settling down in order to enable future generations to flourish in their new homeland. Despite the fact that North African Jews had throughout history been extremely mobile and adventurous in their breadwinning, venturing in earlier centuries around the known world as merchants and sailors,[5] (and also occasionally as pirates), they had always had a home base to return to, a flourishing community with its own institutions and supports. Now, initially at least, many found themselves and their families entirely thrown on their own resources, and from a semi-Middle Eastern, semi-European and traditional Jewish culture, were thrown headfirst into secular Western societies.

The causes of this disruption, which made migration seem the least of all evils, were no less difficult to bear for being relatively clear to define. Scholars differ mainly over where to place the greatest emphasis. The Second World War and the period of decolonization brought to an end the traditional coexistence—*convivence*—of Jewish and Muslim communities in the Middle East. Jews in North Africa even suffered from the Holocaust, though not on the scale of European Jews,[6] the Second World War being the first major disruption of their traditional way of life. Many Jews were interned in concentration camps or labor camps and encountered, to their surprise, the implacable hatred of European antisemitism, arguable worse than anything they had met before in a Muslim environment. Although North African Jewry survived, these events probably marked the beginning of the end of its traditional existence. The war was, however, largely a dramatic incursion into the process which began with colonization and ended with undermining the viability of Arab-Jewish coexistence in North Africa. Most writers seem to agree that the colonial experience (symbolized by the granting of French citizenship to Algerian Jews in 1870) was one of the main causes of the rupture separating Jews from their traditional environment and orienting them towards the new, Western metropolis.[7] At the same time, rival nationalist movements in the region were growing and, as each North African country developed its own movement for independence, the Zionist movement claimed Jewish loyalties.[8] Although some Jewish intellectuals, such as Albert Memmi, supported the cause of political independence for North Africa, the majority saw it ultimately as a threat. Despite their longstanding presence in North Africa, they feared cultural and economic displacement by Muslim nationalist elites, in part because of their recent embrace of French language and culture.

The result of the growing rift between Jews and Muslims in North Africa was the hasty departure, within a few years during the 1950s and early 1960s of most Maghrebian Jews from their ancestral home. The speed with which the exodus took place and the general prohibition against taking belongings or wealth meant that many Jews had to leave almost empty-handed. Culturally speaking also, important segments of the intelligentsia did not resist the impulse of shedding some of the burdens of the past, both visible traces of Maghrebian culture and of their Jewish tradition. They were interested principally in making a living in their new homes in Israel, Europe and North and South America, maintaining their traditions in a low-key and non-engaging fashion, and assimilating into the cultures to which they had immigrated. It was not until about twenty years had passed that older people who had been adults in North Africa and even younger ones with only vague childhood memories began to express in writing their emotional links to this past.

Naturally (after assuring economic survival) much individual and collective digesting of the past, weaving memories through storytelling, had taken place in the meantime, preparing the ground for what came to be recognized as a minor cultural renaissance.[9] The new self-expression of Maghrebian writers often has little in common with their tradition, and the literary revival sometimes bears little relationship to older genres. As modern, Westernized individuals who have mastered the intricacies of Western civilization, they look back on inherited cultures which were both traditional and modernizing in a hybrid and naïve fashion (from today's point of view). Bridging the gap of years, of different geography, culture and language, their novels evoke the landscape of the past with detachment, humor, irony, or sentimental nostalgia. These modern individuals are stating that they once partook of a different identity, collective and traditional: without wishing to compromise their present authentically modern voices, they nevertheless assert that their identity has a unique dimension not shared by others in the East or in the West.

Leaving aside for the moment the quality of the novels, their very existence is a significant cultural fact in modern Jewish literature. The North African Jewish philosophers, political writers and novelists of today write as if within one contemporary Western, particularly French, tradition. One may suggest, however, that their common experience of migration from traditional, Jewish, Maghrebian to modern, Western cultures gives them a critical awareness of the gap between expectation and reality, between the wish to communicate meaning on the one hand and understanding by the recipient on the other, between "signifier" and "signified." The concern with difference, which preoccupies these writers in common, makes it worthwhile to discuss their work within the same context. However, it must be noted that while North African writers emphasize displacement due to their own cross-cultural experiences, contemporary French, and lately Anglo-American, philosophy and literary theory have been emphasizing just such a concern, arrived at, it appears, through the internal dynamics of Western thought.[10]

For example, the preference for analysis over resolution of philosophical problems is shared by the previously mentioned psychologist, sociologist and novelist, Albert Memmi.[11] His love of analysis partly stems, it seems, like most of his writing, from the contradictory loyalties of his childhood, when he participated in Arab, French, and Jewish cultures. Even during the independence period when political passions were at their height, he never condoned violence for the sake of national independence. His analysis of the psychological problems of colonizers and the colonized advocated self-knowledge as the means for overcoming a sense of inferiority; he disagreed with Frantz Fanon and Jean-Paul Sartre, who advocated the use of violence on the part of the colonized in order to achieve psychological freedom.[12]

Jacques Derrida, referred to above, may also have evoked echoes in a parallel aesthetic stance on the part of some Maghrebian Jewish novelists. This influential thinker—who even rejected the idea of philosophical "thought"—cannot be pinned down easily. The widespread influence of his writings (on literary theory, feminism, Deconstruction) further complicates discussion of them within this context. I wish only to name certain qualities of his writing that perhaps connect him to that of the other writers to be discussed: their emphasis on the text, love of analysis and abhorrence of facile resolutions of the terms of dialectical thought, and the constant displacement of terms from one context to another.

The analytical distancing used as a philosophical tool by Memmi and Derrida is paralleled in fiction by Maghrebian Jewish novelists reflecting similar attitudes which grow out of the experience of disruption of traditional relationships, displacement, and migration to wholly new environments. Aesthetic elements, such as open rather than closed forms, blurring of the boundaries between fiction and history, heterogeneous structures reflecting cultural contradictions, the use of elements from oral traditions (such as jokes, proverbs and moral tales), and an abundant use of humor, characterize the novels.

The three novelists whose works are to be used as examples share the fact that they are all writing, in French, what seem to be mostly autobiographical novels. Ami Bouganim, of Moroccan origin, writes about Moroccan Jews who have moved to Israel. Albert Bensoussan, of Algerian origin, writes from a new life in France. Claude Kayat, from Tunisia, has a protagonist who (like himself) moves first to Israel and later to Sweden. Their portrayal of migration, therefore, originates in personal experience, and the aesthetic presentation of it stems from knowledge of the cultural and psychological implications of displacement.

Albert Bensoussan's novel, or fictionalized autobiography, *Frimaldjézar* (1976),[13] is frankly nostalgic for an idyllic childhood world. Its lyricism, humor, and wordplay have helped set the tone for later novels in similar mode. It describes the childhood of a middle-class boy growing up in Algiers during the colonial period, the Second World War, victory, and Algerian independence. Since this world is lost forever, the novelist, from his new home in misty, chilly Brittany, refers to it as Nineveh, the city to which the prophet announces its doom. The city in the novel is not destroyed but rather transformed. Its way of life becomes less carefree, and its multicultural population of colonial times has given way to a much more homogeneous one in the post-independence period. But the parallel with Nineveh of a population of joyful insouciance unaware of what destiny holds seems an apt image for colonial Algiers, at least for the Jews. The name *Frimaldjézar* is related to the word 'frime'—show or fun in French, combined with the Arabic for

Algiers—and much of the happiness of life in this beautiful suburb perched on a hill above the sea comes from enjoyment of superficial, trivial things, such as the smells of spices, the pleasant confusion of the markets, the noisy prayer of the synagogue, and particularly the facile glories of the local opera, playing before a public easily delighted.

Only the author of this autobiographical novel, at the age of ten, somehow foresaw the disappearance of the colonial world:

> Our opera house was our whole life, our city, our addiction. And I was the only one to glimpse in the twilight of my tenth year the horrible things to come, to shiver at the unbelievable lightheadedness of our fluttering and artificial people, aping the manners of the metropolitans. . . .
>
> L'Opéra de chez nous c'était notre vie, notre ville, notre chancre. Et j'étais seul à entrevoir au crépuscule de mes dix ans l'horrible à venir, à frémir de l'incroyable légèreté de notre peuple papillonnant et guindé, singeant les manières métropolitaines. (p. 90)

The child (so we are told) saw the essential unreality of the colonial society, for which the opera constituted its heart. Unlike adults, the child found his world too new, too marvelous, to be taken for granted. His vision was one of the first insights the future writer had of the weakness of the society he was part of. Beneath his joy, lurked what turned out to be a realistic fear of losing that world.

If colonial life was doomed, what alternatives did the Jews of the Maghreb have? One solution, an alternative to migration, might have been to go back to the roots of some Jews in Judeo-Berber tribes, which had lived in the hinterland since before the Islamic invasion of North Africa. Bensoussan evokes these roots in a section of the novel entitled "Pré-histoire." Discussing his grandfather Messaoud, he tries to "Reconstitute our mythology, redraw our family heraldry, using the minute shreds of collective memory which float in the shapeless debris of prehistory." ("Recompenser notre mythologie, redessiner notre écusson de famille à travers les infimes bribes de mémoire collective qui passent dans de vagues débris de préhistoire"). He describes the identity of his "tribe" as "Hebrew, Moghrebi, and soon-to-be French,"— "identité hébraïque, et maugrèbe, et bientôt française" (p. 126).

Bensoussan does refer to the ability of his community to return to the villages in times of danger.[14] He describes a Jewish shepherd perfectly at home in the hinterland and shows the filtered impressions of the world war and the Holocaust. Jews with remote connections to Algeria, or none at all, were coming to take refuge there, bringing rumors of box cars and crematoria. His home became a stopping place for Jews on their way to hide in the countryside. "Il y avait foule à la maison, base de transit pour le retour aux villages" (p. 55) (There were crowds at home, which had become a transit base for the return to the villages).[15] North Africa had thus over the centuries constituted a refuge for Jews in times of danger. However, Bensoussan also recalls origins outside North Africa in "Tolède, Jérusalem en Sépharade" (p. 126) (Toledo, the Jerusalem of Sefarad). This thought reflects the dual ancestry of North African Jews, some of whom must have descended from the ancient Maghrebian Jewish communities and some from those expelled from Spain. With the unprecedented violence, hatred, and bitterness engendered by the civil war in Algeria (1954–1962), the Algerian Jews found themselves expelled along with the French, with whom they had most recently identified. The centuries spent in North Africa thus became another chapter in the history of the exile of the Sephardim, in their migration from one country to another around the Mediterranean basin:

> Our passage through Isbilia, a mere detour. After Toledo, after Spain, and our ancient rootedness in Moghrebian lands, and our long hopping from one side of the Mediterranean to another, farewell Frimaldjézar.[16]

The author himself has left the Mediterranean for a more northerly clime. He experiences pain and nostalgia in his new exile but, as we see, the very contrasts between an idyllic childhood among warm and cheerful Mediterranean people, and his present existence in Brittany, impel him to write novels and memoirs. The impetus for writing thus lies in the 'décalage'—the gap—between past and present, East and West (or South and North), tradition and modernity, the child and the adult. From his distance in time, culture and geography, Bensoussan projects the sense of impending disaster back into the mind of the child that he was:

> And I could see you, faraway Frimaldjézar, just as you might perhaps look at this hour, immersed in your dirty water and your dead rats lapping against the docks, your lizards and your lepers assaulting the Ottoman bastions that a long civilization had been able to muzzle.[17]

He sometimes sees a reminiscence of the same sun in the cold sky of the north, "when the cold comes and stiffens my oatmeal, stifles my inky cries in wool/ quand le froid vient trancher mes avoines, étouffer mes cris d'encre dans la laine" (p. 24). Migration, for Bensoussan, has meant a total physical disconnection from the world of his childhood. Though muffled, it is the pain of separation, not only in climate but also in culture and geography, from a world of the past, which compels Bensoussan to write.

In *Frimaldjézar,* Bensoussan evokes a Sephardic identity through allusion. Other later works of his refer to it even more directly. His personal affinity for Hispanicity is apparent in his professional publications as a professor of Spanish literature on, for example, the Peruvian Mario Vargas Llosa, and on the art of translation.[18] He has published a novel on the *converso* experience: *Marrane ou la confession d'un traître* (1991) and with the same publisher the essays *L'Echelle de Mesrod ou parcours algérien de mémoire juive* (1984) as well as *L'Echelle sépharade* (1993).

Where Albert Bensoussan expresses loss in measured tones of nostalgia, Ami Bouganim's characters in *Le Cri de l'arbre* (1983) lament in strident voices. Rather than one individual living in dignified if solitary exile, we have in Bouganim's novel a whole society of Jews from Morocco thrown into a primitively appointed transit camp or *ma'abara* in Israel in the 1950s. The novel depicts individual characters with vivid colors, and at the same time tries to give the impression of a collective voice of an uprooted community. The implication is that these Moroccan Jews are an organic community which has been removed from its natural environment. The novel implies that the migration of Moroccan Jews was occasioned less by persecution in Morocco than by Jewish religious fervor, the desire to be in Jerusalem rather than a need to leave Morocco. The gap in the novel is not only between the past and the present but also between aspiration and reality, between a villa in Jerusalem and a hut somewhere outside Haifa. In the novel, the Jewish Agency officials who had organized the exodus had apparently made little attempt to make the Moroccans aware of what they might really find on their arrival, but the novel makes fun of the illusions themselves. The tragicomic figure of Mzel, an elderly woman from Marrakesh, in her exaggeration epitomizes the illusions which had led the Moroccan Jews to uproot themselves.

> A villa for each family! After two thousand years of drifting. . . . They were at last about to anchor their destiny in the land of their fathers. For two thousand years, their dreams had led them ceaselessly to Jerusalem—and they landed in a ma'abara! . . . [Mzel] loudly demanded her villa, four or five rooms, a tropical garden, a magic kitchen with one faucet for milk and one for honey.
>
> Une villa et par famille! Après deux mille ans de dérive . . . ils allaient enfin jeter l'ancre de leur destin dans la terre de leurs ancêtres. Pendant deux mille ans, leurs rêves n'avaient cessé de les conduire vers Jérusalem—et ils échouèrent dans une ma'bara! . . . [Mzel] réclamait sa villa à grands cris, quatre ou cinq pièces, un jardin éxotique, une cuisine magique avec un robinet de lait et un robinet de miel. (pp. 10–12)

Though these Jews from Morocco experience many hardships, the culture they brought with them helps them to survive as a group. When they do eventually visit Jerusalem (on a hasty and somewhat disappointing bus tour) and are deposited in a park, they get together to tell stories of the exile in Morocco:

> They sit down under the shade of a fig tree and there, they start scaring Jerusalem with their stories of Mogador. . . . And I can tell you, Jerusalem went pale with jealousy as it listened to the scandalous relations that those Jews had had with exile.[19]

> Ils se retirent à l'ombre d'un figuier et là, ils entreprennent d'effaroucher Jérusalem de leurs récits sur Mogador. . . . Et Jérusalem, vous dis-je, pâlissait de jalousie à l'écoute de la scandaleuse liaison . . . que ces juifs-là avaient eue avec l'exil. (pp. 106–107)

Storytelling is an essential element in their culture, whichever part of Morocco they had come from, whether their background is predominantly French-, Arabic-, or Spanish-speaking. A counterpoint to Mzel is the poetic and romantic figure of Zohra, a Spanish-speaking aristocrat who sings in Judeo-Spanish about exile, about the many exiles in the long history of her people:

> She sings of exile, a nostalgic thickening to her voice, the exile from Jerusalem, the exile from Spain, the exile from Morocco.

> (Elle chante l'exil, un embrun nostalgique autour de la voix, l'exil de Jérusalem, l'exil d'Espagne, l'exil du Maroc.) (p. 12)

It appears that a new layer of exile may have been added to the previous ones, even though, paradoxically, the Moroccan Jews have come home. Unlike in the *mellah* of Morocco, their souls are no longer at rest on Shabbat in the *ma'abara*:

> The Jews scrub their bodies with soap and water but their souls are still stained by a certain nostalgia, a nostalgia for exile . . . nostalgia for a certain mobilization.[20]

Once having been mobilized by the experience of exile, the Maghrebian Jews described here do not find it easy to settle down. They feel frustrated and directionless.[21] Their souls remain those of a Mediterranean, sea-going, and mobile people. In their separate communities in Morocco, they believed that for generations they had been quite comfortable as Jews, despite their exile. According to Bouganim's novel, Israel brings together Jews of very different walks of life, speaking Arabic, French, and Spanish (perhaps also

Judeo-Spanish and Haketia), and in opposition to the common problems they share, makes them realize they are Sephardim. The children even begin to learn Zohra's ballads, implying that a shared culture is developing. This does not seem to be necessarily more modern than those which existed in Morocco, although the few Moroccan Jews who acquire an education do break away from the group. There are references to a budding writer who succeeds in shocking the rest of the community, and one would not be surprised if this were an autobiographical figure of the author.[22] This novelist does have the blessing of the characters in the older generation who wrote and read the *Gazette* of Mogador, the former mouthpiece of the community. The novel reflects a trenchant sense of humor, based (as with Kayat's novel to be discussed later) on cultural contradictions (here between Sephardic and Ashkenazi Jews). It incorporates stories, songs and other elements from an older oral tradition, and its structure is open and heterogeneous, reflecting the incoherence that Bouganim seems to believe the Moroccan Jewish society and culture are going through.

Migration in Bouganim's novel has entailed the uprooting of a community and an attempt to plant it in a new land. This has led to the atrophy of the roots, a relative lack of continuity with the past and of creativity in the present. Communal frustration replaces the nostalgic sadness of an individual now cut off from his community, as found in Bensoussan's novel. Nevertheless, Bouganim's novel is a powerful evocation of a collective psychological transition, unusual among the generally individualistic novels about migration.

Claude Kayat, a novelist, playwright and artist of Tunisian origin, now lives in Sweden, as does the protagonist of his novel *Mohammed Cohen* (1981).[23] The main character's name is, of course, a synthesis of the cultural contradictions implied in being a Sephardic Jew from North Africa. This protagonist happens to have a Muslim mother who married a Tunisian Jew and in order to assuage her father, promised to name her son Mohammed. We thus have the paradox, for the purposes of the novel, of a Jew named Mohammed Cohen.[24] He is naturally faced, for life, with a series of insoluble cultural dilemmas. These he sensibly confronts with a sense of humor which makes for a very amusing, though poignant, novel.

Unlike the protagonist of Albert Bensoussan's book, Mohammed grows up in a country which is already well on the way to independence. He is fully at home in both Muslim and Jewish cultures and, leaving as a sixteen-year-old, his main regret is that he had not learned from his mentor to play Tunisian music (p. 140). The French component of his identity is also important, being personified by his revered teacher, who imparts a love of the French language. It is the latter which consoles Mohammed in his new life, after he migrates to Israel (p. 177). French constitutes his "vie intérieure." He recognizes, though, that had he remained in Tunisia he would have had problems with his Arabic as well. The pain of separation from his country and culture impels him to write his past:

> "In order not to lose my past, I wrote with the despair of a drowning man ... writing gushed out of me, ran like a balm over this wound that would not heal."
>
> Pour ne pas perdre mon passé, j'écrivais avec le désespoir d'un homme qui se noie ... l'écriture jaillissait de moi, coulait comme un baume sur cette plaie constante. (p. 178)

He begins to write "prose, but in order to survive"—"de la prose ... mais pour survivre" without knowing whether he is writing a novel or not. Eventually, helped by a Swedish couple he had known in Tunisia, the protagonist emigrates to Sweden, becomes a teacher, and returns to Tunisia on vacation, where at the end of the novel his Swedish wife gives birth to his first child in the room where he himself was born. The novel is humorous enough for such amazing coincidences to be acceptable, for anything is possible in a world in which someone can be named Mohammed Cohen. The sentimental ending in which he thus temporarily returns to his roots in Tunisia artificially resolves a situation which has been tinged with tragedy, for his mother has been killed by a terrorist bomb in Tel Aviv, and his closest Tunisian Muslim friend, whom he calls his "Siamese twin," is paralyzed after being wounded by an Israeli air raid over Lebanon.

Embodying so many contradictions within one's personality can lead to despair, or to a heightened sense of the bitter, though humorous side of life. The protagonist chooses the latter, and the novel is full of wordplay, jokes, and wry comments stemming from a healthy skepticism. For example, the lesson that travel and migration lead to a mature outlook on life is brought home through a joke, a pun on the fact that the farm where he is a dayworker dispatches its tomatoes overseas when they are only half ripe: "Intended for export, they are sent by boat, for, as everyone knows, travel encourages maturity"—"Destinées à l'étranger, ou les expédie en bateau, car, comme chacun sait, les voyages favorisent la maturité" (p. 172). Migration for Mohammed Cohen, out of a country in which as a child he had felt at home, has been a maturing process. Once he had emigrated to Israel, he was launched on a path of mobility, and the move to Sweden did not constitute another process of uprooting. The mail service is still of vital concern for him, as distance from family is added to distance from friends. The cultural tensions are treated in a light, sometimes deliberately superficial way, as if Mohammed Cohen really does not want to agonize over his predicament. His name, again, sums up the latter perfectly. In Tunisia, among Tunisian nationalists, his last name met with sneers. In his Zionist youth camp, and later on in Israel, it is his first name which is utterly indigestible. Only in Sweden, the most enlightened of countries, no eyebrows are raised. In Kayat's novel it is considered necessary to maintain the humor at all costs, resulting in the portrait of a protagonist with few communal ties, but apparently content with his new home.

Of the three writers, only Bensoussan (who portrays the most middle-class environment) seems totally convinced that emigration from North Africa was the only alternative for Jews, and he devotes much of his writing to painful nostalgia. The other two seem to imply that, fictionally and emotionally, they might have stayed longer, and perhaps the logic by which the communities had been compelled was not a sufficient one. Whatever the reasons for leaving, though, the novels are dealing with the multiple effects of migration in the lives of the protagonists and Jewish communities. The forms of the novel and literary structures chosen tend to be heterogeneous, reflecting underlying cultural contradictions. The novels include elements from oral traditions, and are generally humorous, choosing to portray the disappointing and semi-tragic situations inherent in uprootedness in a comic light. They employ open structures, leaving the future uncertain, and refraining from dictating solutions. Though light in tone, either nostalgic or comic, the novels are generally written with skill, hinting at profound tensions which ultimately reflect the dilemmas of modernity. How far can multicultural individuals identify with particular nation-states? How can one survive in a cosmopolitan and heterogeneous world without asserting one's roots, which in every case involve a return to the culture of one's childhood? What price do individuals have to pay for balancing the irreconcilable demands of mobility and pragmatism with traditionalism, cultural certainties, and emotional security? Moreover, the more traditional times for which one feels nostalgia were usually themselves fraught with the contradictions of colonialism and of Jewish-Arab rivalries.[25] Sometimes in the same camp as, sometimes embarrassed by their similarities with the Arabs, from colonial times already Sephardim had a contradictory, fluid, and transnational identity.

The fact that these novels attempted to grapple with these universal issues means that the novels constitute a phenomenon worthy of attention. After a pause of some twenty-five years, consciousness of Sephardic uprootedness began producing philosophical and imaginative literature reflecting the cultural contradictions of migration by favoring humor and analysis over harmony and reconciliation. In this, Sephardic writers are both quintessentially modern, and mirroring their own particular historical experience.

NOTES

1. An earlier version of this chapter was published in Hebrew as "Hagira Be Romanim Me'et Sofrim Yehudim Me-Tzfon Africa: Bensoussan, Bouganim, Kayat," *Peamim* 35 (1988): pp. 130–40. With thanks to *Peamim* for their permission to reuse in a reworked version.

2. On the paradoxes of relations with the French language, see Jacques Derrida, *Le Monolingüisme de l'autre* (Paris: Galilée, 1996), especially the phrase "Je n'ai qu'une langue, ce n'est pas la mienne" (I have only one language, and it is not my own), p. 13, which is a motif repeated throughout the book.

3. The easier integration in France still holds true historically despite the rise of antisemitism, partially due to a new Islamism, and which has contributed to a new exodus of French Jews to Israel and the United States. For thoughts on why Sephardim did not have much literary production in the United States, see Diana Matza's introduction to the anthology, *Sephardic-American Voices: Two Hundred Years of a Literary Legacy* (Hanover: Brandeis Univ. Press, 1997). See esp. pp. 7–12.

4. Tunisia and Morocco became independent in 1956, Algeria in 1962. By the mid-80s, only a few hundred Jews remained in Algeria, about five thousand in Tunisia, and fifteen thousand in Morocco. The French Jewish community, however, doubled in size between the 1950s and 1980s following the addition of 235,000 Jewish immigrants from the Maghreb; the Spanish Jewish community swelled to 21,000, many from the Maghreb, and Canada absorbed some twenty thousand Maghrebian Jews. Figures are from André Chouraqui, *Histoire des Juifs en Afrique du Nord* (Paris: Hachette, 1985), p. 451. More updated figures may be found in Jewish People Policy Planning Annual Assessments (Jerusalem: Jewish Agency for Israel).

5. This point is made by Chouraqui, ibid., p. 449.

6. The persecution of Jews in North Africa during the Second World War is described in Charles Haddad de Paz, *Juifs et Arabes au pays de Bourguiba* (Aix-en-Provence: Paul Roubaud, 1977), pp. 37–44, and in one of several eyewitness and autobiographical accounts, *Days of Honey: The Tunisian Boyhood of Rafael Uzan* ed. Irene Awret (New York: Schocken, 1984). See also Robert Attal et al., *Regards sur les Juifs de Tunisie* (Paris: Albin Michel, 1979), pp. 182–193, and Paul Ghez, *Six mois sous la botte* (1943; Paris: Manuscript, 2009); Mitchell Serels, et al., *Del Fuego: Sephardim and the Holocaust* (New York: Sephar Hermon, 1995). For analysis of the causes of antisemitism, see Michel Abitbol, *Les Juifs_d'Afrique du Nord sous Vichy* (Paris: Maisonneuve et Larose, 1983). More recently, there have been several new studies. See, e.g., Robert Satloff, *Among the Righteous: Lost Stories of the Holocaust's Long Reach into Arab Lands* New York: Public Affairs, (2006); Aomar Boum and Sarah Abrevaya Stein, *The Holocaust and North Africa* (Stanford: Stanford University Press, 2019); and a recent issue of *Sephardic Horizons* 11:2–3, (Spring-Summer 2021) devoted to the Jews of Tunisia and Libya, https://www.sephardichorizons.org. We must also mention the harrowing and far more tragic experience of Sephardim of the Balkans, particularly Greece, recounted in Isaac Jack Lévy, Rosemary Lévy Zumwalt, *The Sephardim in the Holocaust: A Forgotten*

People (Tuscaloosa: University of Alabama Press, 2020), which includes a section on North Africa.

7. See Edmond Amran El Maleh, "Juifs Marocains et Marocains Juifs," *Les Temps Modernes* 33, no. 375 bis (Oct. 1977), 495, 520, for a view of the process of disconnection. El Maleh pointed out that Mohammed V, the king of Morocco, had prevented the Vichy government from applying anti-Jewish measures in Morocco. He believed that the emigration of the Jews of Morocco was a tragedy brought on by the colonial policy of "divide and rule" and exacerbated by Zionist activities. Abitbol, however, writes that decolonization was the main factor forcing the Jews to leave North Africa. Algeria, in which antisemitism was the main factor, was the exception, Muslim antisemitism being encouraged by the French (*Vichy*, pp. 27–28). In Tunisia it was the decline in French power.

> Cet affaiblissement de la puissance coloniale—en soi générateur de conflits ethniques longtemps sublimés—raviva la volonté d'indépendance de la population musulmane; encouragée par le crépuscule français, celle-ci commença par porter ses coups au maillon le plus faible et même le plus désarmé de la situation coloniale, le Juif dont la promotion sociale avait été précisément l'un des aspects les plus insupportables. (ibid.)

> (This weakening of the colonial power—which in itself was liable to generate ethnic conflicts that had long been sublimated—revived the Muslim population's desire for independence; encouraged by the twilight of the French, Muslims began by targeting the weakest and most defenseless link in the colonial situation, the Jews, whose social ascendancy had precisely been one of the most unbearable aspects of colonialism.)

See also Michel Abitbol, *Le Passé d'une discorde: Juifs et arabes du VIIe siècle à nos jours* (Paris: Tempus, 2003).

8. See Mark Tessler and Linda Hawkins, "The Political Culture of Jews in Tunisia and Morocco," *International Journal of Middle East Studies* 11: 1 (Feb. 1980), pp. 59–86, esp. pp. 64–67. For a literary portrayal of the origins of Zionism in Tunisia in the 1920s, see Ryvel, *L'Enfant de l'Oukala et autres contes de la Hara*, pref. Serge Moscovici, (Tunis: La Kahena, 1931; Paris: Lattès, 1980); the last story, probably written in the late 1920s, describes the impact of a Zionist emissary from Russia on the Jews of Tunis. See my "The Portable Homeland of North African Jewish Fiction: Ryvel and Koskas," *Prooftexts* 4 (1984), pp. 258–59, and Chapter 2 previously.

9. See Lucette Valensi, "From Sacred History to Historical Memory and Back: The Jewish Past," *History and Anthropology* 2 (1986), pp. 283–305, esp. pp. 294–303. The novels reflect, according to Valensi, a common theme of death and loss associated with the migration from North Africa. See also Guy Dugas, *La Littérature judéo-maghrébine d'expression française*, Philadelphia: CELFAN Edition Monographs, 1988; Hélène and Shmuel Trigano, eds., *La Mémoire sépharade: Entre l'oubli et l'avenir* (Paris: In Press, 2000) and Nina B. Lichtenstein, "North Africa, France, and Israel: Sephardic Identities in the Work of Chochana Boukhobza," *Sephardic Horizons* 3:2 (Summer 2013), www.sephardichorizons.org. Also Leïla Sebbar, ed., *Une Enfance juive en Meditérranée musulmane* (Saint-Pourçain-sur-Sioule: Bleu Autour, 2012), esp. pp. 81–87.

10. Or "différance,"' as the Algerian-born Derrida would put it. Derrida's term 'différance' refers to the lag inherent in any signifying act (between speech or writing and meaning). See Jacques Derrida, *Dissémination*, trans. and intro. Barbara Johnson (Chicago: Univ. of Chicago Press, 1981), introduction, p. ix. On displacement, see esp. a 1972 interview entitled "Positions," discussed in the introduction to *Displacement: Derrida and After,* ed. and intro. Mark Krupnick (Bloomington: Indiana Univ. Press, 1983), pp. 5, 12–16; and Shira Wolosky, "Derrida, Jabès, Lévinas: Sign-Theory as Ethical Discourse," *Prooftexts* 2 (1982), 283–302.

11. See e.g., Albert Memmi, "La Vie impossible de Frantz Fanon," *Esprit* 39: 406 (Sept. 1971), pp. 248–273.

12. Frantz Fanon, *Les Damnés de la terre* (1961), *The Wretched of the Earth*, Richard Philcox (trans.), New York: Grove Books, 2005, e.g., "colonialism is not a thinking machine. . . . It is violence in its natural state and it will only yield when confronted with greater violence. . . . Violence is man recreating himself" (Chapters 2, 3, 4, passim). Jean-Paul Sartre, in his introduction to Fanon, merged a philosophical dialectic of colonialism with actual warfare: "Abattre un Européen, c'est faire d'une pierre deux coups, supprimer en même temps un oppresseur et un opprimé: restent un homme mort et un homme libre." (To kill a European is to kill two birds with one stone: there remain one dead man and one free man). *Situations V* (Paris: Gallimard, 1964), p. 183.

13. Albert Bensoussan *Frimaldjézar* (Paris: Calman-Lévy, 1976). Subsequent page numbers quoted in the text refer to this edition. This work won the prize *Prix de l'Afrique méditerranéenne* in 1976. On the porous boundary between Sephardic autobiography and novel, see Jonathan Schorsh, "Disappearing Origins: Sephardic Autobiography Today," *Prooftexts* 27:1 (Winter 2007), 82–150.

14. The next novelist to be discussed, Ami Bouganim, refers in another book, *Récits du Mellah* (Paris: Lattès, 1981), p. 26, to a tendency for Jews in times of plague to take refuge in the countryside. Such an option implies the maintaining of a whole network of relationships with non-Jewish, Arab or Berber villagers, on a permanent basis, ready to be activated. See also the documentary film and book, Robert Satloff, *Among the Righteous: Lost Stories from the Holocaust's Long Reach into Arab Lands* (New York: Public Affairs, 2007), discussing cases of Jews who were rescued or hidden by Muslims sometimes in the hinterland during the Vichy/Nazi/Fascist period.

15. Since the time of the Jewish revolt against the Romans in Cyrene, 155–177 CE, Jews have taken refuge in the interior. See Shmuel Applebaum, "The Jewish Revolt in Cyrene and the Subsequent Recolonization," *Journal of Jewish Studies* 4 (1951), pp. 177–186; and Renzo De Felice, op. cit., p. 4.

16. "Notre passage en Isbilia, simple péripatie. Aprés Tolède, après l'Espagne, et notre séculaire enracinement en terres maugrèbes, et notre long déhanchement d'un part à l'autre de Méditerranée, adieu Frimaldjézar" (p. 185).

17. "Et je te voyais, Frimaldjézar la lointaine, telle que peut-être tu t'enfonce à cette heure dans tes eaux sales et tes rats crêvés au clapotis des docks, avec tes lézardes et tes lèpres à l'assaut des bastions ottomans qu'une longue colonisation avait su museler" (p. 24).

18. See for example *Mémoire et fidélité sépharades, 1492–1992: actes du colloque 1492–1992* (Rennes: Presses universitaires de Rennes, 1993), colloquium coordinated and proceedings edited by Bensoussan. The colloquium included a discussion moderated by Bensoussan on sephardism today: "Le sefardisme d'aujourd'hui." (pp. 183–206). Elisabeth Schousboë in *Albert Bensoussan* (Paris: L'Harmattan, 1991), pp. 34–35, 38–39 discusses Bensoussan's loyalty to "Sepharad."

19. Extensive analysis of Bouganim's work may be found in Najib Redouane, Yvette Bénayoun-Szmidt, eds., *Ami Bouganim: Voix marocaine en Israël* (Paris: L'Harmattan, 2021), see esp. Afaf Zaid, "*Le Cri de l'arbre* de Ami Bouganim," pp. 51–60, for a Moroccan view of Bouganim.

20. "Les Juifs se frottaient pourtant le corps à l'eau et au savon; mais leur âme restait entachée d'une vague nostalgie, nostalgie de l'exil, nostalgie d 'une certaine mobilisation" (p. 51).

21. Ami Bouganim, *Le Cri de l'arbre* (Tel Aviv: Editions Stavit, 1983; 1999). References are to the 1983 edition: "Comment nous dépêtrerons-nous de ces sables mouvants dans lesquels nous nous sommes enlisés et vers quelles rives dirigerons-nous la galère sur laquelle nous avons embarqué notre Histoire?" (p. 188) (How shall we untangle ourselves from these quicksands into which we have sunk and toward which shores shall we guide the ship on which we have embarked our History?)

22. Bouganim became an educator in Israel and has published books on pedagogy, on Herzl (1998), Spinoza (2000), Yeshayahu Leibowitz (1999); on documents relating to the history of Israel (*Sites et sources*, 1988, 2004, 2005); on Jerusalem, and on the city of Tel Aviv (2009). His publications give the impression that as an individual he has definitely put down roots in Israel, since the 1980s. An indicative work is *Le juif egaré*, a study of diasporic Jewish philosophy that concludes by emphasizing the paramount value of the land of Israel in Jewish identity (Paris: Desclée de Brouwer, 1990). A chapter by Bouganim in Leïla Sebbar, *Une Enfance juive en Méditerranée musulmane* (Saint-Pourçain-sur-Sioule: Bleu Autour, 2012), entitled "Le Berceau de Dieu," expresses his continuing nostalgia for Mogador/Essaouira: "Je n'ai cessé de . . . reconstituer avec une rare précision ses décors et ses sites dans mes rêves. J'ai laissé l'enfant là-bas; je suis resté de là-bas. Le prix de l'émigration serait un cocon de chenille qui n'aurait pas donné de papillon et où se conserveraient mes souvenirs. . . . " (pp. 74–75) (I have continued to . . . reconstitute with great precision in my dreams its appearance and its sites. I left my childhood there; I am still from there. The price of emigration is a silk cocoon which has not yet given up its butterfly and where my memories are kept. . . .)

23. Claude Kayat, *Mohammed Cohen* (Paris: Seuil, 1981). Quotations and page numbers are from this edition. The novel has been translated into English as *Mohammed Cohen: The Adventures of an Arabian Jew*, trans. Patricia Wolf (New York: Bergh Publications, 1989). Claude Kayat has subsequently published several more novels, one being the excellent *La Synagogue de Sfax: roman* (Paris: Punctum, 2006). An article by Debbie Barnard well describes the insoluble and tragicomic issues of identity in *Mohammed Cohen*. See "It Ain't Easy Being Me: Violence and Identity in Claude Kayat's *Mohammed Cohen*," *CELAAN Review: Review of the*

Center for the Studies of the Literatures and Arts of North Africa special issue *Jews of Tunisia* 7:1 & 2 (Spring 2009), pp. 85–97.

24. Fictional names embodying cultural contradictions have been used by other North African novelists. One example is the hero of Albert Memmi's first novel, La Statue de sel 1953; rev. ed., pref. Albert Camus (Paris: Gallimard, 1966), whose name is Alexandre Mordechai Benillouche, described by Memmi as reflecting respectively his French, Jewish and Berber heritages. Mohammed Cohen the Jew has a 'Siamese twin' in his Muslim friend Hassan who attends his Bar Mitzvah classes in his place. See Moncef Khemiri "*Mohammed Cohen* ou la fraternité à l'épreuve de l'Histoire" *La Tunisie dans la littérature de langue arabe et de langue française* (Tunis: L'Or du Temps, 2001), pp. 189–204.

25. Johann Sadock, in "Anti-Arab and anti-French Tendencies in post-1948 Oriental Jewish Literature Written in French," mentions a little Jewish boy in Bensoussan's *Frimaldjézar* who wanted to become an Arab shoeshine boy, a *yaouled*, even though the other boys threw their brushes at him; p. 250 in Hafid Gafaïti et al., *Transnational Spaces and Identities in the Francophone World* (Lincoln: Univ. of Nebraska Press, 2009), pp. 243–63. 'Oriental' Jews could also view themselves as 'Sephardi' Jews, but according to another author in the same collection, 'Sephardi' was just one of the overlapping identities of Algerian Jews. See Sarah Sussman, "Jews from Algeria and French Jewish Identity," ibid., pp. 217–42.

Chapter 5

Modernity and Beyond

Sephardim have always been the most modern of Jews in their outlook. Baruch Spinoza is credited with introducing modern skepticism toward religion (at great pain to himself) in the seventeenth century. Shmuel Trigano has a chapter on "L'Invention sépharade de la modernité juive" in his voluminous anthology, *Le Monde sépharade* (2006).[1] Several authors in Yael Halevi-Wise's collection show how Sephardism itself helped Ashkenazi Jews to undertake the transition to modernity, as the image of sophisticated, worldly yet fully Jewish Sephardim during the Spanish Golden Age became an ideal for modern European Jews, especially in Germany or Britain.[2]

In the post-war twentieth century, the turmoil of history prompted Francophone Sephardim, especially in North Africa, to adopt European (largely French) philosophical currents and embrace Existentialism, authenticity, realism and *engagement,* which they have found useful as tools in their soul-searching and painfully sincere autobiographical fictions (autofictions). The earliest novels by Albert Memmi helped to point the way for both Muslim and Jewish Maghrebian writers in the first half of the 1950s. *La Statue de sel* (1953) is still anthologized and quoted to this day as an authentic portrayal of the plight of the colonized and of working class Jews whose culture was an amalgam of Arab, indigenous Jewish, and French colonial elements, enabling them to identify with both the oppressors and the oppressed. The novel portrays the intellectual growth of a young man from a poor background who experiences, like the majority of Tunisian Jews at the time, the harshness of the Nazi occupation, Muslim antisemitism, and French duplicity. Memmi transposes to his hometown riots and killings of Jews that actually occurred in Baghdad (1941) and Libya (1945 and 1948), rather than Tunisia, using some poetic license to make his point.

The first-person narrator is Alexandre Mordechai Benilouche, whose name represents the threefold cultural identity (Jewish, French, Arab-Berber indigenous) of the author. The novel has a frame, in that we first encounter the narrator sitting for his university exams in Western philosophy, and symbolically rejecting Western civilization (while sabotaging his future academic career) by using the examination time to begin writing this confessional autobiography. At the end of the novel, he takes ship for Argentina. The novel was awarded the prestigious Prix de Carthage and has inspired much study.

Naim Kattan of Baghdad, who also wrote in French, documented the coming of age of a similar young man, though of a more comfortable background, in Iraq. His novel *Adieu Babylone* (1975) records the terrible *farhud* (pogrom) that took place in Baghdad under similar circumstances to those of Libya, when a hiatus of control in the city, and a slow response on the part of British forces, enabled murderous anti-Jewish riots to take place. Such momentous historical events make for compelling reading and need no artistic embellishment. Similarly, the novel records the narrator's transition from hoping to participate, though a Jew, in the new nation-state of Iraq, to estrangement under trauma, and the protagonist's eventual leaving for ever the country of his birth.

In the case of both Memmi and Kattan, the implicit audience for the novel is a French-educated or Western-educated one. Both authors write in a direct, unadorned style, allowing situations, relationships, and conflicts within the individual and between the individual and surrounding circumstances to speak for themselves. To achieve this effect, of course, there is more art than meets the eye. Their rebellions are simultaneously against the traditional Jewish setting, the European colonial elite, and Muslim society that never did accept Jews as equals. The two authors have definitely been aware of each other, and Memmi has published a short essay about Kattan, also referred to in Chapter 4.[3] The latter, for his part, had published one year earlier an essay entitled "Le Séfaradisme" in which he claimed a spiritual community with Jews from other Muslim countries.[4] Memmi saw Kattan, as he saw himself, as a chronicler of lost civilizations. Moreover, both writers spoke their respective forms of Judeo-Arabic as their first language.[5] As young men, members of the Jewish minority, the narrators of each of these novels,[6] set in the 1940s and early 1950s, are acutely aware of social differences and the potential for embarrassment when norms are breached.

Kattan's novel contains a telling description of one of his Muslim friends' holding a birthday party for himself. An ordinary event for Westerners, but he explains that in Middle Eastern societies at that time, most people did not know when their birthday was, or even sometimes how old they were. The Muslim friend decides to hold his twentieth birthday party, even though he must have been twenty-three or twenty-four. The friends had always met previously in cafés, never in each others' homes. It turns out that his house does not have a proper address, so they have to ask for the house at his brother's shop on the corner. Inside the house, in its central patio, two women in black veils huddle, and turn their backs on the visitors. Up in the host's room, which has a narrow iron bed, he explains that this is not really his bedroom, just his study, obviously not true. He says he will call the maid to bring tea, and one of the women in black (most likely his mother, though not introduced) brings the tea. The Jewish narrator reflects sadly on the Iraqi level of self-deception, where an educated young man feels it necessary to lie about his mother. After a while, they repair to the neutral ground of the café where they can all behave naturally again.

Albert Memmi's protagonist, a student in the French *lycée* of Tunis, cultivates a slightly uncomfortable friendship with a Jewish boy (Henri) from a much higher class and wealthier circumstances, though in the end he accepts their differences and Henri's lack of serious commitments. He is ill-at-ease in the rather empty social gatherings of wealthy young Jews, and especially uncomfortable about the events' charitable purposes (to benefit the poor Jews of the *hara*). He also sincerely supports the Tunisian independence movement, belongs to a mainly Arab nationalist anti-colonial group, and has a Muslim friend with whom he forces himself unsuccessfully to maintain links after a "pogrom" takes place and his best Jewish friend dies (see Chapter 4). He is pained and alienated by the Muslim friend's inability to empathize. Such uneasy cross-ethnic and cross-class relationships are the stuff of both Memmi's and Kattan's autofictions. They both have a penetrating eye for the embarrassing, pained awareness of cultural difference in colonial and newly post-colonial situations. As in the Spanish writer Ortega y Gasset's phrase, "Soy yo y mi circumstancia" (I am myself and my circumstances), these novels accurately portray the interactions of the Jewish protagonist living in a Middle Eastern colonial predicament and how he or she is shaped by this situation.

The *doyen* of Francophone Sephardic novelists, Albert Cohen, after a long hiatus in his literary career, and perhaps even being inspired, one might hazard, by younger writers such as Memmi, returned to the field with his *Belle du Seigneur*, which he had been writing and rewriting, and which was finally published in its first edition in 1968, and translated into English in 1995. This lengthy study, ostensibly of a doomed love affair between Solal, a Jewish high official of the League of Nations, and his colleague's non-Jewish wife, is grounded in psychological realism, and even more in Cohen's bitter satire. Overcome by desperate love, and disillusioned at the League of Nations' inability or unwillingness to rein in Hitler, he abandons his post. The two lovers take off together, living in hotels, their love affair eventually felled by tedium and despair. With no possible future open to them, no professional or social context, they commit suicide together. This takes place against the background of mounting antisemitism in Switzerland and France, as the Nazi threat increases. The contradictions of Sephardic identity, and the extreme contrast between the traditional and the modern in Jewish life, crop up early in the novel in the shape of Solal's colorful and embarrassing relatives from Greece who insist on visiting their important nephew in Geneva. Apart from this humorous interlude, the novel (in my view) is largely somber, and Sephardic identity is subsumed into a Jewish one, in the face of European antisemitism. In view of the threat of the Holocaust, this novel presents an even more untenable social situation for its protagonist than Memmi's or Kattan's post-war settings. The novel does contain the stream of consciousness, or hallucinations, of the main character, as he sees visions of Charlie Chaplin and Hitler, and reminiscences of his childhood, but this seems more like Surrealism, or a bad dream, than humor. In fact, one critic sees this stream of consciousness as a deliberate strategy to out-Proust Marcel Proust and out-Wolff Virginia Wolff in a parody of modernism and the stream of consciousness technique.[7] Albert Cohen and Edmond Jabès experienced similar traumas upon their arrival in France. Cohen's early encounter with antisemitism is recounted by Esther Bendahan in her thesis and book, *Sefarad es también Europa*. A flagrant verbal attack on him as a ten-year-old boy marked him for life and in a way inspired him to be a writer, in a kabbalistic sense to repair the world.[8]

The Holocaust in its horror has often confounded realist writers, who are confronted with a reality far worse than their worst nightmares. Edmond Jabès of Egypt likewise did not find realism adequate for his fictions. In his work, the traumas of history (experienced personally or absorbed as a memory living and inherent in his surroundings) have led to the abandoning of realism for a more poetic prose style.[9] His symbolic, lyrical novels abandon narrative in favor of a series of questions.

Jabès left Egypt in 1957 as a result of Gamal Abdul Nasser's economic persecutions, imprisoning of many Jews, and expulsions of virtually the whole community, whose members had to leave their millennial home in Egypt almost empty-handed.[10] Once in France, he is said to have experienced a second trauma: in the land where he had expected to find freedom and equality, Jabès was shocked soon after his arrival to encounter antisemitism, in the shape of antisemitic graffiti on a wall.[11] Whether or not this was the entire motivation for the development of his life's new direction, it certainly deeply affected this perhaps relatively naïve and idealistic young man from Egypt, encountering Europe for the first time beyond his French-language education in Egypt. His writing turned from poetry to poetic prose, from the trauma of leaving Egypt to the trauma of the Holocaust, the subject of all his subsequent novels.[12] The seven-volume *Le Livre des questions* (1963–1973) was followed by another seven-volume series, *Le Livre des ressemblances* (1976–1987). The author's concern with the subversion of language and narrative is subservient to his discussions of Judaism and the relation of Jews to the Book.[13] Aimé Israel-Pelletier suggests that the melancholy of his books, the sense of mourning, arises from the unresolved mourning for leaving Egypt.[14] Like many other Sephardim, Jabès felt that his personal suffering and loss were insignificant compared with the suffering experienced by Ashkenazim in the Holocaust. His personal loss is thus suppressed, subsumed into the general Jewish tragedy of the Holocaust. *Le Livre des questions* tells the tragic story of a young couple, Yukel and Sarah, who had survived the death camps and had returned, a story that one would have expected to represent a happy outcome. However, she eventually succumbs to madness, and dies after twelve years in a psychiatric clinic, and he seems about to commit suicide, seeing only death in his future. Yukel himself had written "The Book of Sarah and Yukel." He stops writing and heads south to the Mediterranean after she dies. "Scorpions stung Sarah's eyes, vultures ransacked her forehead, while the bitter water and black fruit delivered her lover to death" (p. 234),[15] and even to Israel where he seeks the desert, "I have told of the desert through the indestructible memory of the void whose every grain is a tiny mirror. . . . If grass is the question of life sand is perhaps the answer" (pp. 234–235).[16] Their relationship is commented upon and discussed in Talmudic fashion by a sort of chorus of rabbis across the ages (and their students), a conversation consisting mostly of questions, few of which ever receive answers.[17]

Just as the lovers' relationship is tragically aborted, so language also subverts meaning in Jabès' works. This aspect of his writing was seized on by the Deconstructionists, among whom Jacques Derrida was prominent and especially interested in Jabès. Exile and uprooting in Jabès lead to the consideration of the book as the author's only dwelling place or homeland. Derrida (who met him in Paris) was himself a Sephardic exile from Algeria, where he had experienced the war years, the Vichy government's stripping of Algerian Jews' French citizenship and its eventual restoral, and the trauma of Algeria's war of independence which led to the Algerian Jews' exile to France along with the French *pieds-noirs*. Many have noted the Jews' ancestral connection to Algeria dating back millennia before the colonial period, and predating the Arab invasion of North Africa in the seventh century. All of this was swept away in 1962 in "a day"—*Mille ans, un jour*—as Edmond Amram El Maleh would say later about the Jewish presence in Morocco. Jacques Derrida, viewed humorously as a Jewish saint by his fellow Algerian and Deconstructionist, Hélène Cixous,[18] though one of the most prominent theorists of Deconstruction in France, and without practicing religion in the least, was nevertheless grounded in Algerian Jewish traditions.[19] He recounts the experience of the Torah scrolls being removed from the Ark in his childhood synagogue in Algeria, and the meaning of the veil (curtain) concealing the writing, *l'écriture,* and says that a child who has witnessed this can arrange there all the bits of his life.[20] The analytical method of Deconstruction, the taking apart and putting back together of a text in new ways, lead us to the

Derridean concept of 'displacement' of the subject. Derrida believed that so-called 'thought' is often merely textual displacement. Displacement, of course, whether textual or in person, can readily be related to Jabès' all-pervading theme of exile. Mark Krupnick states that Derrida prefers "textual displacement" to the "evaluation of thought."[21] "Displacement is an exile from older certitudes of meaning and selfhood, a possibly permanent sojourn in the wilderness" (p. 5).

Cixous takes Derrida's Deconstruction one step further and produces a feminist Deconstruction. Derrida and Cixous, both born in Algeria, experienced the disconcerting decentering of having their French citizenship (granted to all Algerian Jews since the mid-nineteenth century) revoked due to the Vichy regime's antisemitic legislation. Both experienced it in dramatic ways: Cixous, as a toddler, was expelled from the "Garden of Eden," the French playground she attended, and Derrida was expelled from the French high school. Though neither writer was religious, Cixous as a female experienced a deeper alienation from the traditional synagogue rites. By the late fifties and early sixties, having had their French citizenship restored after the war, they both found themselves virtually expelled from Algeria, the land of their birth, to France.[22] All these rejections, as they felt, honed both writers' taste for cultural contradictions over harmony. Thus it is not surprising that two of the leading theorists of Deconstruction are Algerian Sephardic Jews who have experienced the disjunctions and disconnections in the flesh.

Cixous describes the crushing feeling of exclusion at the age of three, when she experienced antisemitism in Algeria in the French nursery school she was enrolled in, and her feeling of being expelled from the garden of French childhood.[23] Derrida was expelled from school as a Jew in Algeria at the age of eleven, and wrote in 1999 of how his instinct to approach texts from the side, his interest in minor works, non-canonical cultural heritage, details, footnotes to the main argument, digressions, might be a response to this initial trauma.[24]

One might add that in both Derrida and Cixous, punning is paramount. Cixous' book on Derrida, *Portrait of Jacques Derrida as a Young Jewish Saint*, is a prime example. She describes him thus:

> He is the dry-witted prince of the Jews, the scoffer, the mocker, what a word that is! The heart-word the word of words at the heart of the matter, the Derrider of eloquence and all its eloquence.[25]

Cixous speaks also of parallels in their personal experiences, "the archives of what he calls 'my nostalgeria' and that I call my 'algeriance'" and of "circumconniving in the languages of translinguistic sport" (p. 5).

Cixous writes dexterously of the mixture of languages in her home in Algeria. Her mother was Ashkenazi and her refugee grandmother from

Germany knew hardly any French. Her Algerian Sephardic father picked up bits of many languages, and thus in her home Arabic, Spanish, French, Hebrew, Berber, and German merged to form a family language she calls "German Charabia" or "Algharbiya."[26]

The use of diglossia or triglossia is a frequent technique of uprooted, cosmopolitan Sephardic writers in their fiction. Though such techniques are probably not very popular with publishers (whose eye on monolingual markets for literary production most likely discourages such authorial indulgences), post-modern writers, not only Jewish ones, have sometimes succeeded in imposing an idiosyncratic, personal multilingualism, in small amounts. One of the foremost diglossic writers was the Jewish Moroccan writer, Edmond Amram El Maleh. As the streets of Maghrebian cities echoed once with many languages, so his writings echo this former multilingual mix of Arabic, Spanish, and French.

Jews were not the only ones to be multilingual. The approach of Muslim Maghrebian writers (both Arabs and Berbers) to this issue is markedly different from that of Jewish writers, though. Arab and Berber Francophone writers have seen multilingualism as a tearing, a schism within their identity. Kateb Yacine, according to Abdelkebir Khatibi, eventually gave up writing in French, as being the language of the colonizer, and had his plays translated into colloquial Arabic. He himself, though, was not able to write directly in Arabic and, having voluntarily deprived himself of French, lapsed into silence toward the end of his life.[27] Jewish writers such as Derrida, Cixous, and El Maleh have been more comfortable with multilingualism and, as Cixous' essay on Oran shows, even actually missed it after the end of the colonial period. The reasons are perhaps not hard to find, in the Jewish tradition of using Hebrew for sacred purposes and the language of the nation where one lived for secular purposes. Though Cixous gave up her father's desired classes in Hebrew and Arabic after his death, she immediately embarked on learning English and German, two languages that she felt a personal need for. Derrida laments the cultural forces that have led to his having only one language, which he feels is really not his own.[28]

Edmond Amram El Maleh celebrates the multilingual voices of Tangiers. Arabic, Spanish, English, and perhaps even other parallel ways of communicating such as Haketia (which draws on Ladino/Judeo-Spanish, Castilian, Hebrew, and Moroccan Arabic) or Berber mingle with French in his novels on almost every page. His diglossia does not clarify but adds to the impression of Tangiers as a cosmopolitan city, a spatial technique. In a city like this, it is not unusual for the inhabitant as well as the tourist not to understand everything they hear on the street. The other languages add to the impression of diversity and dissonance, in a place where no one person could understand everything that is being said. In Chapter 1 we referred to Elias Canetti's travelogue, *Voices of Marrakesh*. Canetti listens to the traditional storytellers in the public square, notes their clothing, gestures and tones, writes of them with great respect, but understands hardly a word of what they say. In Canetti's case we might say that this is a pose, the Nobel-prize-winning writer's unexpected homage to the primitive origins of his craft, but in the case of El Maleh it is perhaps part of the Moroccan indigenous writer's attempt to weave everything he can into the texture of his narrative, an attempt to bring to life through the reader's senses the multilayered texture of his city, home to birds, animals, and many human ethnic groups, each with its own language, assailing our ears in turn. El Maleh even makes fun of Canetti, asking what he could be looking for, among the people of Marrakesh, whom he did not understand.

Though Sephardim had embraced French with alacrity, and incorporate diglossia into their French-language writings, other non-Francophone Sephardic writers have also used diglossia. One example is the Israeli Hebrew-language writer, A. B. Yehoshua,[29] whose *Mar Mani,* as it proceeds backward in time, includes more and more words from the Sephardic language, Ladino or Judeo-Spanish. What is the actual effect of this technique for readers? Obviously, those few who still know the Sephardic language feel comfortable and at home the more these words increase, and are delighted to encounter these familiar terms. For the majority of readers, though, these words increase the effect of strangeness, alienation from the past. The strange behavior of the slightly unhinged main character, Avraham Mani, in the oldest narrative set in Athens in the early 1800s, composed of one side of a conversation with the elderly rabbi's wife, Dona Flora, whom he calls *rubisa*, is reinforced by his use of a language probably unfamiliar to his readers (Yehoshua writes for the average culturally literate Israeli reader, rather than for a minority of Sephardim who understand Ladino/Judeo-Spanish). As he recounts his conversation with his dying rabbi, he is trying to emphasize his extreme respect for the rabbi, while having apparently given him some shocking news that actually brought about the rabbi's death. Terms such as *pisgado* [heavy person, deadweight] (the rabbi's teasing term of endearment for him) thus have a double meaning and are likely to alienate the reader and increase the sense of strangeness. Yehoshua, as a consummate novelist, is doing this deliberately, of course, and this book will be discussed again in Chapter 6.

It cannot be said that diglossia creates a sense of strangeness for the well-known Mexican novel (also a film), *Novia que te vea*[30] [May I see you a bride], by Rosa Nissán. A young girl's gradual growth into maturity within the traditional community of Mexican Sephardim, and her encounters with modernity, employ terms from Ladino. Since the novel is in Spanish, and Ladino terms are likely to be comprehensible to Spanish-speakers, this is not likely to provoke alienation in those reading the original Spanish, in fact it may be a major source of interest for the reader. The English-language translation by Dick Gerdes is another matter. Here the American publisher did not venture to include the Ladino terms, but had them all translated and dropped the original Ladino altogether. This timidity of the publisher deprives the reader of the sense of another language, the diglossia being one of the salient artistic features of this novel. In English, the Ladino words might have had the same effect as in Yehoshua's novel, one of distancing, a sense of strangeness, but a little exoticism might also have been welcome to the English-language reader, who is not reading only for the plot. With the growth within the United States of Latino/Latina literature in recent decades, North American readers may be getting used to the idea of diglossia, at least in some sectors of the reading public. Diglossia reflects the untidiness of the post-modern world—there are more and more places where it is increasing, where monolingualism is being complicated by bi-or trilingualism, and bilinguals and trilinguals are becoming more reluctant to speak only one language.[31] Language is not always used solely for its meaning: witness the innumerable uses of the Hebrew language by American Jewish organizations, such as synagogues with their inscriptions, or associations with their logos. Often it is the artistic aspect of the calligraphy and Hebrew script that is the point, and whether or not everyone fully understands the meaning is less paramount. Commercial enterprises might use French, Spanish, or Italian in their titles for their effect of sophistication, regardless of whether the customers fully understand. Popular singers sometimes sing in another language, or have bilingual lyrics for their songs, to the delight of their fans. Likewise, in a novel that includes diglossia, the foreign-sounding words, perhaps not fully understood by the reader, are there for aesthetic or historical effect, whether of familiarity or strangeness, as well as for their meaning.

One North African Jewish writer who is by no means post-modern, but was writing in the 1920s and 30s, and who used diglossia while obviously ignorant of Spanish, is the Algerian novelist Elissa Rhaïs. In her French-language novel *L'Andalouse,* the main protagonist, Dolorès, a Spanish woman of Tangiers, converses with her fellow-Spaniards in a strange sort of jargon, obviously there for aesthetic effect. Born in Algeria, into a family with Moroccan Jewish connections, Elissa Rhaïs later moved to the metropolis of Paris, where she became a popular novelist writing on exotic settings in North Africa. Either she or her main publisher, Plon, cultivated an exotic image for the author, too. Her name is a pseudonym, her real name being Rosine Boumendil, and it has even been suggested that she was an imposter, not having written the novels herself, but having forced her more fluent young nephew to write them. It is an interesting phenomenon that several Maghrebian Jewish writers have used pseudonyms. One can think of Ryvel (Raphaël Lévy) in Tunisia, and even Albert Memmi's texts where autobiography is concealed behind an alter ego or narrator. Was this a result of the shifting of identities for Jews beginning in the colonial period, where, especially in Algeria, Jews might have different persona for interacting with different ethnic groups or professional circles? Much has been written on this by Benjamin Stora, Albert Bensoussan, and others.[32] North African Jews became adept at living in different worlds (and having a different name in each). To return to Albert Memmi, his narrator Alexandre Mordechai Benilouche uncomfortably straddled three civilizations, and was totally at home in none of them. This sort of compartmentalization became easier for later generations, especially North African Jews who have grown up in France, and straddling several cultures is a typically post-modern position. In the colonial period and in North Africa, indigenous Jews wanted to become French, but since they have moved to France or elsewhere, they have come to appreciate and long for the experiences of traditional life in the old country where, as Derrida said, they could stick together all the pieces of themselves.

There are several coping techniques. A return to religion (Claude Kayat in distant Sweden says that he yearns to attend a synagogue practicing the Tunisian rite—the tunes, the order of prayers, the atmosphere, all obviously recreating his Tunisia for him)[33]; participation in specific ritual events such as Lag B'Omer or other pilgrimages, either by returning to Djerba or joining a celebration somewhere in the suburbs of Paris, or attending Djoha festivals, or having recourse to humor to lessen the pain of what has been irretrievably lost. There is a rich vein of humor in North African Jewish literature, and though direct lines are hard to trace, it might owe something in a literary sense to Albert Cohen's assumption of Charlie Chaplin's role as the "Great Dictator," as well as Cohen's other extravagant characters. Albert Memmi's hero in *Le Désert*, for example, in telling his life story, often ends up looking ridiculous, and poking ironic fun at himself. The heroes of these novels set in modern times find themselves in humorous situations because they are trying to conform to too many codes at the same time, resulting in what has been termed incoherence. Whereas Memmi's protagonist in the early *La Statue de sel* was often painfully embarrassed, other writers, such as Annie Fitoussi, or Marco Koskas, have treated life among these conflicting cultural codes with more lightheartedness. Claude Kayat's earlier novel, *Mohammed Cohen*, about the identity of an Arab Jew whose father is Jewish and his mother Muslim, and who actually makes Aliyah (immigrates to Israel), elaborates this comical premise in a lighthearted way, though with serious undertones. His later novel, *La Synagogue de Sfax*, about the last Jew of the provincial town of Sfax, begins on a light note but ends in pure tragedy. Jokes, humor, self-deprecating stories, are all coping mechanisms used in fiction as in real life to deal with a history that was tragic for the parents and grandparents, but now for the younger generation evokes bemusement. Andre Aciman of Egypt, though writing in English, evinces a Proustian sensibility, but manages to make the exploits of his Sephardic families on the eve of their expulsion surprisingly funny ("pathologically Sephardi" as the Ashkenazi relative describes them), while tragic at the same time.

The transition to modernity and beyond, experienced in extreme forms by Sephardim who left a traditional lifestyle in a non-Western country for a new life in the West or in Israel, has been the hallmark of the second half of the twentieth century, and up to the present. There are many stopping places along this trajectory, and thus an immense number of personal adaptations or compromises between the two poles. The writers discussed in this chapter have incorporated the dilemmas that almost all Sephardim experience, conjuring out of them literary works of compelling interest, humor, and high aesthetic level.

NOTES

1. Shmuel Trigano, *Le Monde sépharade* (Paris: Seuil, 2006), vol. 1, *Histoire*, pp. 243–278. See also in the same volume, Gérard Nahon, "La Transition de l'histoire sépharade vers la modernité" (pp. 723–744) and Shmuel Trigano, "L'Invention sépharade du sionisme moderne," pp. 861–878. See also the collection, edited by Paloma Díaz-Mas and María Sánchez Pérez, *Los sefardíes ante los retos del mundo contemporáneo: Identidad y mentalidades* (Madrid: CSIC, 2010, esp. the introduction, pp. 11–29).

2. See especially Yael Halevi-Wise, "Postscript: Rebecca Goldstein's *Spinoza*," in Halevi-Wise, pp. 275–283.

3. Albert Memmi, "Naïm Kattan, mon semble, mon frère," in Jacques Allard, ed., *Naïm Kattan: L'Écrivain du passage* (Montreal: Hurtubise, 2002), p. 91. He asks the question of whether North Africa and the Middle East are now just a dream for Sephardim, and the answer is "Mais non, puisqu'il existe des écrivains-chroniqueurs comme Naïm Kattan."

4. Naïm Kattan, "Le Séfaradisme," pp. 93–100 in Kattan, *L'Écrivain migrant: Essais sur des cités et des hommes* (Montreal: Hurtubise, 2001). Notice that both of these books came out with the same publisher.

5. For Kattan, see Naïm Kattan, "Jewish of Arab Origin and Culture," *Covenant Global Jewish Magazine* 1:1 (Nov. 2006) www.covenant.idc.ac.il/en/vol1/issue1/kattan_print.html For Memmi, see Albert Memmi, "Who is an Arab Jew?" reproduced on www.Jimena.org. Memmi's original statement appeared in print in a chapter of *Juifs et arabes*, (Paris: Gallimard, 1974), trans. into English as *Jews and Arabs* (Chicago, O'Hara, 1975).

6. Albert Memmi, *La Statue de sel* (Paris: Corrêa, 1953) trans. Edouard Roditi as *The Pillar of Salt*, latest edition Boston: Beacon, 1992. Kattan's novel is *Adieu*

Babylone (Montreal: La Presse, 1975). In Eng, *Farewell Babylon: Coming of Age in Jewish Baghdad* Trans. Sheila Fischman (London: Raincoast, 2009).

7. Steven Bowman, "The Languages of Albert Cohen," pp. 445–451 in David Bunis, ed., *Languages and Literatures of Sephardic and Oriental Jews* (Jerusalem: Misgav Yerushalayim, 2009). Ref. is to p. 448. Bowman also says that Cohen's language is a Jewish language, "Jewish, if you will, by the nature of the parody he successfully deploys." (p. 448).

8. Esther Bendahan, *Sefarad es también Europa: El otro en la obra de Albert Cohen.* Zaragoza: Prensas de la Universidad de Zaragoza, 2016. I consulted the PDF of this PhD thesis (University of Zaragoza, 2014), on Albert Cohen, with profound thanks to Esther Bendahan. It contains an interview with Shmuel Refael Vivante, author of a dramatic adaptation for the stage of another of Cohen's novels, *Le Livre de ma mère.* Refael states that he considers Cohen, despite not writing in a Sephardic language, to be a Sephardic writer since his themes, his settings (such as his mother's Sephardic home) are much more Sephardic than European. European identity was a mask that his late mother removed from her face, he says. Thus it seems to me that Refael sets up an opposition between 'Sephardic' and 'European,' and would not agree with Bendahan on the point made in her title (see PDF, pp. 400–404, esp. p. 403).

9. Ammiel Alcalay describes his work thus: "The work of Jabès, a hybrid of surrealism and postmodernism, in a curious way provides one of the most ambitious responses by any writer attempting to come to terms with the deep internal schism that occurred as ancient Middle Eastern Jewish communities found themselves cast adrift at the end of an era" p. 106 in Reeva Spector Simon et al., eds., *The Jews of the Middle East and North Africa in Modern Times* (New York: Columbia Univ. Press, 2003), chapter entitled "Intellectual Life," pp. 85–112.

10. On the difficult conditions under which they had to leave Egypt, see Maurice Mizrachi, "Growing up under Pharoah" online at Historical Society of Jews from Egypt website. Aimée Israel-Pelletier, in "Edmond Jabès, Jacques Hassoun, and Melancholy: The Second Exodus in the Shadow of the Holocaust," *MLN* 123:4 (Sept. 2008), pp. 797–818, writes "In 1957, Jabès was a successful poet and stockbroker. . . . Threats, intimidation, and humiliation were the strategies used to make men comply. Jaron writes: 'The government was not necessarily cooperative. One day officials would restrict him from leaving his home to go to work, and the next day they would confine him to his apartment: 'ce fut comme ça, jusqu'à la fin,' Jabès related. 'J'ai essayé de sauver quelque chose . . . Enfin, n'importe quoi, je n'ai rien pu sauver'" (p. 804). Also Raphaël Sigal, "Edmond Jabès et l'Egypte," paper delivered at the Netanya Academic College Conference on Francophonie, April 2008.

11. Interestingly, Jabès does not mention this incident in his more recently published interview recounting how his family settled in France. See "Paris," in Aurèle Crasson and Anne Mary, eds., *Edmond Jabès* (Paris: Hermann, 2012). Jabès says about arriving in Paris "Ce ne fut pas, à proprement parler, un soulagement, mais plutôt la révélation de mon destin profond: La confirmation aussi du destin collectif juif." However, he had written about it in *Livre des questions*, vol. 1. See Eric Benoît, "Edmond Jabès et les chemins de l'écriture," pp. 33–45 in Crasson and Mary. This author describes several traumas: his sister's death, his getting lost in the Sinai Desert

in a sandstorm and almost perishing, his departure from Egypt and loss of his library, and the encounter with French antisemitism (pp. 33–34).

12. Here are some critical interpretations of Jabès that I have found useful: Ammiel Alkalay, *After Jews and Arabs: Remaking Levantine Culture* (Minneapolis: Univ. of Minnesota Press, 1993), pp. 59–69; Shira Wolosky, "Derrida, Jabès, Levinas: Sign-Theory as Ethical Discourse," *Prooftexts* 2, pp. 283–302; Shlomo Elbaz, "*Le Livre des Questions*: 'Prise de conscience d'un cri,'" in Elbaz et al., *Jabès: Le Livre lu en Israël* (Paris: Point hors ligne, 1987) (an anthology of Israeli scholars writing on Jabès); Rosemarie Waldrop, *Lavish Absence: Recalling and Rereading Edmond Jabès* (Middletown, Conn.: Wesleyan Univ. Press, 2002). Israel-Pelletier writes that "Jabès does more than express solidarity with the Jews of Europe. . . . He identifies with their plight while recognizing he escaped their fate and the world's 'indifference'" (2008, p. 799).

13. See Edward Kaplan, "Jabès, Edmond," p. 371 in *Blackwell Companion to Jewish Culture* (1987).

14. See earlier, note 10.

15. "Le scorpion a piqué le regard de Sarah et le vautour a vidé son front, tandis que l'eau amère et le fruit noir rendent son amant à la mort." *Le Livre des questions*, Vol. 3, *Le Retour au livre,* p. 98.

16. "J'ai dit le désert à travers l'indestructible mémoire du néant dont chaque grain est le minuscule miroir. . . . 'Si l'herbe est la question de la vie, le sable en est, peut-être, la réponse. J'aurais, alors, consacré mon existence à harceler le désert'—Reb Mitri" ibid., pp. 98–99.

17. "'The Jew answers every question with another question'—Reb Léma" Edmond Jabès, *The Book of Questions* trans. Rosemarie Waldrop (Middletown Conn: Wesleyan Univ. Press, 1976), p. 116 (this section is entitled "The Book of Yukel"). See my short discussion of Jabès and the Holocaust in "Sephardic Literary Responses to the Holocaust," in Alan Rosen, *Critical Interpretations of Literature of the Holocaust* (Cambridge: Cambridge University Press, 2013).

18. Hélène Cixous, *Portrait de Jacques Derrida en jeune saint juif* (Paris: Galilée, 2001).

19. See Wolosky (cit.), who emphasizes the predominance of writing over orality in both Jabès and Derrida (p. 288). Also Ammiel Alcalay, cit., p. 61.

20. Anyone one who has attended one of the synagogues whose congregants are of North African origin, perhaps in France or in Israel, has witnessed the intense joy and awe that accompany the Torah as it is carried out to be read.

21. Mark Krupnick, *Displacement: Derrida and After* (Bloomington: Indiana Univ. Press, 1983), p. 11. Derrida was speaking in an interview entitled "Positions," made in 1972. He stated "Thought is the illusory autonomy of a discourse or a consciousness whose hypostasis is to be deconstructed."

22. On the social and psychological effects on Algerian Jews in general, see Benjamin Stora, *Les Trois exils: Juifs d'Algérie* (Paris: Pluriel, 2012), esp. on Jacques Derrida, pp. 87–88. Derrida himself describes his expulsion from school due to the Vichy *Statut des Juifs*, and his sentiment in later life of being an outsider, what he calls a marrano, a member of a reviled and outlawed minority.

23. See Christa Stevens, "Judéités, à lire dans l'oeuvre d'Hélène Cixous," *International Journal of Francophone Studies* 7:1–2 (2004), pp. 81–93.

24. Ibid., Stora quotes from Derrida's *La Contre-allée* (Paris: La Quinzaine littéraire, 1999), p. 44.

25. Hélène Cixous, trans. Beverley Bie Brahic, *Portrait of Jacques Derrida as a Young Jewish Saint* (New York, Columbia University Press, 2004), p. 1.

26. See Cixous' essay "The Names of Oran," in Anne-Emmanuelle Berger, ed., *Algeria in Others' Languages* (Cornell: Cornell Univ. Press, 2002), pp. 184–194.

27. Abdelkebir Khatibi, trans. Whitney Sanford, "Diglossia: In Memory of Kateb Yacine," in Berger, ed., op. cit., pp. 157–160. See also Réda Bensmaia, trans. Whitney Sanford, "Multilingualism and National 'Character': On Abdelkebir Khatibi's 'Bilangage,'" ibid., pp. 161–183.

28. Jacques Derrida, *Le Monolinguisme de l'autre* (Paris: Éditions Galilée, 2016).

29. Yehoshua does have a strong connection with French culture. He lived in France for four years, soon after completing his studies, working, studying French and reading French literature. His mother's family were *olim* from Morocco (information from Jeannette Rosilio Spier, his first cousin) and therefore he may even have heard some French at home. Nevertheless, he claims that it was an American writer, Faulkner, who has had most influence on him outside Hebrew writers such as Agnon. Bernard Horn, in *Facing the Fires: Conversations with A. B. Yehoshua* (Syracuse: Syracuse University Press, 1997), p. 3, states that "Occasionally, a French pronunciation or word will slip in, partly a product of four years in France in the mid-60s as the general secretary of the World Union of Jewish Students."

30. Rosa Nissán, *Novia que te vea*, (Mexico City: Planeta, 1992); trans. Dick Gerdes, *Like a Bride; and Like a Mother* (Albuquerque: Univ. of New Mexico Press, 2002). In my view, these English titles lose the element of a blessing or an exhortation from the older generation that was included in the Spanish/Ladino phrases "Novia que te vea" and "Hisho que te nazca." Yael Halevi-Wise, discussing how Mexicans receive this writing, states that "Nissán's playful linguistic hybridity adds a charming ethnic ring to her narrative." See "A Taste of Sepharad from the Mexican Suburbs: Rosa Nissán's Stylized Ladino in *Novia que te vea* and *Hisho que te nazca*," p. 185 in Margalit Bejarano and Edna Aizenberg, eds., *Contemporary Sephardic Identity in the Americas: An Interdisciplinary Approach* (Syracuse: Syracuse Univ. Press, 2012. The English edition of the novels includes a preface by Ilan Stavans, who mentions a certain flatness when Nissán's book does not include her phrases in Ladino.

31. When I was first married, I was intrigued to listen to the conversations of my husband's family, Sephardim from Libya, as many sentences would include three or four languages—Italian, Arabic, English, and perhaps some Hebrew. When we traveled in Tunisia, the relatives there added French to this mix. For an originally monolingual English speaker, all of this was quite puzzling, but I did appreciate the rich mixture of cultures.

32. E.g., Benjamin Stora, *Les Trois exils: Juifs d'Algérie* (Paris: Pluriel, 2011).

33. My email interview with Claude Kayat in *Sephardic Horizons* 1:3 (2011), https://www.sephardichorizons.org/Volume1/Issue3/TunisianJewishNovelists.html.

Chapter 6

A Return into History

After modernity, and post-modernism, where do we go from here? Besides displacement and discontinuity, there has also been a less-recognized trend among Sephardic writers to delve back into the past. Perhaps the most prominent writer to have adopted this technique is the Israeli A. B. Yehoshua, with his Hebrew-language novels on the Sephardic past. Another is the Mexican writer Angelina Muñiz-Huberman, with her short stories set in Spain and Mexico, both before and after 1492, her novel of sixteenth century Jewish exiles from Spain, attempting to reach the Holy Land (*Tierra adentro*, trans. as *Mystical Journey,* 2011), and her novel on Jewish pirates of the Caribbean (*Los Esperandos: Piratas Judeoportugueses . . . y yo,* 2017). Around 1992, there was a spate of novels in English and Spanish related to events surrounding 1492, and it continues. But there are also several Francophone novelists who have turned to history with considerable effect, including Albert Memmi, in *Le Désert* (1977); the Tunisian-origin Nine Moati (1937–2021) in *Les Belles de Tunis* (1983) and *La Passagère sans étoile* (1989); Patrick Modiano (1945-, Nobel Prize 2014) in many of his novels haunted by the Nazi occupation of Paris; Clarisse Nicoïdski (1938–1996) in *Couvre-feux* on the same period; Didier Nebot, *Le Chemin de l'exil* (1992) on the exile from Spain in 1492; Colette Fellous (1950-), especially *Avenue de France* (2001); Gisèle Halimi (1927–2020) on the eighth-century Jewish-Berber queen, *La Kahina* (2006); Jacob Cohen (1944-), in a family history of abduction, *Du danger de monter sur la terrasse* (2006); and Eliette Abécassis (born 1969) with *Sépharade* (2011).

A number of novels by Sephardim deal with recent history, as we see, but not very many have dealt with more remote periods in history. A. B. Yehoshua is the author of two extraordinary Hebrew-language historical novels, *Mr. Mani* (1990) and *A Journey to the End of the Millennium* (1998). The first traces the adventures and misadventures of a Sephardic family over the generations, proceeding back in time to the early nineteenth century. The second is set entirely in the distant past in the years just before the turn of the first Christian millennium and was published, appropriately, just before the second millennium. One thus might have expected Yehoshua's later novel[1] that refers to Spain in its original Hebrew title (*Hesed sefaradi*, Spanish kindness) (2010) to be a historical novel involving Sephardim in Spain, perhaps set just before or just after 1492, a time when historically Spanish kindness toward the Jews was notoriously lacking.[2]

Its English title, *The Retrospective,* is a clearer reference to one of the main themes of the novel, a modern-day film festival devoted to the life's work of one director, held at a film school in the Spanish city of Santiago. The aging director is Israeli, and he attends together with his lady friend, who has been the star of his films ever since his first attempts at filmmaking. The Hebrew title refers to an important theme of the book. Perhaps indirectly, since the film is about repentance, it alludes to a modern Spanish atonement for the mistreatment and injustices done to the Jews over the centuries through the expulsion and the ravages of the Spanish Inquisition. A. B. Yehoshua shows his attunement to history as he takes the protagonists to such places as a village on the outskirts of Jerusalem (the village being from 1948 to 1967 ruled by Jordan) where, between 1967 and the recent past, Israelis could visit freely. Thus one of his films was shot in the railway station next to the village. Now the novel's characters return to find the station demolished and the village on the other side of a fence, under Palestinian administration, a vivid bringing to the fore of the march of history. In Spain, with its many mementos of the past, history is inescapable for Jews, and the last scene of this novel is a dreamlike trip back in time to meet Don Quixote and Dulcinea in person, no less, while the main issue of the novel finds resolution. Thus, though *The Retrospective* is set in the present, it is moored to the past with many cords. Since Yehoshua's focus is the well-being of Israel, his homeland, his novels of necessity are historiographic, or "historiosophic," in the term that Yael Halevi-Wise uses. The spatial and cyclical dimensions are also unavoidable.[3]

Angelina Muñiz-Huberman has also expressed a return to the Sephardic past in both prose and poetry. Her prose writing suggests an almost magical ability to identify with people living in the distant past, such as a Spanish Jewish mystic, or a deposed Aztec princess married to one of the Spanish conquistadors, but still secretly identifying with elements of her former religion (like many former Jews who remained in Spain or traveled to Mexico, and perhaps to what became the southwestern United States, the Mexican Indian princess has been forcibly converted). These characters come to life uncannily in her pages, as do the characters of *Tierra adentro*, her novel of a group of pilgrims which includes a Jew who has left Spain and is secretly trying to make his way to Jerusalem,[4] or Oseas, the philosophical pirate-cook of her latest novel, *Los esperandos*.[5]

Many other historical novels about the history of the Sephardim, of varying ambition and scope, in other languages such as English or German, and by non-Sephardic or non-Jewish writers, might have been brought in as examples, for the persecution and expulsion of the Sephardim from Iberia has served as a metaphor or trope for many of the ills and prejudices of modern history.[6] An example of this latter might be the Spanish novelist, Antonio Muñoz Molina and his novel *Sefarad* (2001), which makes a connection between the suffering of Iberian Jews over about four hundred years from the expulsion and Spanish and Portuguese inquisitions, and the suffering of Jews at the hands of the Nazis and their allies during the Holocaust (the connection of course being European antisemitism).

Historical novels may involve a journey backward in time, with revelations of successively more distant periods, as does Yehoshua's *Mar Mani*, or a more straightforward historical narrative, perhaps covering one lifetime, or a series of generations, in chronological order. A cyclical view of history may be manifested, or a linear progression. Whichever technique is chosen, the author must have a firm belief in the past's ability to illuminate the present.

The Desert: Or, The Life and Adventures of Jubair Wali al-Mammi (Le Désert ou La Vie et les aventures de Jubaïr Ouali el-Mammi),[7] the Tunisian Jewish writer Albert Memmi's fourth novel, first published in 1977, attempts through fiction to reintegrate a traditional civilization with modernity. Drawing on the techniques of North African oral literature and Oriental genres, Memmi proposes a value system and world view which consciously echo, with modern overtones, medieval North African philosophy. The structure and technique of the novel transform Memmi's nostalgic evocation of his cultural roots into a cyclical vision of the past and a view of how the wise man relates to the community.

In *Le Désert*, Memmi gave his imagination free rein. He applied himself fully as an artist (or, as he preferred to say, a traditional craftsman) to creating an imaginative artifact. Through *Le Désert*, Memmi also tried to open up a new field for the North African novel: going beyond autobiography or contemporary problems, he set out to embody the historical imagination. One of his strategies in *Le Désert* is to approach traditional genres which celebrate the exploits of peoples and their legendary heroes.

Le Désert takes up the story of a fictitious earliest ancestor who was a companion of the Jewish-Berber queen, la Kahéna, and purports in its preface to be the promised continuation of the chronicles of Le Royaume-du-Dedans, begun in *Le Scorpion*. The narrator, the long-exiled prince of the kingdom, now defeated by Tamerlane,[8] offers his tale in response to an inquiry from the conqueror, holding court in Damascus, as to how his own realms might be saved from the same fate. The aging al-Mammi sees his duty to respond as an opportunity to spin a story, which happens to be an account of his own adventures. Al-Mammi implies that, through wise governance of his realms and impulses, Tamerlane may prevent his own empire from falling to another conqueror in turn. *Le Désert* thus resembles Memmi's earlier novels in taking the form of a fictional autobiography.[9] But the relation between actual events and fiction is richer and more complicated here than in any of his earlier novels. The key to Memmi's aesthetic in *Le Désert* seems to lie in his idiosyncratic use of historical events.

Memmi explains his attitude to chronicled history as follows: "Historical facts serve me less as facts than as detonators, catalysers" ("Les faits historiques ne me servent pas tellement comme faits mais comme détonateurs, catalyseurs").[10] From the earliest pages the novelist, or rather fictional narrator, takes pains to fix the setting in time and place for readers who may not be familiar with it: "In the far north of Touat, between Tamentit and Sbe-Guerrara, there existed a small independent kingdom" ("dans l'extrême nord du Touat, entre Tamentit et Sbe-Guerrara, il a existé un petit royaume indépendant. . . . ") (pp. 14–15 and 11–12, with a map of the region in southern Morocco). This quotation is lifted almost directly from a scholar's historical study, but the information is misleading as "historical fact": like Borges' ironic literary scholarship, these references are reliable mainly as landmarks in the world of the novelist's imagination. Memmi had thoroughly read in available sources on a small Jewish kingdom which existed in that area,[11] but his novel derives equally from Muslim and Jewish history. The original source of information, and the one to which all subsequent scholars refer, is in fact the work of the Muslim historian of the fifteenth century, Ibn Khaldun.[12]

The life of Ibn Khaldun also provided the pattern for the novel's hero. The fictional al-Mammi, courtier, politician and chronicler of his times, is based fairly closely on the historical Ibn Khaldun, who met Tamerlane in 1401.[13] But the novel establishes a fictional connection between the destruction of the kingdom and al-Mammi's encounter with Tamerlane in 1400, which has no parallel in the case of Ibn Khaldun:

> It was in 1392, after a decisive assault by Tamerlane, followed by an almost total massacre of the population, that the Kingdom of Within ceased to exist. Eight years later, in 1400 to be exact, in the city of Damascus which had been sacked in turn by the same conqueror, al-Mammi was paying obeisance to the victor. (p. 1, Eng. trans.)[14]

More importantly, the fascinating biography of Ibn Khaldun, indeed material for a historical novel, foreshadows several events and attitudes in *Le Désert*. They include Ibn Khaldun's diplomatic mission to Pedro the Cruel in Spain, his fear for his life in Tamerlane's presence, and his desire to flatter the conqueror while impressing him with his own knowledge and wisdom.

The figure of Ibn Khaldun is particularly appropriate in Memmi's novel for several reasons: his dual roles as actor in and chronicler of history; the tension between the active and the contemplative life; his unique imagining of a logic to history while living in the midst of turmoil; the diplomatic cunning he is forced to employ merely to survive; and lastly, that he was Muslim rather than Jewish, which allows *Le Désert* to reflect the close historical experience of the two religions in North Africa. Thus, the historical material, i.e., Ibn Khaldun's biography and the facts he and others provide, is the catalyst for Memmi's imaginative constructions. These have a superficial resemblance to facts but a purpose which is basically novelistic, the celebration in literature of the cultural past. Another critic of Memmi's *oeuvre*, Lia Brozgal, also cautions us to distinguish as best we can between apparent facts in Memmi's writings and interviews, and his agenda as a novelist, an autobiographer, and creator of autofictions.[15]

The complex, well-balanced and careful construction of *Le Désert* brings into Western focus the cultural dilemmas of Maghrebian life and fiction. From the point of view of the novelist's art, because of its limited and precise aim, it is even more successful than Memmi's earlier novels. His previous novel, *Le Scorpion* (1969) was more complex technically, applying a new theory of writing in colors,[16] and incorporating a portion of a novel similar to *Le Désert*, begun by one of his characters. The framework of the later novel is not as purely North African or Middle Eastern as it might appear at first sight, but the subject matter combines some genuinely indigenous concerns of Memmi's original culture with philosophical elements shared by East and West, or North and South. His techniques owe much to North African oral folktales. The form of wisdom thus stressed is a largely personal interpretation of his ancestor's wisdom but is integrated successfully into the novel. Memmi is concerned with both literary experiment and preservation of his tradition, transposed into the novel. Paradoxically, this fact also places *Le Désert* within the tradition of historical vision and cyclical return of the modern post-romantic novel. While this novel draws on many sources both Western and Eastern, *Le Désert*'s basic impulse to breathe new life into the forms and history of Maghrebian Arab-Jewish identity is this author's most original contribution to the genre.

While Memmi is interested more here in the Maghreb than in the culture of Jews originating from Spain, Patrick Modiano, the 2014 winner of the Nobel Prize for Literature, despite having ancestors from the Iberian Peninsula who settled in Greece, is apparently marginal to Sephardic literature in a different way. Modiano is a name of Italian origin, meaning "from Modena," and so his ancestors from Iberia probably passed through Italy on their way to Greece. His father was a Sephardic Jew originating from Salonika in northeastern Greece and who may have immigrated, perhaps fled, to France (again via

Italy) during or prior to the Second World War. The tragic fact is that 95–98 percent of the Jewish population of Salonika perished during the Holocaust. Modiano's mother was an actress of Belgian, non–Jewish origin, and Patrick Modiano himself in the past has generally preferred not to be identified as a Jewish writer.[17] Though Modiano is not halakhically Jewish (since his mother was not Jewish), nevertheless the concerns of his novels, dealing frequently with the period of Nazi occupation, and the moral compromises people like his father had to make in order to survive, align him with Jewish and specifically Sephardic writers, notably with Primo Levi and his "gray zone." When considering the Holocaust period in history, the lacunae of memory often intervene, especially since many prefer to forget a painful period when survival was paramount. Thus, Modiano's writing often deals with the lack of inherited memory, the uncertainty created in the minds of a younger generation by non-communicative, alienated parents, victims of unknown traumas. Relationships that are cut off, either by lack of empathy, by death, by forgetting, or by other types of loss, dominate his novels. *La Rue des boutiques obscures* (1978, translated as *Missing Person*, 2005) is a prime example of such themes, and is allied with his father's experiences.

Absent from Modiano's fiction are references to his father's family's original Ladino/Judeo-Spanish-speaking culture. The main character in *La Rue* does obtain a job through a friend with the embassy of Panama in Paris on the basis of speaking Spanish, and so tries to pass as a Latin American. His Judeo-Spanish or Ladino of Salonika would soon have betrayed him as Jewish for anyone really listening, but "saved by Ladino" is a nice trope and even the subject of a film about the Holocaust years.[18] This part of the novel also recalls, though not explicitly, the activity in Paris of Mauricio Fresco, a Sephardi of Turkish origin who was a Mexican diplomat in occupied Paris[19] during the war years. And indirectly to historical efforts to grant Spanish citizenship to some Sephardic Jews during the war years. Modiano does not bring up allusions to these. Modiano's character, at that time named Pedro, senses that the Nazis are closing in on him, asking questions, so he decides to flee with his wife or girlfriend, the non-Jewish Denise Coudreuse, leading to disaster when they are betrayed on the Swiss border. But the events do not unfold logically, according to cause and effect: everything is fragmented, implicit, unexplained, and doubtful. The main part of the novel deals with the attempts of this character (later dubbed 'Guy' by his boss) to piece together his life story, including his name, before that event. Nothing in this superficially simple narrative is certain, since the narrator has lost all memory of his past. A series of improbable, somewhat mythological events lead him along as he attempts to reconstruct his real identity, and in the end all we really know are his "trous de mémoire" (memory gaps) that he confesses to an old friend. A study points out all the (no doubt deliberate) coincidences between the narrator Guy Roland's story and Homer's *Odyssey*. Denise Coudreuse, for example, may have improbably provided some kind of thread that may have saved his life.[20]

Thus, there is much artistry in every aspect of the novel, which mimics a detective story. Several characters have more than one name, for example, as appropriate for various aspects of their lives. Just as those who fought for the Resistance would have a nom de guerre, as well as a series of aliases, so those who were fleeing the Nazis, like the main character, adopted pseudonyms. Our character was known by some as Pedro Stern, by others as Pedro McEvoy when he was a diplomat (this name evokes the sound of the word "decoy"). Several names, such as that of his best friend, Freddie Howard de Luz, combine different languages and cultures. Only "Guy Roland" is an extremely simple, generic, fully French name, but it turns out to have been made up for him by his detective agency boss since "Guy" could not remember his real name. If he were actually a Jew from Salonika who had lost his memory because of a wartime trauma, he would probably not have been originally called Pedro, either, as this is an unusual name for a Jew. "Guy" in French as in English, may connote just a man, someone without identity, just as Ulysses calls himself Nobody: the first words of Modiano's novel are "Je ne suis rien" (I am nothing).[21] Little has been established by the end of the novel despite his insistent searching, sparing no cost. Guy has many hard-sought conversations in which he fails to ask the right questions that will get him the answers he craves. Either he pretends to know more than he really does, hiding behind a wall of presumptive knowledge, and thus cannot ask, or he pulls back at the last minute. This is the case with his last appointment, with perhaps the very *passeur* (people-smuggler) who betrayed him, leaving him for dead, and making off with Denise, who has never been heard from again. Guy apparently does not really want to know the terrible truth and prefers to remain in the dark.

The title of the novel underlines the chiaroscuro technique of this fiction. The "Rue des boutiques obscures" is the French version of the evocative name of a street in Rome (Via delle Botteghe Scure, Street of the Dark Cellars)[22] that may have once been Guy's address (perhaps after fleeing from Greece) but the novelist does not tell us. The dark cellars can refer to the dead brain cells of Guy's memory that can never be revived or penetrated. They are also the events that, despite professing to wish to know, Guy would really prefer to remain in the dark about, as knowing the truth might be too traumatic for his restricted and emotionally arid present state of mind.

The title of the novel exemplifies one of Modiano's major obsessions: how urban topography reflects the minds of city-dwellers. He is the ultimate preservationist. He frequently decries the demolition of buildings and streets, the "decapitating" of trees, in his city of Paris. The city is closely tied to one's own identity. Documents of identity are often defective, expired: they ultimately fail us (as in his search for the life and death of Dora Bruder, who disappeared in the Holocaust, in the documentary novel of that name). His investigations into his own identity, such as *Un Pedigrée* (a recounting of his staggeringly dysfunctional family life as a child and adolescent[23]) are cast in the form of novels. Both father and mother neglected him, constantly farming him out to friends, sending him off to harsh, abusive boarding schools for "les enfants mal-aimés," (unloved children) until on graduation his father tried to make him enroll in the army, which he managed to avoid. Shortly after, his father disappeared for good, while his mother, an actress who was always "sans un sou" (out of cash) would accost him on the street for money. Literature was his solace and writing his salvation. He seems to have felt that his generation has been a "lost generation" of French youth in the 1950s and 1960s. They aimlessly wander the streets of Paris, along streets that begin nowhere and lead to nowhere; the heroine of *Dans le café de la jeunesse perdu*,[24] Louki, imagines streets as ending in a cliff from which she dreams of jumping off, and she does indeed commit suicide eventually. Modiano's post-war characters are lost in a fog of youthful purposelessness, the labyrinths of Parisian streets through which they trudge, usually at night, reflecting their states of mind. People lose the ones they love, relationships are cut off by deliberate disappearances, fear of the Gestapo or the post-war draft haunts them, and trauma can be inherited from father to son.

Paris's generally dingy appearance and weather in *La Rue* are rarely penetrated by sunshine; only when Guy visits Denise's former roommate is there some bright light from a chandelier and a hallway light and, when he leaves, even some sunshine. The brilliance of the deadly snow scene blinds him, and he loses consciousness, though he somehow survives. Thus, the contrast of light and darkness constantly presses in on Guy. Many of his childhood friends, despite the period of insouciance that he remembers before the war, have unhappy stories: Gay Orlov, the Russian Jewish refugee, commits suicide as she never wants to grow old; Guy's friend Freddie de Luz disappears to Hawaii where his solo sailing vessel washes up empty, just before Guy catches up with him after twenty years; the novel ends as Guy contemplates once more Gay's childhood photo at a beach, and suddenly realizes she is crying, probably as she does not want to leave the sunlight. Guy comments that such are our lives, a brief moment in the light, and then we are swallowed up by darkness. Modiano's novels are a continual meditation on the same themes, many of which involve history: the Holocaust, the Nazi occupation, the collaboration of French citizens, and Jewish victims' attempted flights to safety, all inspired by loss and a dysfunctional family life.

Another Holocaust-themed semi-autobiographical novel written and published in France is Clarisse Nicoïdski's *Couvre-feux* [Curfew] (1981). The author returns to her early childhood, when as a toddler in a family that had fled to France, she was in semi-hiding from the occupying Nazis in the city of Lyon. The songs and sayings of Judeo-Spanish infuse her view of the world, and the poetry and fiction of Clarisse Nicoïdski return us to the world of Judeo-Spanish or Ladino-speaking Sephardim. In this case the author's family was from the Balkans and she writes Ladino poetry in the particular dialect that we find in the songs of the singer-composer Flory Jagoda and others from the former Yugoslavia. In *Couvre-feux* we have a child's-eye view of the Nazi occupation, and its terrors, interspersed with the older generation's Ladino phrases. The shut-in and extremely bored four-year-old, innocently malicious, knows what will bring fear to her mother's eyes and asks such questions as "*Maman*, do the Nazis really exist?" Her mother reacts with a stream of Ladino prayers and curses and insists that they touch some garlic to fend off the evil eye. The mother is susceptible to asthma and has a very bad attack that evening. The fear and the asthma have both entered her lungs and she mumbles incoherently, scaring her daughter. The novel is to some extent tragicomic, though, as the fears of the mother are not realized, and the whole family survives the war in hiding. Eventually the child is entrusted to an expensive Dickensian-style school/orphanage, where children are whipped and obliged to attend mass, but after the war the parents gradually come back to reclaim the children. The little girl's misunderstanding of what it is that threatens them leads to ironic humor. For example, we often hear the phrase "Les Nazis, la Gestapo, la milice et toute la bastringue" ("The Nazis, the Gestapo, the militia, and the whole merry-go-round/the whole quadrille"—although this is not an exact translation of this final word, which is evocative of low-life and rowdiness, and we know that the threats facing these Jews amounted to far more than the bad manners or drunkenness that this word immediately implies). There is diglossia in Ladino/Judeo-Spanish, especially prayers, as well as insults and curses on the Nazis. Judeo-Spanish is "la langue des parents" (the parents' language) and little Judith is amazed at the orphanage to hear other children's parents using a different language. Her mind is constantly asking questions, and her ears ("elle a l'oreille qui traine partout") are always flapping, but in the absence of explanation she often comes to the wrong conclusions: she thinks "la Gestapo" must be a horrible old witch, that the Nazis eat Jewish children, that the *couvre-feux* is something like a fire engine, or fire truck. What is real is the fear, which causes a particular sensation in the pit of her stomach, and the realization that even after Liberation and several days of celebration, the fears and nightmares do not go away so easily. The last scene is somewhat carnivalesque—at a school ceremony in memory of the heroes of the Resistance who lost their lives, the little girl is secretly playing with matches, and inadvertently sets fire to the long and beautiful black lace mantilla that the schoolmistress is wearing in mourning for her husband. This novel is path-breaking for Sephardic novels of the Holocaust in the sense that it combines a lyrical, surrealistic view of war and Holocaust with the use of diglossia from the Sephardic language.[25]

A similarly ambitious historical novel is Nine Moati's *Les Belles de Tunis* (1983, with a reprinting in 1984 and new editions in Tunis in 1999 and 2004).[26] It covers four generations in a Jewish family of Tunis, following the lives of the women in sympathetic and sensitive detail. Moati describes both the *touansa* (indigenous) and the *grana* or *gorni* (of Spanish or Italian origin) Jewish groups, which did not fully merge until the 1940s. Judging from her Italian-sounding name, her family would have been part of the latter group, since *gorni* means "Livornese," families that immigrated to Tunisia from Livorno, particularly in the eighteenth and nineteenth centuries, for purposes of trade.[27] Even earlier, these families had fled Spain or Portugal for Livorno, a city where *conversos* were encouraged to settle and which had no ghetto. For several centuries, they maintained links with Iberia and would return there for business. The prosperity they brought to Tuscany was highly valued by the ruling Medici. The Livornese Jews' trading networks embraced much of the Mediterranean and extended as far as India. These culturally European Jews tried to introduce European civilization, such as the use of the toothbrush, as the novel describes, to the indigenous Tunisian Jews, but deep cultural rifts separated the two groups for many decades. Like Elissa Rhaïs, but without the need for subterfuge, Nine Moati had a penchant for Orientalism.[28] That is, as a novelist Moati had a painterly eye, seeing aspects of visual beauty in what might have struck other Tunisians as ordinary. She obviously admired the work of the British Orientalist painter, J. F. Lewis, and one of his paintings ("Life in a Harem," 1858) graces the jacket of her novel. A recent, sociological book-length study of Judeo-Maghrebian literature reproduces many of the jackets of recent novels and points out the continuing strong attraction of Orientalism to writers, publishers, and the public they appeal to.[29] The scrutiny of such non-literary elements of a book as the cover/jacket illustration is known as study of the "para-text" and can be fruitful. A later novel by Moati bears the title *L'Orientale* and is the story of a Frenchwoman who fell in love with Lewis the painter himself. An interview with Moati published in www.harissa.com (website of Tunisian Jews, "les Tunes"), emphasizes the Oriental decor of her home,[30] and in recognition of the visual potential of her writing, several of her novels have given rise to television versions. A work on Orientalist painting, the art book entitled *The Shafik Gabr Collection: Masterpieces of Orientalist Art* (2012) attempts to put Orientalism in a new, more positive light, as the Egyptian collector believes that European Orientalist art, through its expression of curiosity about the Other, can be conducive toward East-West understanding. Nine Moati's historical writing, as well as her wartime novel, *La Passagère sans étoile*,[31] presents us (without irony) with heroines who are beautiful, courageous, and good, and has attracted a loyal coterie of French-language readers, not all in France. The fact that the latest edition of her novel was published in Tunis suggests that, although her work is Orientalist in tone, it may also help to serve the purpose of mutual understanding, enabling Tunisian Muslims in some measure to understand sympathetically the past of the Jewish community of Tunisia.

The year 1992, as noted earlier, inspired many historical novels on the period leading up to and following the expulsion of 1492. Didier Nebot, a French Jew (of Algerian origin), projects back to the fate of the fictional Benavista family. Nebot writes in French of the land of his distant ancestors, Spain, and the fate of the Benavistas during the difficult century preceding 1492.[32] In his historical novel, *Le Chemin de l'exil* (1992), two brothers born near Toledo, one a faithful but persecuted Jew, the other a *converso*, figure prominently. A love of the landscape of Spain is a keynote, though the faithful brother's descendants are eventually forced to choose exile, taking refuge in the Muslim lands of the Maghreb. There is an implicit alliance between Jews and Muslims, who suffered similar collective fates in Spain (a choice of forced conversion or exile) at roughly the same time. Louise Larlee has pointed this out, as well as an incipient parallel between Spain of the fifteenth century and France of the late twentieth century (Larlee, pp. 8–9).

A somewhat rosy-tinted view of Jewish life and Jewish-Muslim *convivencia* (coexistence) puts the novel in alignment with Nine Moati's *Les Belles de Tunis* (1983), a "Jewish girl imprisoned in the harem" plot twist is reminiscent of the Algerian Elissa Rhaïs (or of the Book of Esther) and the cold, implacable hostility of Castilian Old Christians reminds us of Albert Memmi's Castile episode in *Le Désert* (1977). The frontier country, marking the border between Christian and Muslim realms up to 1492, the lives of *conversos/marranos* as wealthy but despised social pariahs, paralleled by persecuted Jews and Muslims left behind as the frontier moved southward, are somewhat reminiscent of today's socially marginalized in postcolonial France. The Sephardic author's clear sympathy or nostalgia for a hypothetical Jewish-Muslim symbiosis is shown not only in the structure of this novel but also in the different focus of two of his subsequent works.[33] After many dangers, the surviving Jewish member of the Benavista family lands on North African soil, and is greeted by a local Muslim in the closing lines of the novel:

> An adolescent of more or less his own age was smiling at him. He had olive skin, black eyes, and he was speaking in an incomprehensible language. He was an Arab, an Arab of Algeria. He extended a friendly hand to David. "Salam

Aleikum," he said. And David, understanding that he had been saved, replied, "Shalom."[34]

This novel's somewhat rosy-tinted view of Jewish-Muslim relations in North Africa demonstrates a need in some historical novels to provide a "happy ending." Perhaps that is often the purpose of a historical novel: to amend and improve on the tragic chaos of history.

Colette Fellous, a novelist of Tunisian origin, takes a spatial and visual approach, in a complex and hallucinatory novel, *Avenue de France* (2001).[35] Her transitions from present-day Paris to Tunis of a century or more ago are fascinating. In a Paris street, the first-person narrator hears a sudden cry that provokes in her an imaginative return to her childhood in Tunis and enables her to encounter her grandfather when he was fourteen years old. Historical trends and exact locations' change over time both come to life in the novel. The grandfather decides at that precise moment in 1879 that he must learn French and privilege it over his own Judeo-Arabic in order to survive and succeed. Soon after, in 1881, came the French protectorate and the colonial period with all it meant for Tunisian Jews and their cultural transition. His granddaughter, the novel's narrator, is able to stroll down the "Avenue de France" (later Avenue Bourguiba) and meet her ancestors as they adapt to French culture and broaden their horizons beyond Tunis, transforming themselves into Europeans. This is how she slides into the past:

> I have the good fortune to be there, on this late morning in 1879, and meet the eyes of my grandfather. His eyes sparkle, he is fourteen years old, and this is an important day . . . our eyes meet. . . . All the words that he has used up to now to live and grow, to look at and tame the things that surround him, have collapsed at one blow. I raised my arm to stop him, but it was too late, history was marching ahead in leaps and bounds, his decision was taken, the decision for all of us, as well.[36]

The cry from the Paris street turns out to have been a visceral cry from a woman with mental problems, but on a novelistic level it is the trigger to unleash the historical imagination. The author's ancestors appear at different stages in history, caught up in their mundane lives of childhood, courtship, family life, with all the material trappings of each period. Colette Fellous has a deep sense of love for the people involved in their innocently trivial concerns, as the clock advances toward the times of war and brutality, followed by exile. However, in the present day, the narrator feels that she and her brother, who now live in France, are cut off from their Tunisian roots by their lack of Arabic. Her visiting brother, after a trivial incident on a street in Tunis, and accusations in a police station against which he cannot defend himself because he knows no Arabic, is prevented from renewing his Tunisian passport ever again. Just as the half-mad woman in the Paris street screams because of some unspecified injury against her, the narrator's heart is torn by an unspecified crime, perhaps that of unjust exile.

Gisèle Halimi, a prolific writer and journalist, lawyer, and feminist advocate of Tunisian Jewish origin, reaches back much further into Judeo-Maghrebian history to create her novel *La Kahina* (2006).[37] The name "Kahina," as readers may know, is a feminine form of "cohen." This portrait of a supremely powerful woman, the legendary priestess and soothsayer, is based, we are told, on an enormous amount of research. Halimi is not the first to research the Kahena: Albert Memmi's 1977 novel included a male figure, al-Kahin, a similarly doomed Judeo-Berber resistance leader against the Arab-Muslim takeover of North Africa, as did Roger Ikor in 1979 and, in 1998, Didier Nebot (both female figures).[38] A Jewish publishing house in Tunis between the wars was named Éditions La Kahéna, and there is even a play about her. Despite researchers' efforts (noted in the six-page bibliography and the footnotes to Halimi's novel), we know very little about the historical figure, and so the legendary Kahena provides fertile ground for novelists. The female figure who dominates this novel is sexually passionate, an infallible seer of the future, a generous enemy who liberates the prisoners she takes in battle instead of executing them. Legend has it that she was betrayed to the Arabs by her two sons; in the novel, she also adopts an Arab prince, a prisoner who should have been executed. He becomes her slave, but at the same time communicates her battle plans and movements through an intermediary to the enemy. Though a brilliant and charismatic commander, she loses the loyalty of her own people through a cruel preventive scorched earth policy, is inexorably harassed and hunted down until in the ultimate scene she is captured, decapitated, and her proud head, a slight, scornful smile still playing about its lips, is sent to the caliph, who cannot understand how a mere woman had given his forces so much trouble. This tragic and powerful story, the defeat of the last Jewish-Berber resistance against Islam and the invading Arab forces in approximately 700, before they forged ahead to rule the rest of the Maghreb and conquer southern and central Spain in 711, needs little aesthetic adornment to engage the attention of readers, especially the Jewish public at which it is aimed. To enhance the mythical relevance of this tale, Gisèle Halimi also tells us that the story was told to her as a child by her father and uncles. The feminist aspect only enhances its appeal to us, as we have a female leader defending her beleaguered people against colonizing, marauding foreign armies which impose an alien culture and religion on those they have defeated.

Jacob Cohen's novel set in Morocco, *Du Danger de monter sur la terrasse* (2006),[39] evokes ancient Jewish fears while emphasizing how, even through trauma and tragedy, domination and dhimmitude, Jews and Muslims of Morocco are still inexorably linked. The ending is a slight comfort to those who have suffered rather than a happy one, though some happiness may come of it. To explain, this powerful novel which is set a generation ago and in the present, tells the story of a Moroccan Jewish family, whose little girl was kidnapped and forcibly converted to Islam. She is married off into an orthodox Muslim family in the medina, cut off from her family, only streets away from where she grew up, and leads a sheltered and dutiful life devoted to her mother-in-law, husband, and daughter.

The Jewish family cannot stop mourning the loss of their daughter who, on the morning of the holiday of Sukkot, had gone up to their terrace to admire their *sukka* once more. The terrace in this Moroccan city was theoretically a safe place where women could do their laundry and children could play without the need to venture on the street. However, it was possible to cross the close-set rooftops as far as the Muslim quarters, and vice versa. Jews feared incursions from the medina across the roofs. Perhaps even the legendary Jewish martyr Solika la Tzadika had been captured on a rooftop and, refusing conversion to marry a prince, was executed in Fez in 1834.[40] The little girl in the novel had been cautioned not to go up to the roof. The Jews' worst fears were realized once more, and the family, powerless at the time of this novel, simply did not speak of this tragedy.

The author's ingenious plot comes to the rescue, though. The girl's father, a jeweler, had fashioned identical precious stones for his two children, his son and his daughter, and she was wearing it when abducted and converted. She gives it to her Muslim daughter, Khalidja, who in keeping with more modern views, and on her mother's insistence, many years later is allowed to go to France for her education and professional training. The Jewish family had moved to Paris years before, where lack of fear and infinite freedoms allow their own next generation (the younger brother's son) much liberty, even the liberty to date a Muslim woman. The reader may guess how fate and a skillful plot line bring the two young people, unbeknownst first cousins, together. The novel ends with the weeping (from joy) of Khalidja's mother, about to travel to France to visit her daughter and probably the boyfriend, with the permission of her Muslim husband. History, thus, can intrude via fiction even on modern Sephardic families. The implication is that, despite injustice and the imbalanced power relationship, Jews and Muslims in a sense had formed one big family in Morocco.

A similar conclusion may be reached concerning the novel, *Sépharade* (2011), by Eliette Abécassis,[41] a romantic novel that bills itself (or is billed by the publisher) as "le grand roman du monde sépharade." It involves a search for identity on the part of a young Sephardic woman living in France, a return to Moroccan roots, a traditional Moroccan Sephardic wedding, and the intrusion of a curse via the evil eye, which means that she can never unite with the love of her life. The novel is supposed to encompass the history of Moroccan Jews from Iberia and the expulsion, the inquisitions, the survival of their beliefs and culture in Morocco and elsewhere, up to the present day. Like other cultural artifacts (novels and films), it takes a particular aspect of Sephardic culture (Moroccan) and projects it as the ultimate version, whereas there are actually multiple versions of Sephardic identity that claim similar legitimacy and "last word" status for its practitioners as the "real" Sephardim. Possibly each country of origin lays claim to its own version.

The foregoing discussion of the return into history among Sephardic Francophone writers, lengthy though it is, highlights the importance of the trend. Whether the history they deal with is distant or of yesterday, the past has served them constructively in their efforts to express, through their novels, Sephardic identity and its lineage.

Technical virtuosity, like that of A. B. Yehoshua, is generally less important to francophone writers than a personal recounting of events in history, from Memmi's alter ego's fictional autobiography, to Moati's, Nicoïdski's and Nebot's family autofictions, often highlighting events in the story of a family over generations. The families are usually intended to be emblematic of other Sephardic families too. Their culture exists outside of established institutions other than the family (the exception is Modiano whose characters, lacking family and continuity, are disconnected in the extreme). The cyclical idea, that history tends to return and repeat itself, often embodied in the form of historical novels, is always there, though, in the shared ambition of most of these writers to evoke and breathe life into a personal and communal Sephardic identity.

NOTES

1. A. B. Yehoshua, *The Retrospective* (New York: Doubleday, 2013). See also my interview with the author," Interview with A. B. Yehoshua" in *Sephardic Horizons* 3:1 (Spring 2013), https://sephardichorizons.org/Volume1/Issue2/Articles_V1I2/Yehoshua.html.

2. Yael Halevi-Wise, *The Retrospective Imagination of A. B. Yehoshua*, (University Park: Pennsylvania State University Press, 2021), suggests that '*Hesed Sefaradi*' may (also) refer to *Sephardic* kindness, in forgiving the Spanish and Portuguese for their persecution, and in bringing about a Sephardic rapprochement with these countries in recent times. See also Yael Halevi-Wise, "Where is the Sephardism of *Hesed Sefaradi/The Retrospective?*" *Sephardic Horizons* 4:1 (2014), https://www.sephardichorizons.org/Volume4/Issue1/WhereSephardism.html.

3. See Yael Halevi-Wise, *The Retrospective Imagination of A.B. Yehoshua*, Chapter 2 on spatiality, "Mapping A.B. Yehoshua's Worldview," (pp. 16–51) and Chapter 7 on

historicity, "Love under the Burden of History," (pp. 145–160). Halevi-Wise analyzes Yehoshua's complex and multidimensional opus with multidimensional critical tools, appropriate to Yehoshua's complexity.

4. Angelina Muñiz-Huberman, *Tierra adentro* (Mexico City: Joaquin Mortiz, 1977). The main character, Rafael, born in Toledo in the mid-sixteenth century, escapes the inquisition and undertakes a lengthy and arduous pilgrimage to the Holy Land, ending up in Safed.

5. See Sandra M. Cypess, review of Angelina Muñiz-Huberman, *Los Esperandos: Piratas Judeosportugueses . . . y yo* (Madrid: Sefarad Editores, 2017). *Sephardic Horizons* 11:1 (Winter 2021). https://www.sephardichorizons.org/Volume11/Issue1/Cypess.html.

6. See Yael Halevi-Wise, *Sephardism* (Stanford: Stanford Univ. Press, 2012) esp. the Introduction, "Through the Prism of Sepharad: Modern Nationalism, Literary History, and the Impact of the Sephardic Experience," pp. 1–34.

7. An earlier, much longer version of this portion of the chapter was previously published in *Philological Quarterly* 61:2 (Spring 1982), pp. 193–207. With thanks to the editors of *Philological Quarterly* for permission to reproduce. It also formed the basis of the Translator's Preface to my translation of this novel (Albert Memmi, *The Desert*, Syracuse: Syracuse University Press, 2015). Other studies of the novel are Isaac Yetiv, "Du *Scorpion* au *Désert*: Albert Memmi Revisited," *Studies in Twentieth-Century Literature* 7:1 (1982), pp. 77–82; ibid.,"From Ethnocentrism to Humanism: Albert Memmi's *Le Désert,"* *International Fiction Review* 16:2 (1989), pp. 128–131; Dalia Kandiyoti, "The Possibilities of History: *The Desert* and North African Jewish Identity," *The European Legacy* 1:4 (1996), pp. 1452–58; and Lia Nicole Brozgal's "Blindness, the Visual, and Ekphrastic Impulses: Albert Memmi Colours in the Lines," *French Studies* 64:3 (2010), pp. 317–328 (pp. 324–25 discuss the illustrations). See also Afifa and Samir Marzouki, *Individu et communautés dans l'oeuvre littéraire d'Albert Memmi* (Paris: L'Harmattan, 2010), pp. 15–16, and Chapter 8.

Albert Memmi, *Le Désert ou La Vie et les aventures de Jubaïr Ouali el-Mammi* (Paris: Gallimard, 1977; Gallimard Folio, 1989). Trans. Judith Roumani (Syracuse: Syracuse Univ. Press, 2015). Subsequent references are to the French 1977 edition and the English 2015 edition.

8. Tamerlane in reality never reached as far as North Africa, and certainly not southern Morocco, where al-Mammi's kingdom is situated.

9. A relatively new term for this in literary criticism is 'autofiction' and, for writing by a Jewish author, 'autojudeography.' See Thomas Nolden, "A la recherche du judaïsme perdu: Contemporary Jewish Writing in France," pp. 118–38 in Vivian Liska and Thomas Nolden, eds., *Contemporary Jewish Writing in Europe: A Guide* (Bloomington: Indiana Univ. Press, 2008), esp. pp. 125–26. According to Nolden, the term was invented by Robert Ouaknine.

10. Unpub. taped interview by Jacques Roumani, based on my list of questions, conducted at Memmi's home in Paris, Dec. 4, 1977.

11. Memmi stated in the interview "J'ai fait le maximum de lectures possible. . . . " They may include Haim Hirschberg, *A History of the Jews in North Africa* (1965; tr. Leiden: Brill, 1974); Nahum Slouschz, *Travels in North Africa* (Philadelphia: Jewish

Pub. Soc., 1927); André Chouraqui, *Marche vers l'Occident: Les Juifs d'Afrique du Nord* (Paris: Presses universitaires, 1952), esp. p. 34: "Dans le Touat enfin, à l'extrême nord, au Gourara, entre Tamentit et Sba Guerrara, les historiens arabes nous rapportent l'existence d'un petit royaume juif, dans un pays où la langage et la race des Zenata berbères se sont conservées intactes. . . . " This seems to be the source for "Ce qu'en disent les historiens" *Le Désert,* pp. 11–12. Memmi would not have been aware, in the mid-1970s, of Jacob Oliel's research, as the latter's first book on the subject was not published until 1994. See Jacob Oliel, *Les Juifs au Sahara: le Touat au Moyen Age* (Paris: CNRS, 1994) and idem, *Les Juifs au Sahara: une presence millénaire* (Quebec, Côte-St-Luc: Editions Elysée, 2007).

12. Memmi may have referred to the French translation, *Histoire des Berbères et des dynasties musulmanes de l'Afrique septentrionale,* 2 vols. Trans. W. M. de Slane (1847–51; rpt. Paris: Guithner, 1968).

13. Walter J. Fischel, *Ibn Khaldûn and Tamerlane: Their Historic Meeting in Damascus, 1401 A.D.* (Berkeley and Los Angeles: U. of California Press, 1952); *Ibn Khaldûn in Egypt* (Berkeley and Los Angeles: U. of California Press, 1967).

14. "C'est en 1392, après un assaut décisive de Tamerlan, suivi d'un massacre à peu près complet de la population, que le Royaume-du-Dedans cessa d'exister. Huit ans après, en 1400 exactement, dans la ville de Damas, mise à sac à son tour par le même conquérant, El-Mammi présentait ses hommages au vainqueur" (p. 12).

15. Lia Brozgal, *Against Autobiography: Albert Memmi and the Production of Theory* (Lincoln: University of Nebraska Press, 2013).

16. See Guy Dugas, "Quelques compléments á propos de l'écriture colorée chez Albert Memmi," *Sephardic Horizons* 5:3–4 (Summer-Fall 2015), https://www.sephardichorizons.org/Volume5/Issue3-4/Dugas.html.

17. But see Bailey Trela, "The Jewish Half-Lives of Patrick Modiano: The Nobel Laureate on the Paper Trail of Evanescent French Jews, in *Family Record*," *Tablet Magazine* Sept. 6, 2019. https://www.tabletmag.com/sections/arts-letters/articles/patrick-modiano-family-record. As his writing career progressed, Modiano became more and more involved with the elusive Jewish origins of his family.

18. *Saved by Language: The Story of Moris Albahari*, dir. Bryan Kirschen and Susanna Zaraysky, 2015.

19. His story is told in Devi Mays, *Forging Ties, Forging Passports: Migration and the Modern Sephardi Diaspora* (Stanford: Stanford University Press, 2020). See also my review in *Sephardic Horizons,* 11:2–3, www.sephardichorizons.org/Volume11/Issue2-3/Roumani.html#_edn2.

20. See Charles O'Keefe, "The *Odyssey* and Signs to the Rescue: Escaping the Labyrinth and Enjoying Gaps in Patrick Modiano's *Rue des boutiques obscures,"* in *Nottingham French Studies* 45:1 (Summer 2006), pp. 16–26. Also Devila Cooke and Colin Nettelbeck, "Modiano in the Feminine: *A nous deux Madame la Vie,"* *Nottingham French Studies* 45:1 (Summer 2006), pp. 39–53, for a more general discussion of the relationship between his life and work, especially the early emphasis on male characters, and the emergence of female protagonists in his later works, as he came to terms with the relative influences of his parents in his life. Much new material has come out since Modiano won the Nobel Prize for Literature in 2014.

21. O'Keefe, idem.

22. The actual street in Rome is a very mundane and busy downtown thoroughfare, with nothing mysterious about it.

23. *Un Pedigrée* (2005) may be found in Patrick Modiano, *Romans* (Paris: Gallimard, 2013), pp. 829–890. Another autobiographical novel is *Livret de famille* (1977), ibid., pp. 205–333, dedicated to the memory of his brother, Rudy, who died as a child and had been the only real family for him.

24. 2007. See ibid., pp. 895–981. This novel is full of streets that lead nowhere, or that lead to eternity, such as the street that passes through the middle of the Montparnasse cemetery, at the end of which the narrator Roland has the illusion that he will find his dead beloved: "Elle était plutôt une zone frontière. . . . Quand nous arrivions au bout, nous entrions dans un pays où nous étions à l'abri de tout. . . . J'ai eu un moment l'illusion qu'au-delà du cimetière je te retrouverais. Là-bas, ce serait l'Éternel retour" (p. 975).

25. See more at: Judith Roumani, "The Holocaust in Sephardi-Mizrahi Literature: A Review of Some Responses in Prose," http://www.sephardichorizons.org/Volume4/Issue2/Roumani.html.

26. Nine Moati, *Les Belles de Tunis* [The beauties of Tunis] (Paris: Seuil, 1983), republished Tunis: Cérès, 1999, 2004, with a special introduction by the author for the Tunisian reading public. There is no translation into English but an Arabic translation is apparently in preparation.

27. For details on their history see Francesca Trivellato, *The Familiarity of Strangers:The Sephardic Diaspora, Livorno, and Cross-Cultural Trade in the Early Modern Period* (Newhaven. Yale University Press, 2009).

28. See my *"Elissa Rhaïs:* Enslaved Imagination in Colonial Algeria," *CELFAN Review* 2:1 (Nov. 1982). Many of her novels are set in a pre-colonial or early colonial time in North Africa, before the pervasive French influence of her own day (the 1920s).

29. Ewa Tartakowsky, *Les Juifs et le Maghreb: Fonctions sociales d'une littérature d'exil* (Paris: Presses universitaires François-Rabelais, 2016), pp. 122–132.

30. Yaël König, "Rencontre avec Nine Moati," n.d., https://harissa.com/D_Arts/rencontreavecninemoatty.htm.

31. Nine Moati, *La Passagère sans étoile* [The passenger without a star] (Paris; Seuil, 1989) which could even be classified as a Holocaust novel. The star in the title has a double meaning, as 'guiding light' and the Jewish star, since the heroine, being from Livorno and Tunis, is almost never suspected of being Jewish, enabling her to return to German-occupied Paris and work in the Resistance.

32. Didier Nebot, *Le Chemin de l'exil* (Paris: Presses de la Renaissance, 1992). For an in-depth analysis, see Louise Larlee's "Représentations littéraires de l'histoire sépharade dans *Le chemin de l'exil de Didier Nebot*: MA thesis, McGill University, 2009.

33. Didier Nebot, *La Kahéna: Reine d'Ifrikia* (Paris: Carrière, 1998) and a historical essay, *Les Tribus oubliées d'Israël: L'Afrique judéo-berbère, des origines aux Almohades* (Paris: Romillat, 1999).

34. Un adolescent de son âge à peu près lui souriait. Il avait le teint mat, les yeux noirs, il parlait un langage incompréhensible. C'était un Arabe, un Arabe d'Algérie. Il tendit une main amicale à David.
"*Salam Aleikum*," lui dit-il.
Et David, comprenant qu'il était sauvé, répondit: "Chalom" (p. 316).
This discussion of Nebot is based on my chapter in Yael Halevi-Wise, *Sephardism* (Stanford: Stanford Univ. Press, 2012), pp. 232–233.

35. Colette Fellous, *Avenue de France* (Paris: Gallimard, 2001). Born in Tunisia and living in France since the age of seventeen, she has authored about twenty novels.

36. J'ai la chance d'être là, en cette fin de matinée de 1879, pour croiser le regard de mon grand-père. Ses yeux scintillant, il a quatorze ans et c'est un grand jour . . . nos yeux se croisent. . . . Tous les mots qu'il utilisait jusque-là por vivre et grandir, pour regarder et apprivoiser les choses qui l'entouraient, ont chuté d'un coup. J'ai levé mon bras pour l'arrêter, mais c'était trop tard, l'histoire marchait à grandes enjambées, sa décision était prise, celle de nous tous aussi (pp. 110–111).

37. Gisèle Halimi, *La Kahina* (Paris: Plon, 2006).

38. See Joelle Allouche-Benayoun, "Gisèle Halimi, La Kahina," *Clio: Histoire, femmes, et sociétés* 30 (2009), http://journals.openedition.org/clio/9502. There are at least a dozen novels with the same title by a wide array of authors.

39. Jacob Cohen *Du danger de monter sur la terrasse* (Casablanca: Tarik Editions, 2006).

40. The story of Solika has inspired novels and a play. See "'Solika,' A Play Performed at the Jerusalem Theater by the Beersheva Theater Company," reviewed by Judith Roumani, https://www.sephardichorizons.org/Volume8/Issue3&4/Solika.html.

41. Eliette Abécassis, *Sépharade* (Paris: Albin Michel, 2011). Her prolific output and translations into many languages have made her one of the most popular French novelists.

Conclusions

Sephardic literature in modern times has migrated in many senses—from oral elements to written literature, from traditional to modern ways of life, and all the way to post-modern, from East to West, or alternatively from South to North, from southern Europe and the southern coast of the Mediterranean, to northern Europe and North America (without forgetting South America), from Islamic lands to Christian countries and to the Jewish state, from forgetfulness to remembering, and from traumas to partial healing.

It has migrated from a fixation on the present to evocations of the past, from tradition to modernity and beyond, and back into History. Despite their deep interest in the past, Sephardim have become and remain a significant cultural voice in Israel, in France, and in other countries too, particularly in the French-speaking world, *la francophonie*. Our study of the novels by Sephardim originating in some half dozen countries, around the Mediterranean and Middle East, and who have migrated to another half dozen countries, while expressing themselves in French, the language of a third country (a language that many learned in the schools of the Alliance Israélite Universelle), shows significant similarities among the writers. A future volume, perhaps, can do justice to Sephardic fiction writers in other languages, such as Spanish, Ladino/Judeo-Spanish, or English. Acquiring modern French culture and language is not, however, the only bond between the writers I have examined: they also stem from Jewish communities that have similar histories and have suffered similar disruptions. Whether or not they have any actual ancestral connections to Iberia, and whether they use Ladino/Judeo-Spanish or not, the overarching tradition (*nusach*, *halakha*, and *minhagim*) that they share is a Sephardic one, reaching back before Spain to the Middle East and in particular Babylonia. Jewish communities that had been entrenched since before the advent of Islam were everywhere uprooted in modern times and their members launched willy-nilly on a process of accelerated modernization and migration. They tell their stories of the end of traditional symbiosis or *convivence* in Muslim lands and of the extreme disruptions of modern history that have buffeted them.

Though newer, gathering manifestations of antisemitism in France[1] may, according to many analysts, portend the end or at least the decline of a flourishing Jewish culture in France, perhaps this will not be so in the far-flung francophone diaspora world. The love affair that Jews have had with French culture since long before Avraham Galante decided to write his *Histoire des Juifs de Turquie* in French (in Istanbul, in 1940) may be eroding in France, or perhaps it is merely moving to other shores. Israel has a vibrant francophone community composed of Sephardim from Mediterranean and Arab countries, and Sephardic communities have been reestablishing themselves there in modern, Israeli versions of their old communities in Muslim and Christian countries. The European Jewish intelligentsia traditionally has been Francophile, many Sephardim from North Africa and the Mediterranean have moved to Canada and the United States, and there are or have been pockets of Sephardim in French-speaking Africa. The legacy of gratitude for Napoleon's perceived benevolence toward Jews, reinforced by the Crémieux Decree of 1860 and the impact of the Alliance Israélite Universelle, survived the Dreyfuss Affair as well as the Vichy government's and French individuals' collaboration with Nazi deportations, the temporary loss of their French citizenship for the Algerian Jews, and De Gaulle's later less than friendly pronouncements about Jews and Israel. Though perhaps not desired, either by non-Jews or by the Jews already resident in France (Paris was characterized as "Vilna on the Seine") French Jewish life has been greatly enriched by the arrival of Sephardim in the fifties, sixties and seventies due to the end of colonialism and the end of Jewish life in Muslim lands. The extreme and traumatic events that have assailed French-speaking Sephardim in modern times also inspired them to a flourishing literary activity, particularly in prose. One (maybe paradoxical) example is the survival of Ladino or, as it is called in French (and sometimes in other languages, too), Judeo-Spanish. In Belgium, France, and Israel (and even in the United States to some extent) classes in the Sephardic language are flourishing. The survival of the language after the Holocaust is largely due to such writers and broadcasters as the Israeli author Isaac Ben-Rubi, whose Ladino/Judeo-Spanish novel of the Holocaust, *El Sekreto del mudo* (1953) was translated into French as *Le muet de Auschwitz*,[2] and scholar-poets like Haim-Vidal Séphiha, the champion of Judeo-Spanish and its teaching in French-speaking lands. A bilingual dictionary in French and Judeo-Spanish prepared by Isaac Nehama, and bilingual periodicals such as *La Lettre sépharade* or *Los Muestros* also have attested to the liveliness of Sephardic culture and its synergy with the French language. Other secular francophone manifestations are, to give just a few examples in addition to the novels discussed herein, the annual Djoha Festival in Paris, and cinema such as Jewish-Muslim collaborations in Tunisia (*Un été a la Goulette,* 1996, and *Villa Jasmin,* 2009) and the

2012 film by Hélène Trigano, *Fragments de la mémoire sépharade*. Another important and popular Jewish-Muslim-French collaboration is the animated film *Le Chat du rabbin* directed by Joann Sfar in 2011.[3] A recent film, *El Hara* (2017, directed by Margaux Fitoussi and Mo Scarpelli), explores the poor Jewish district in Tunis in which Albert Memmi grew up. In the religious sphere, events such as "pélerinages," pilgrimages originally performed in North Africa with local Jewish saints' tombs as their destination, are now performed in Parisian suburbs with a parking lot as the destination.[4] Several prominent modern-day Israeli Sephardic rabbis, possible contenders for the position of Rishon l'Zion, chief Sephardic rabbi, are of French education and rabbinical training. Historically, in the early twentieth century, the French-language press flourished almost everywhere there were Sephardim to be found: *Le Journal de Salonique* (the longest-lived French-language periodical in the Ottoman Empire), *La Voix juive* (Alexandria), *La Tribune Juive* and *La Revue Sioniste* (Cairo), *La Nation* of Salonika (in French and Ladino, voice of the Club des Intimes, alumni of the French school) and *La Justice* and several others published in Tunis[5]—all attest to the overwhelming importance of French in these Jewish communities, continuing into the mid-twentieth century. The journals ceased publication either due to the Holocaust, wartime difficulties, accusations of Zionist activity, or the gradual diminishing of their readership as Jews left these countries permanently.

Perhaps because Sephardim have largely settled successfully into their new homes, their history and travails are little known outside the French sphere.[6] Their fiction embodies the pain of upheavals of many kinds. The skillful fictionalized accounts, often autobiographical, enliven these processes of modern history, which otherwise are viewed by Westerners, including Ashkenazi Jews, as exotic and remote.

The French-language Sephardic writers discussed in this book often remained faithful to the oral sources of Sephardic culture and incorporated many elements from oral literature into their writings. They embodied in their fictions the idea of a portable homeland of their unique cultures, one that could be taken with them, as the imperatives of modern history made life more precarious in their original physical homes. When the sudden ruptures came, and they were forced to leave, they were already well equipped with both a French culture and the memories of their traditional upbringings and identity to survive successfully in modern Western societies. Just as Albert Camus, a third-generation Algerian, part French, part Spanish, speaking a French-based patois that drew on several languages, saw his Mediterranean idyll coming to an end (if it had ever existed),[7] so Albert Memmi, whose first language was Judeo-Arabic, who had worked for and applauded Tunisian independence, and was an admirer of Habib Bourguiba, found it impractical to stay on in the new country that had no space for its minorities, even those that had been there longer than Arabs. The Jewish writers took with them their portable homeland, consisting perhaps of a few beloved objects which, like Proust's madeleines, could inspire their writing, and they took an originally oral culture of storytelling, with stock figures like the wise clown Djoha, proverbs, traditional stories and a preference for oral literature. Traditional divisions between men's and women's storytelling could still be traced, though with much irony, even in a new Western society such as France. These elements and techniques were skillfully woven into their modern fictions. Thus, after a hiatus of a few decades, they were often able to bring about the rebirth of a greatly transformed Tunisian Jewish culture, for example, in France and in Israel. One can posit a literary lineage from Ryvel's early twentieth century tales of the *hara* of Tunis, to Albert Memmi's use of oral tales, and to Marco Koskas' late twentieth century semi-humorous, semi-sad tales of Jewish life in the provincial town of Nabeul. The more humorous and fantastic elements employed in women's storytelling are reflected in the writing of Annie Fitoussi. Albert Bensoussan, and Edmond Amran El Maleh, though with different approaches, both embody oral elements in their writing. Hovering over these more modern writers are the figures of Elias Canetti, with many oral elements and his admiration of the public storyteller, and above all Albert Cohen, whose larger-than-life characters such as Mangeclous, according to several critics, are the pure voice of Sepharad for the new generation. For women Sephardic writers the work of Elissa Rhaïs and of Blanche Bendahan (both of Algeria)[8] have provided models or inspiration.

The end of historic symbiosis (if it ever really existed) and the sudden ruptures of History fostered a spate of autobiographical novels. Migratory writing interlaced cultures and world views without glossing over the inconsistencies. Naim Kattan of Iraq, Claude Kayat of Tunisia, Albert Bensoussan of Algeria, and of course the doyen of the autofiction, Albert Memmi, used their fascinating if painful personal experiences on the margins of modernity to help create the novel of migration. It is interesting that the Mediterranean itself has not figured more prominently in these fictions though other seas, such as the Atlantic Ocean and Indian Ocean have figured as the cultural space of transition in other literatures of migration.[9] But for Sephardim, the cultural issues began long before and have continued long after the voyages by air or sea.

From Didier Nebot's imagining of the expulsion from Spain, an archetype for more recent expulsions, to Giorgio Bassani's portrayal of what must have seemed like the end of Jewish life in Italy during the Shoah, to Naim Kattan's farewell to Iraq, Albert Memmi's and Marco Koskas' departure from Tunisia, and Andre Aciman's reluctant leave-taking from Egypt, emotional pain is sometimes masked under humor, but always present. Algerian Jews, already imbued with French culture, seem to regret more of the physical characteristics of Algeria—the sunshine, the connection with the land—whereas Sephardim from other countries took with them a particular folkloric culture and set of religious practices, things more easily transportable.[10] The pain not only of leaving one's native soil, but also of losing a traditional culture, which might be devalued and denigrated in the new home, is expressed in the collection of childhood memories by Jewish writers brought together by a Muslim writer, the Algerian Leïla Sebbar, in her *Une Enfance juive en Meditérranée musulmane* (2012), which represents an admirable imaginative leap of empathy on her part. Over the last few decades, consciousness of Sephardic uprootedness in the writing of Sephardim themselves, for example Ami Bouganim, Albert Bensoussan, and Claude Kayat began producing philosophical and imaginative literature reflecting the cultural contradictions of migration by favoring humor and analysis over harmony and reconciliation.

Sephardic writers passed quickly from modernity to post-modernity, their later writing expressing the cultural contradictions not in resolution or synthesis but in deliberate highlighting of disharmony, bilingualism/diglossia, non-linearity, shifts in tone and genre, fractured writing, and other symptoms of the post-modern predicament. Their life stories of uprootedness prepared them thoroughly for the post-modern condition. A focus on the Holocaust, exile and mourning, expressed in surrealist and poetic prose by Jabès, on displacement and punning by Derrida and Cixous, on multilingualism and diglossia by El Maleh, on tragicomic, ironic characters recalling those of Albert Cohen in Annie Fitoussi, Marco Koskas or Claude Kayat: all these elements express an extreme sensitivity among Sephardic writers to post-modern forces.

Perhaps because literary explorers have become exhausted with all this post-modernity, a countertrend, the return of the wave, has been a turn back into History, with attendant techniques such as cyclical writing. Two relatively early historical novels by Sephardim, Muñiz-Huberman's *Tierra adentro* and Albert Memmi's *Le Désert* (both from 1977), as well as A. B. Yehoshua's *Mar Mani* (1992), have perhaps inspired other writers. Nine Moati presents Tunisian Jewish history through an Orientalist lens, like her popular Algerian predecessor of the 1920s and '30s, Elissa Rhaïs. One should also mention the Holocaust-themed historical novels of Nine Moati and of Patrick Modiano. Memmi's novel successfully evokes the past of the Jews of North Africa, while Didier Nebot focuses on an "out of Spain" theme of the expulsion. Historical novels, in bringing a period to life, sometimes draw on traditional genres such as oral storytelling, thus circling back to the origins of Sephardic literature discussed in chapter one. Historical novels are also by nature cyclical, in taking us back into the past, but as they make this past relevant to our present, they deposit us back in the current moment.

An interest in history leads us to the question of "memory" and attendant issues. In Europe, "lieux de mémoire," the preserving of cultural heritage sites, evident for all Jews in Holocaust sites, memorials, museums, etc, or for Sephardim in Red de Juderías/ Rutas de Sefarad tracing and identifying old Jewish communities in Spain, is of great importance. Many other manifestations, such as the preservation of old synagogues in places where there are no longer Jews, are viewed as essential.[11] They are important for Jewish identity, and for non-Jews constitute an educational, cultural, historical, artistic, and touristic asset. In Spain the re-integration of the Jewish aspect into Spanish culture has been an essential element in post-Franco modern Spanish identity. For Sephardim expelled from Muslim lands, however, in most cases all this is increasingly impossible. Exceptions that we hope will continue to be available are such sites as the La Ghriba Synagogue in Djerba, Tunisia, and heritage tours to Morocco concentrating on Jewish sites such as saints' tombs, or in Turkey a Jewish Museum and tours of a series of Sephardic synagogues in Istanbul and Izmir. The Moroccan government has announced a new program of restoration of Jewish sites, particularly old synagogues, and cemeteries. The joyful processions, such as the marking of Lag B'Omer in Djerba, hard for even well-wishing governments to police, have been toned down or canceled for security reasons (we have already noted the recreation of a North African pilgrimage in the suburbs of Paris). Thus, Sephardim until now have had little in the way of sites of memory. Many, especially older people, were traumatized by their departure, and did not want to remember it or their lives beforehand, in a similar way to suppression of Holocaust memories. Novels, as well as other genres such as film or art, or religious practice, can help to unlock the memories and lead toward partial healing. Thus, though Jews are not only the people of the book and would benefit greatly from access to actual Jewish sites, the new novels can partially fill a void.

Discussions of Jewish diaspora have traditionally focused on the diaspora of Jews scattered from ancient Israel, after the destructions of the First and Second Temples. Diaspora theory today includes approaches to other diasporas of other peoples (see for example Emanuela Trevisan Semi, *Diaspore: esempi, storici e modelli interpretative*, 2008) and the nuances identified, such as a greater or lesser connection with the original mother country, greater or lesser linguistic, religious and social integration into the new homeland, are now being applied to the Jewish diaspora, for example in the 2008 article by Jonathan Ray about Sephardim as a sub-ethnic group.[12]

The issue for Sephardim, it seems to me, is that there are or have been several motherlands, whether motherlands that have rejected their Jews, like Iberia or Muslim countries, the new adopted motherland of France (the Jews of Algeria holding French citizenship were "repatriated" in 1962 to a motherland they had never lived in), or the ancient, refound motherland of Israel.[13] All these motherlands have been problematic in one way or another, and perhaps the ideal of "Sepharad," a non-geographical homeland of the heart, has been the least problematic only because it has been the least material one.

Literature, and the publishing industry, in recent decades have shown more tolerance than before for bilingualism and diglossia. Novels that reflect Sephardic cultural reality need also to reflect the reality of multilingualism. They do this often by inserting diglossia—terms in other languages—that arouse among readers either a sense of familiarity, or of exoticism, depending on the reader's particular linguistic background. Generally, the use of these terms is sparing and does not interfere with the flow of the French language. It helps us to glimpse the complex multilingual reality of the past, where different generations within a family were more comfortable with one language rather than another, and so even family conversations had to be multilingual. Diglossia can also illuminate social relationships, showing how, for example, the poorer Jews speaking the "pitiful patois" of the *hara* of Tunis (Memmi's phrase) related to each other and to French culture: for after all what they were speaking could just as well have been described as a rich and colorful folk dialect of Judeo-Arabic, eliminating the negative stereotype that Memmi's generation heard in their own and their parents' speech patterns. The same might have been said about descriptions of Judeo-Spanish as being a corrupted jargon that the Turkish Jews should rid themselves of expeditiously in favor of a European language, as many intellectual leaders, such as David Fresco and his Istanbul periodical, *El Tiempo*, advocated. Thus, novels and other print media have reflected historical social attitudes to language. An overvaluation of the correct, standard French of the academy has led in the past to devaluation, impoverishment and erosion of other Jewish linguistic traditions among Sephardim.

Traumas of various kinds provoked by the disruptions of exile have sometimes been displaced or shifted, causing some Sephardic Francophone writers, such as Edmond Jabès of Egypt, to devote their creative energy to writing Holocaust literature. Others who write historical novels, such as Didier Nebot, evoke the 1492 expulsion from Spain as a way of mediating the expulsions experienced in modern times. Feelings of relief at delivery from danger, appreciation of the greater freedom Jews enjoy in Western societies, are always complicated by nostalgia for the place, climate and language in which one grew up and for the traditions of the past. Ambiguity in facing these issues directly can lead to authors' transposition of their fiction into another time and place: the five-hundred-years-ago expulsion from Iberia, or the Holocaust as experienced in Europe, but to a lesser extent in North Africa or Iraq.

The authors' relationship to the French language is an issue where there is little ambiguity. Sephardim made French their own, in all the countries where they had access to French language schools, whether Alliance Israélite schools or the state-run schools of Algeria. Together with the language came a new mentality: modernity, rationalism, and the chance to better oneself through education. Such an opportunity wooed Sephardim away from their traditional languages—Judeo-Spanish or Judeo-Arabic—and in the case of Judeo-Spanish even soaked into the other language, so that still today many French elements can be identified in it. Thus, in that sense Sephardim had been mentally preparing themselves for leaving Middle Eastern lands for several decades, perhaps a couple of generations. The eventual arrival in France was much harder for certain people, such as older adults, than for others. France itself had many disappointments in store for the idealists: witness Jabès's turn to Holocaust literature as he encountered antisemitism, Bensoussan's depressingly chilly Brittany, Annie Fitoussi's emotionally paralyzed lawyer, and Andre Aciman's account of his grandparents' extremely traumatic first encounter with Paris (one hopes, exaggerated for literary effect). The quaint French and antiquated manners of these would-be French citizens, loyal before they even arrived, met rude awakenings. Behind these realistic events hover the idealistic and ridiculous characters invented by Albert Cohen. And so the lure of the French language was a sword that cut two ways: it empowered Sephardim to embark out to a wider world, and Sephardic writers to a wider readership, while it separated them from their indigenous roots, made staying on impossible and departure unavoidable.

In contrast, for Muslim (Arab and Berber) writers of the same generation, French was the language imposed on them by the colonizer, a burden from which they needed to free themselves after independence. This was the reason for the intense linguistic Arabization campaigns that took place, with their own inherent paradoxes involved. Which form of Arabic to choose, whether to suppress other indigenous languages such as Berber languages in the interest of national uniformity, these are the issues that have plagued Muslims since independence. Because of this opposite approach, there has been extremely little cooperation in joint literary endeavors between Muslims and Jews. Political factors (basically regarding Israel) have also been overwhelming in the relationship, or lack of one, between Jews formerly of Arab countries and Muslims.[14]

Just as the age-long relationship of *convivencia* between Jews and Spaniards died, so the age-old symbiosis between Jews and Muslims in the Middle East was disrupted and destroyed. That the Sephardim survived these events and reestablished themselves elsewhere does not mean that the events were not traumatic and tragic for many. The distance of a few decades still allows us to glimpse their pain. Whether one prefers to use the more neutral term "exodus" or the more fraught term "expulsion," the result was the same.

Sephardim, whether from Iberia or North Africa and the Middle East, would be entitled to view their history as one of a series of betrayals. They were expelled from Iberia at the end of the fifteenth century, or forcibly converted, then exiled again in the twentieth century from Muslim lands. Israel has disappointed many, and France is not living up to their idealized image. Though such has been the fate of the collective, on an individual level, most have adapted to new homes, learned new languages and cultures, and shown incredible resilience, showing themselves to be both traditional and modern at the same time. Their creative writers, mainly novelists, have dramatized the costs to individuals in incredible journeys of uprooting, migration and adaptation, through which tradition has been a shield for many and a way of coping with new worlds. The power of the French language has served as an essential tool of modernization and success for many Sephardim. I have concentrated here on North Africa, with briefer references to Sephardic francophone literature in the rest of the Middle East, and I offer to readers this short but I hope enlightening analysis of the issues raised in selected texts of modern francophone Sephardic literature.

NOTES

1. See Michel Gurfinkiel's article, "You Only Live Twice: Vibrant Jewish Communities were Reborn in Europe after the Holocaust: Is there a Future for them in the 21st Century?" http://mosaicmagazine.com/essay/2013/O8/, as well as many other discussions of the phenomenon.

2. Isaac Ben-Rubi, *El sekreto del mudo*, (Tel Aviv: Lidor, 1953). French version, trans. André Chedel, *Le Muet d'Auschwitz* (Paris: La Pensée Universelle, 1973).

3. As a series of graphic novels, it was published in French by Delcourt from 2002 to 2020 and the first five books in English by Pantheon in 2007–2008, and has been translated into many languages. In 2004 and 2005 it was presented in French onstage, while the animated film in French appeared in 2011.

4. See Laurence Podselver, "Le pèlerinage du Maarabi à Sarcelles: un pèlerinage transposé du judaïsme tunisien," in Hélène and Shmuel Trigano, eds., *La Mémoire sépharade: Entre l'oubli et l'avenir* (Paris: In Press, 2000), pp. 205–215.

5. On all of these periodicals, see entries in Norman Stillman, ed., *Encyclopedia of Jews in the Islamic world.* (Leiden: Selected Brill, 2010).

6. On the psychological trauma of the uprooting during the 1950s and 1960s, expressed in other languages, see e.g., David Meghnagi, who talks about the Jews of Libya, "June 1967: I still feel the anguish," www.brogi.info/2011/02/

libia-1967-il-pogrom-degli-ebrei-david-meghnagi-ricorda.html. In London, zoom lectures organized by Harif Organization of Jews from MENA have been doing an excellent job of spreading information about such topics as the exile of the Jews of Iraq and other Middle Eastern countries, from those who experienced the events.

7. "He believed in the existence of a Mediterranean culture not confined to any particular nationality, nor to any nationalism, except 'the nationalism of sunshine' . . . and this culture, fragrant and balmy, was his own." Paul Berman, "Mother Justice: What Camus Understood about our Situation," (review of Albert Camus, ed. Alice Kaplan, trans. Arthur Goldhammer, *Algerian Chronicles* (Boston: Belknap Press, 2012), p. 44, in *New Republic* (Aug. 19, 2013), pp. 42–46.

8. See Milena Pressman, "L'Émancipation de la femme juive nord-africaine dans les romans d'Élissa Rhaïs et de Blanche Bendahan," *Archives Juives* 48:2 (2015), pp. 67–83.

9. See Vilashini Cooppan, "Net Work: Area Studies, Comparison, and Connectivity," *PMLA* 128: 3 (2013), pp. 615–621.

10. A point made by Guy Dugas, "[Compared with Algeria] en Tunisie . . . et au Maroc . . . [the Jews] préserveront un peu mieux la symbiose judéo-arabe, particulièrement sensible au niveau des traditions communes et du rapport des langages et dialectes." Dugas, "La Littérature francophone des Juifs d'Algérie, vecteur de leur modernité," pp. 137–153, in Shmuel Trigano, ed., *L'Identité des Juifs d'Algérie: Une Expérience originale de la modernité* (Paris: Editions du nadir, 2003), p. 139.

11. The European phenomenon of synagogues without Jews has been noted by Ruth Ellen Gruber in particular, in *Virtually Jewish: Reinventing Jewish Culture in Europe* (Berkeley: California University Press, 2002). Mois Benarroch may not approve of Spain's efforts to create Rutas de Sefarad: he has a probably autobiographical writer (visiting Spain from Israel) complain that he cannot understand why, as a Sephardic Jew, he is supposed to enjoy visiting the empty *juderías* of Spain from which his people were expelled five hundred years ago. See *La trilogía tetuaní*, Pt. 1, *En las puertas de Tánger* (San Bernardino: Createspace, 2021).

12. Emanuela Trevisan Semi, *Diaspore: esempi storici e modelli interpretative* (Verona: Casa Editrice Il Ponte, 2008); see esp. the typology in Chapter 3, "Come pensare le diaspore," pp. 73–92. Jonathan Ray, "New Approaches to the Jewish Diaspora: The Sephardim as Sub-Ethnic Group," *Jewish Social Studies: History, Culture, Society* n.s. 15:1 (Fall 2008): 10–31.

13. Or even the United States, an adoptive motherland that traditionally does not ask questions, at least in the formulation of Emma Lazarus and her poem "The New Colossus."

14. One exception is Sebbar's 2012 book, another is Alek Baylee Toumi, *Maghreb divers: Langue française, langues parlées, littératures et représentations des Maghrébins, à partir d'Albert Memmi et de Kateb Yacine* (New York: Peter Lang, 2002). Yet others are Najib Redouane's introductory editorial to a special issue on "écrivains judéo-maghrébins" *International Journal of Francophone Studies* 7 (1–2) (2004), pp. 3–4, and the books he has edited on Jewish authors of the Maghreb, such as Ami Bouganim and Albert Memmi; and Dora Carpentier Latiri's guest editing of a special issue, "Juifs de Tunisie/Jews of Tunisia" of the journal *CELAAN* 7: 1 & 2

(Spring 2009). In the 1960s, Memmi had been the general editor of an influential series of anthologies of different genres in Maghrebian literature, published by the École Pratique des Hautes Etudes, in association with Mouton and Présence Africaine. He was also the recipient of the prestigious Prix de Carthage (awarded by Tunisia) and presided over a conference in Morocco on Jewish-Muslim relations in 2010.

Bibliography

Abdel-Jaouad, Hédi. "Isabelle Eberhardt: Portrait of the Artist as a Young Nomad," in Françoise Lionnet and Ronnie Scharfman eds. *Post/Colonial Conditions: Exiles, Migrations, and Nomadisms.* Yale French Studies 82 (1993). Vol. 2, 93–120. Also New Haven: Yale University Press, 1993.

Abécassis, Éliette. *Sépharade*. Paris: Albin Michel, 2011.

Abeddour Youness. "Review of Nina B. Lichtenstein, *Sephardic Women's Voices: Out of North Africa.*" Sephardic Horizons 7:3–4 (Summer 2017) https://www.sephardichorizons.org/Volume7/Issue3&4/Rev_Abeddour.html.

Abitbol, Michel. *Les juifs d'Afrique du Nord sous Vichy*. Paris: G.-P. Maisonneuve & Larose, 1983.

Abitbol, Michel. *Le Passé d'une discorde: Juifs et arabes du VIIe siècle à nos jours*. 1999. Paris: Tempus, 2003.

Aciman, André. *Out of Egypt: A Memoir*. New York: Farrar, Straus and Giroux, 1994.

Aciman, André. *The Proust Project*. New York: Farrar, Straus and Giroux, 2004.

Aciman, André. *False Papers: Essays on Exile and Memory*. New York: Picador, 2009.

Aciman, André. *Letters of Transit: Reflections on Exile and Memory*. New York: The New Press, 1999.

Aizenberg, Edna, and Margalit Bejarano, eds. *Contemporary Sephardic Identity in the Americas: A Collection of Interdisciplinary Studies*. Syracuse: Syracuse Univ. Press, 2012.

Alcalay, Ammiel. "1938: Beirut to Jerusalem via Damascus/ An Itinerary for Edmond Jabès." *After Jews and Arabs: Remaking Levantine Culture*. Minneapolis: Univ. of Minnesota, 1993. 59–69.

Alcalay, Ammiel. "Intellectual Life." *The Jews of the Middle East and North Africa in Modern times*. Reeva S. Simon, Michael M. Laskier, and Sara Reguer, eds. New York: Columbia Univ. Press, 2003. 85–112.

Allard, Jacques, ed. *Naïm Kattan: L'Écrivain du passage*. Montreal: Hurtubise, 2002.

Allouche-Benayoun, Joëlle. "Gisèle Halimi, La Kahina," *Clio: Histoire, femmes, et sociétés* 30 (2009). http://journals.openedition.org/clio/9502

Anderson, Benedict. *Imagined Communities* 1983, rev. ed. London: Verso, 2006.

Ansaldo, Marco. "La vera storia dei Finzi-Contini." *La Repubblica*, June 13, 2008. http:ricercar.repubblica.it/repubblica/archivio/repubblica/2008/06/13/r2-la-vera-storia-dei-finzi-contini.

Arkin, Ronda Angel. "Claiming Angels." *Sephardic Horizons* 2:1 (Winter 2012). https://www.sephardichorizons.org/Volume2/Issue1/Arking.html.

Ascher, Gloria. "Jew, Turk, Frenchman, American: Sephardic Identities in Alfred Ascher's Judeo-Spanish Diario." *Sephardic Horizons* 3.2 (2013): n. pag. https://www.sephardichorizons.org/Volume3/Issue2/Diario.html

Attal, Robert and Claude Sitbon, eds., *Regards sur les juifs de Tunisie*. Paris: Albin Michel, 1979.

Awret, Irene. *Days of Honey: The Tunisian Boyhood of Rafael Uzan*. New York: Schocken, 1985.

Azquinezar, Susana. "Contes Séfarades." *Mémoire et fidélité séfarades, 1492–1992: Actes du colloque 1492–1992, Cinquième centenaire de l'expulsion des juifs d'Espagne, 23–24 novembre 1992, Université de Rennes 2 Haute-Bretagne*. Ed. Albert Bensoussan. Rennes: Presses universitaires de Rennes, 1993. 197–206.

Balbuena, Monique. "Diasporic Sephardic Identities: A Transnational Poetics of Jewish Languages." Diss. University of California, 2003.

Balbuena, Monique. "A Symbolist Kinah? Laments and Modernism in the Maghreb." *Iggud: Selected Essays in Jewish Studies Vol. 3, Languages, Literatures, Arts*. Ed. Tamar Alexander. Jerusalem: World Union of Jewish Studies, 2007. 67–84.

Balbuena, Monique. *Homeless Tongues: Poetry and Languages of the Sephardic Diaspora*. Stanford: Stanford Univ. Press, 2016.

Balbuena, Monique. "Ladino in US Literature and Song." *Cambridge History of Jewish American Literature*. Cambridge: Cambridge Univ. Press, 2016, pp. 297–319.

Bango, Isidro. *Remembering Sepharad: Jewish Culture in Medieval Spain*. Madrid: SEACEX, 2004.

Bar-Itzhak, Haya, and Aliza Shenhar. *Jewish Moroccan Folk Narratives from Israel*. Detroit: Wayne State Univ. Press, 1993.

Barnard, Debbie. "It Ain't Easy Being Me: Violence and Identity in Claude Kayat's *Mohammed Cohen*." *CELAAN Review: Review of the Center for the Studies of the Literatures and Arts of North Africa, Special Issue Jews of Tunisia* 7:1&2 (Spring 2009): 85–97.

Bassani, Giorgio. *Il giardino dei Finzi-Contini* (Turin: Einaudi, 1962); *The Garden of the Finzi-Continis*. Trans. William Weaver. New York: MJF, 1983.

Bassani, Giorgio. "Una lápide in via Mazzini [A Plaque on Via Mazzini]." In *Cinque storie ferraresi* (1956); *Five Stories of Ferrara*. New York: Harcourt Brace Jovanovich, 1971. 77–111.

Ben 'Achir, Bou Azza. *Edmond Amran El Maleh. Cheminements d'une écriture*. Paris: L'Harmattan, 1997.

Ben Aziza, Wafa. "Nouvelles expressions judéo-maghrébines entre mémoire et Histoire: une écriture en évolution. *Expressions maghrébines*. 13:2 (Winter 2014): 47–60.

Ben Ur, Aviva. *Sephardic Jews in America: A Diasporic History*. New York: New York Univ. Press, 2009.
Benarroch, Mois: *Bufanda blues*. Madrid: Lulu.com, 2012.
Benarroch, Mois. *La trilogía tetuaní: En las puertas de Tánger, Lucena, Llaves de Tetuán*. Madrid: Lulu.com, 2021.
Benbassa, Esther, and Aron Rodrigue. *The Jews of the Balkans*. Oxford: Blackwell, 1995.
Benbassa, Esther, ed. *Les Sépharades en littérature; Un Parcours millénaire*. Paris: Presses de l'Université Paris-Sorbonne, 2005.
Bendahan, Blanche. *Mazaltob*. Oran: L. Fouque, 1958.
Bendahan, Esther. *Sefarad es también Europa: El otro en la obra de Albert Cohen*. Zaragoza: Prensas de la Universidad de Zaragoza, 2016.
Bendahan, Esther. *Si te olvidara, Sefarad*. Madrid: La Huerta Grande Editorial, 2020.
Benichou Gottreich, Emily, et al., eds. *Jewish Culture and Society in North Africa*. Bloomington: Indiana Univ. Press, 2011.
Bensmaia, Réda. "Multilingualism and National Character: On Abdelkebir Khatibi's 'Bilangage.'" Trans. Whitney Sanford. *Algeria in Others' Languages*. Ed. Anne-Emmanuelle Berger. Ithaca: Cornell Univ. Press, 2002. 161–83.
Bensoussan, Albert. *Frimaldjézar: Roman*. Paris: Calmann-Lévy, 1976.
Bensoussan, Albert. *L'échelle de Mesrod, ou Parcours algérien de mémoire juive*. Paris: l'Harmattan, 1984.
Bensoussan, Albert. "Aude, Adrienne, Rebecca, Rachel: L'Image de la femme dans l'oeuvre d'Albert Cohen." *Nouveaux Cahiers* 91:1 (1987–88).
Bensoussan, Albert, ed. "Débat: Le Séfaradisme d'aujourd'hui." *Mémoire et fidelité séfarades 1492–1992*. Rennes: Presses Universitaires de Rennes, 1993. 183–90.
Bensoussan, Albert. *Échelle sépharade*. Paris: L'Harmattan, 1993.
Bensoussan, Albert. *Pour une poignée de dates*. Paris: Nadeau, 2001.
Bensoussan, Albert, and Joël Leick. *Mes Algériennes*. Neuilly: Al Manar, 2004.
Bensoussan, Albert, and Michel Tyszblat. *Dans la véranda*. Neuilly: Al Manar, 2007.
Berman, Paul. "What Camus Understood about the Middle East." *The New Republic* 12 Aug. 2013.
Berque, Jacques. *De l'impérialisme à la décolonization*. Paris: Minuit, 1965.
Blot, Jean. *Albert Cohen*. Paris: Ballard, 1986.
Borovaya, Olga. "*Le Journal de Salonique*." *Encyclopedia of Jews in the Islamic World*. Ed. Norman A. Stillman. 2010. www.Brillonline.
Boudhiba, Abdelwahab. *L'Imaginaire maghrébin*. Tunis: Maison tunisienne de l'édition, 1977.
Bouganim, Ami. *Récits du Mellah*. Paris: J.C. Lattès, 1981.
Bouganim, Ami. *Le Cri de l'arbre*. Tel Aviv: Editions Stavit, 1983; 1999.
Bouganim, Ami. *Le Juif égaré*. Paris: Desclée de Brouwer, 1990.
Bouganim, Ami. *Theodor Herzl: Le Dernier messie*. Paris: Nadir, 1998.
Bouganim, Ami. *Le Testament de Spinoza*. Paris: Editions du nadir, 2000.
Bouganim, Ami. *Sites et Sources*. Jerusalem: Department for Jewish Zionist Education, The Jewish Agency for Israel, 1988; 2004; 2005.
Bouganim, Ami, and Moti Milrod. *Tel-Aviv sans répit*. Paris: Autrement, 2009.

Boum, Aomar and Sarah Abrevaya Stein, eds. *The Holocaust and North Africa.* Stanford: Stanford Univ. Press, 2019.

Bourget, Carinne. *The Star, the Cross and the Crescent: Religions and Conflicts in Francophone Literature from the Arab World.* Lanham, MD: Rowman and Littlefield, Lexington Books, 2010.

Bouskila, Daniel. "A Sephardic S. Y. Agnon." *Jewish Journal* (April 2013): n. pag. https://jewishjournal.com/news/115766/.

Bowman, Steven. "The Languages of Albert Cohen." *Languages and Literatures of Sephardic and Oriental Jews.* Ed. David M. Bunis. Jerusalem: Bialik Institute, 2009. 445–51.

Bravo, Anna. "Social Perception of the Shoah in Italy." *The Jews of Italy Memory and Identity.* Ed. Bernard D. Cooperman. Bethesda: Univ. Press of Maryland, 2000. 381–400.

Brozgal, Lia N. "Blindness, the Visual, and Ekphrastic Impulses: Albert Memmi Colours in the Lines." *French Studies* 64:3 (2010): 317–28.

Brozgal, Lia N. *Against Autobiography: Albert Memmi and the Production of Theory.* Lincoln: Univ. of Nebraska Press, 2013.

Brozgal, Lia. "Memmi's Novels, in Practice and in Theory." *H-France Salon.* 13:4 (2021).

Bunis, David. "The Changing Faces of Sephardic Identity as reflected in Judezmo Sources." *Neue Romania* 40 (2011), 45–75.

Campoy-Cubillo, Adolfo. *Memories of the Maghreb: Transnational Identities in Spanish Cultural Production.* New York: Palgrave Macmillan, 2012.

Camus, Albert. *Noces: Les essais XXXIX 1938.* Paris: Gallimard, 1950.

Camus, Albert. *Algerian Chronicles.* Trans. Arthur Goldhammer. Ed. Alice Kaplan. Cambridge, MA: Belknap of Harvard Univ. Press, 2013.

Canafe, Nergis. *The Jewish Diaspora as a Paradigm: Politics, Religion and Belonging.* Istanbul: Libra Kitapçılık, 2014.

Canetti, Elias. *Die Stimmen von Marrakesch* (1967). *The Voices of Marrakesh: A Record of a Visit* (1967*)*. Trans. J. A. Underwood. London: Marion Boyars, 1978.

Canetti, Elias. *Die gerette Zunge: Geschichte einer Jugend* (1977). Trans. Joachim Neugroschel. *The Tongue Set Free.* New York: Continuum, 1979.

Canetti, Veza. *Gelbe Strasse* (1989). *Yellow Street.* Trans. Ian Mitchell. New York: New Directions, 1991.

Canetti, Veza. *Schildkröten* (1999), *The Tortoises.* Trans. Ian Mitchell. New York: New Directions, 2001.

Canetti, Veza. *Gedulde bringt Rosen* (1992*). Viennese Short Stories.* Trans. Julian Preece. Riverside, CA: Ariadne, 2006.

Carpentier Latiri, Dora. Introduction to Special Issue, "Juifs de Tunisie/Jews of Tunisia." *CELAAN* 7: 1 & 2 (Spring 2009), 5–8.

Chetrit, Joseph, Jane Gerber, and Drora Arussy, eds. *Jews and Muslims in Morocco: Their Intersecting Worlds.* Lanham, Md: Lexington Books, 2021.

Cheyette, Bryan. *Diasporas of the Mind: Jewish and Postcolonial Writing and the Nightmares of History.* Newhaven: Yale University Press, 2013.

Chocrón, Isaac. *Rómpase en caso de incendio.* Caracas: Monte Ávila, 1975.

Chouraqui, André. *Marche vers l'Occident: Les Juifs d'Afrique du Nord.* Paris: Presses Universitaires de France, 1952.
Chouraqui, André. *Between East and West: A History of the Jews of North Africa.* Trans. Michael Bernet. Philadelphia: JPS, 1968.
Chouraqui, André. *Histoire des Juifs d'Afrique du Nord.* Monaco: Du Rocher, 1998.
Cixous, Hélène. *Les Rêveries de la femme sauvage.* Paris: Galilée, 2000.
Cixous, Hélène. "The Names of Oran." *Algeria in Others' Languages.* Ed. Anne-Emmanuelle Berger. Ithaca: Cornell Univ. Press, 2002. 184–94.
Cixous, Hélène. *Portrait de Jacques Derrida en jeune saint juif.* Paris: Galilée, 2001. Trans. Beverley Bie Brahic. *Portrait of Jacques Derrida as a Young Jewish Saint.* New York: Columbia Univ. Press, 2004.
Cohen, Albert. *Les Valeureux.* Paris: Gallimard, 1969.
Cohen, Albert. *Carnets 1978.* Paris: Gallimard, 1979.
Cohen, Albert. *Belle du seigneur* (1986). Trans. David Coward. *Belle du Seigneur.* New York: Viking, 1995.
Cohen, Annie. *Bésame mucho.* Paris: Gallimard, 1998.
Cohen, Jacob. *Du danger de monter sur la terrasse.* Casablanca: Tarik Editions, 2006.
Cohen, Julia P., and Sarah A. Stein. "Sephardic Scholarly Worlds: Toward a Novel Geography of Modern Jewish History." *Jewish Quarterly Review* 100:3 (2010): 349–84.
Cohen, Mark R. "The Origins of Sephardic Jewry in the Medieval Arab World," *Sephardic and Mizrachi Jewry from the Golden Age of Spain to Modern Times.* Ed. Zion Zohar. New York: New York Univ. Press, 2005, pp. 23–39.
Cole, Peter. *The Dream of the Poem: Hebrew Poetry from Christian and Muslim Spain, 950–1492.* Princeton: Princeton Univ. Press, 2007.
Cooperman, Bernard, et al., eds. *In Iberia and Beyond: Hispanic Jews Between Two Cultures.* College Park, MD: Univ. of Maryland, 1991.
Cooperman, Bernard, et al., eds. *The Jews of Italy Memory and Identity.* Bethesda: University Press of Maryland, 2000.
Crasson, Aurèle, and Anne Mary, eds. *Edmond Jabès.* Paris: Hermann, 2012.
Cupo, Rosy. "Giorgio Bassani in Other Languages." 2016. https://www.newitalianbooks.it/giorgio-bassani-in-different-languages/.
Cypess, Sandra Messenger. "Review of Angelina Muñiz-Huberman, *Los Esperandos: Piratas judeoportugeses . . . y yo.*" *Sephardic Horizons* 11:1 (Winter 2021). https://sephardichorizons.org/Volume11/Issue1/Cypess.html
Danon, Vitalis. *Ninette de la rue du Péché* (1938). Trans. Jane Kuntz. Lia Brozgal and Sarah Abrevaya Stein, eds. *Ninette of Sin Street.* Stanford: Stanford Univ. Press, 2017.
David, Danielle. "Identité perdue, identité retrouvée, identité." *CELAAN Review: Review of the Center for the Studies of the Literatures and Arts of North Africa.* 7:1 & 2 (2009): 122–34.
De Rambures, Jean-Louis. "Albert Memmi, conteur arabe." *Le Monde,* 16 Dec. 1977: 17.
Decter, Jonathan. *Iberian Jewish Literature: Between al-Andalus and Christian Europe.* Bloomington: Indiana Univ. Press, 2007.

Déjeux, Jean. *Djoh'a: Héros de la tradition orale arabo-berbère hier et aujourd'hui* (Sherbrook: Naaman, 1978).
Deleuze, Gilles, and Felix Guattari. *Kafka: Toward a Minor Literature*. Trans. Dana Plan. Minneapolis: Univ. of Minnesota Press, 1986.
Denis, Michel. "Synthèse." Ed. Albert Bensoussan. *Mémoire et fidélité séfarades, 1492–1992: Actes du colloque 1492–1992, Cinquième centenaire de l'expulsion des juifs d'Espagne, 23–24 novembre 1992, Université de Rennes 2 Haute-Bretagne.* Rennes: Presses universitaires de Rennes, 1993. 191–96.
Derrida, Jacques. *Dissémination* (1972). Trans. Barbara Johnson. Chicago: University of Chicago Press, 1981.
Derrida, Jacques. *Le Monolinguisme de l'autre*. Paris: Éditions Galilée, 2016.
Díaz-Más, Paloma. *Sephardim: The Jews from Spain* (1983). Trans. George Zucker. Chicago: University of Chicago, 1992.
Díaz-Más, Paloma, and María Sánchez Pérez, *Los Sefardíes ante los retos del mundo contemporáneo: identidad y mentalidades*. Madrid: Consejo Superior de Investigaciones Científicas (CSIC), 2010.
Dib, Mohammed. *Qui se souvient de la mer*. Paris: Seuil, 1962.
Dugas, Guy. *Albert Memmi: Écrivain de la déchirure*. Sherbrook: Naaman, 1984.
Dugas, Guy. *Littérature judéo-maghrébine d'expression française*. Philadelphia, PA: CELFAN Editions, 1988.
Dugas, Guy. *La Littérature judéo-maghrébine d'expression française: Entre Djéha t Cagayous*. Paris: L'Harmattan, 1991.
Dugas, Guy. "Écrivains séfarades d'expression française." *Mémoire et fidélité séfarades, 1492–1992: Actes du colloque 1492–1992, Cinquième Centenaire de l'expulsion des juifs d'Espagne, 23–24 novembre 1992, Université de Rennes 2 Haute-Bretagne*. Ed. Albert Bensoussan. Rennes: Presses universitaires de Rennes, 1993.
Dugas, Guy. *Albert Memmi: Du Malheur d'être juif au bonheur d'être sépharade*. Paris: Alliance Israélite Universelle, 2001.
Dugas, Guy. "La Littérature francophone des juifs d'Algérie: Vecteur de leur modernité." *L'Identité des juifs d'Algérie: Une Expérience originale de la modernité*. Ed. Shmuel Trigano. Paris: Éditions du nadir, 2003. 137–53.
Dugas, Guy. "Le français, langue de mémoire de la diaspora sépharade: Cohen, Derrida, Cixous et Cie." *L'Espace francophone, une mosaïque de langues et de cultures, Papers of the international conference, "Le Français, instrument de conservation et de transmission de la mémoire dans les réalités francophones."* Ed. Simonetta Valenti. Aosta: Le Château, 2010, pp. 55–69.
Dugas, Guy. "Fantaisie, littérature mémorieuse, iconophilie: Retour sur quelques concepts discutables." *Expressions maghrébines* 13:2, Winter 2014, 139–152.
Dugas, Guy. "Quelques compléments á propos de l'écriture colorée chez Albert Memmi." *Sephardic Horizons* 5:3–4 (Summer-Fall 2015). https://www.sephardichorizons.org/Volume5/Issue3-4/Dugas.html.
Dugas, Guy, ed. *Albert Memmi: Portraits*. Paris: CNRS, 2015.
El Maleh, Edmond A. "Juifs Marocains et Marocains juifs." *Les Temps modernes* 33: 375 (1977).

El Maleh, Edmond A. *Aïlen ou la nuit du récit*. Paris: Maspero, 1983.
El Maleh, Edmond A. "La Mère-Méditerrannée," *Peuples méditerranéens* 30 (Jan.-March 1985).
El Maleh, Edmond A. *Mille Ans, Un Jour*. Paris: La Pensée Sauvage, 1986.
Elazar, Daniel Judah. *The Other Jews: The Sephardim Today*. New York: Basic, 1989.
Elbaz, André E. *Folktales of the Canadian Sephardim*. Toronto: FitzHenry and Whiteside, 1982.
Elbaz, Mikhaël and Abraham Serfaty. *L'insoumis*. Paris: Desclée de Brouwer, 2001.
Elbaz, Robert. "L'Écriture de la mémoire chez Albert Bensoussan," *International Journal of Francophone Studies* 7:1–2 (2004): 35–49.
Elbaz, Shlomo, Lionel Cohen, eds., et al. "Le *Livre des questions*: 'Prise de conscience d'un cri,'" *Jabès: Le Livre lu en Israël*. Paris: Point Hors Ligne, 1987. 45–52, 139–148.
Elbaz, Vanessa Paloma. "Review of David Wacks, *Double Diaspora in Sephardic Literature." Sephardic Horizons* 6:2, (Spring 2016). https://www.sephardichorizons.org/Volume6/Issue2/Elbaz.html.
Eliany, Marc. Intro. Annette B. Fromm. *Jewish Folktales from Morocco: Tales of Seha the Sage and Seha the Clown* (Lanham, Md: Lexington, 2021).
Fanjul García, Serafín. *Literatura popular árabe*. Madrid: Editora Nacional, 1977.
Fanon, Frantz. *Les Damnés de la terre* (1961), *The Wretched of the Earth*. Trans. Richard Philcox. New York: Grove Books, 2005.
Fargion, Liliana P. "Persecution of Jews in Italy, 1943–1945." *The Jews of Italy: Memory and Identity*. Ed. Bernard Dov Cooperman. Bethesda: Univ. Press of Maryland, 2000, 443–54.
Fatih, Zakaria. "The Aesthetics of Fragmentation, or a Way to Read El Maleh," *Expressions maghrébines* 13:2 (Winter 2014), 125–137.
Fellous, Colette. *Avenue de France*. Paris: Gallimard, 2001.
Fergusson, Francis, John McCormick, and George Core. *Sallies of the Mind*. New Brunswick, NJ: Transaction, 1998.
Fink, Guido. "Growing up Jewish in Ferrara: The Fiction of Giorgio Bassani, a Personal Recollection." *Judaism*. (Summer-Fall: 2004).
Fischel, Walter Joseph. *Ibn Khaldun and Tamerlane, Their Historic Meeting in Damascus, 1401 A.D. (803 A. H.): A Study Based on Arabic Manuscripts of Ibn Khaldun's "Autobiography."* Berkeley: University of California, 1952.
Fischel, Walter Joseph. *Ibn Khaldun in Egypt; His Public Functions and His Historical Research, 1382–1406: A Study in Islamic Historiography*. Berkeley: Univ. of California, 1967.
Fitoussi, Annie. *La Mémoire folle de Mouchi Rabbinou, le rabbin le plus pauvre du ghetto le plus misérable de Tunis, plus fort que Mussolini, bien plus fort encore que la mort*. Paris: Mazarine, 1985.
Fitoussi, Margot, and Mo Scarpelli, dir. *El Hara*. Documentary film. 2018.
Fitoussi, Margot. "The Architecture of Home in the Works of Albert Memmi." *H-France Salon*. 13:4 (2021), 1–7.
Fonrobert, Charlotte E. "The New Spatial Turn in Jewish Studies." *AJS Review* 33:1 (2009): 155–64.

Gafaïti, Hafid, ed. *Transnational Spaces and Identities in the Francophone World.* Lincoln, Nebraska: Univ of Nebraska, 2009.

Galante, Avraham. *Histoire des juifs de Turquie.* Istanbul: Editions Isis, 1940.

Gampel, Benjamin. "Does Medieval Navarrese Jewry Salvage Our Notion of Convivencia?" In Bernard Cooperman, *In Iberia and Beyond: Hispanic Jews between Two Cultures.* College Park:, MD: Univ. of Maryland, 1991.

Gaon, Solomon, and M. Mitchell Serels. *Del Fuego: Sephardim and the Holocaust.* New York: Sepher-Hermon, 1995.

Garih, Albert. "Review of Corrie Guttstadt et al., *Mémorial des Judéo-Espagnols déportés de la France: Muestros dezaparesidos"* Paris: Éditeur Muestros Dezaparesidos, 2019. *Sephardic Horizons* (11:1) Winter 2021. https://www.sephardichorizons.org/Volume11/Issue1/Garih.html

Gerber, Jane. *The Jews of Spain: A History of the Sephardic Experience.* New York: Free Press, 1992.

Gerber, Jane. *Cities of Splendour in the Shaping of Sephardi History.* London: Littman Library of Jewish Civilisation, 2020.

Gerber, Jane. "Review of Dalia Kandiyoti, *The Converso's Return: Conversion and Sephardi History in Contemporary Literature and Culture."* *Sephardic Horizons* 11:2 (Summer 2021) dhttps://sephardichorizons.org/Volume11/Issue2–3/Gerber.html.

Ghazi, Fherid. *Le Roman et la nouvelle en Tunisie.* Tunis: Maison Tunisienne de l'Édition, 1970.

Ghez, Paul. *Six mois sous la botte.* 1943. Paris: Manuscript, 2009.

Giroud, Françoise. *Deux et deux font trois.* Paris: Grasset, 1990.

Gittes, Katherine S. "The Canterbury Tales and the Arabic Frame Tradition." *PMLA* 98:2 (1983): 237–51.

Goitein, S. D. *Jews and Arabs: Their Contacts through the Ages.* New York: Schocken, 1955.

Green, Henry. *Sephardi Voices.* Audiovisual archive. https://sephardivoices.com.

Gruber, Ruth Ellen. *Virtually Jewish: Reinventing Jewish Culture in Europe.* Berkeley: California University Press, 2002.

Gurfinkiel, Michel. "You Only Live Twice: Vibrant Jewish Communities were Reborn in Europe after the Holocaust: Is There a Future for Them in the 21st Century?" *Mosaic Magazine: Advancing Jewish Thought* (2013): n. pag. *MOSAIC: Advancing Jewish Thought.* Bee Ideas, LLC, Aug. 2013.

Haddad de Paz, Charles. *Juifs et Arabes au pays de Bourguiba.* Aix-en-Provence: Paul Roubaud, 1977.

Halimi, Gisèle. *Fritna.* Paris: Plon, 2008.

Halimi, Gisèle. *La Kahina.* Paris: Pocket, 2008.

Halevi-Wise, Yael. *Interactive Fictions: Scenes of Storytelling in the Novel.* New York: Praeger, 2003.

Halevi-Wise, Yael, ed. *Sephardism: Spanish Jewish History and the Modern Literary Imagination.* Stanford: Stanford Univ. Press, 2012.

Halevi-Wise, Yael. "Postscript: Rebecca Goldstein's Spinoza." *Sephardism: Spanish Jewish History and the Modern Literary Imagination*. Ed. Yael Halevi-Wise. Stanford, CA: Stanford Univ. Press, 2012. 275–83.

Halevi-Wise, Yael. "A Taste of Sepharad from the Mexican Suburbs: Rosa Nissán's Stylized Ladino in *Novia que te vea* and *Hisho que te nazca*." *Contemporary Sephardic Identity in the Americas: An Interdisciplinary Approach*. Ed. Margalit Bejarano and Edna Aizenberg. Syracuse, NY: Syracuse Univ. Press, 2012. 184–201.

Halevi-Wise, Yael. "Where Is the Sephardism in A. B. Yehoshua's *Hesed Sefaradi/ The Retrospective?*" *Sephardic Horizons* 4:1 (Winter 2014), n. pag. https://www.sephardichorizons.org/Volume4/Issue1/WhereSephardism.html.

Halevi-Wise, Yael. *The Retrospective Imagination of A. B. Yehoshua*. University Park: Pennsylvania State Univ. Press, 2020.

Halfon, Eduardo. *El boxeador polaco* (2008). *The Polish Boxer*. Trans. Daniel Hahn. New York: Bellevue Literary, 2012.

Halkin, Hillel. *Yehuda Halevi*. New York: Nextbook/Schocken, 2010.

Heschel, Abraham. *The Earth Is the Lord's*. New York: Henry Schumann, 1952.

Hirschberg, H. Z. *A History of the Jews in North Africa*. Leiden: Brill, 1974.

Horn, Bernard, and Abraham B. Yehoshua. *Facing the Fires: Conversations with A.B. Yehoshua*. Syracuse, NY: Syracuse Univ. Press, 1997.

Hyman, Paula E. *The Jews of Modern France*. Berkeley: Univ. of California Press, 1998.

Ibn Khaldun. *The Muqaddimah: An Introduction to History*. Ed. and trans. N. J. Dawood and Franz Rosenthal. Princeton, NJ: Princeton Univ. Press, 2005.

Ibn Khaldun. *Histoire des berbères et des dynasties musulmanes de l'Afrique Septentrionale*. Ed. William MacGuckin Slane and Paul Casanova. Paris: P. Geuthner, 1968.

Igel, Regina. "Review of Margalit Bejarano and Edna Aizenberg: *Sephardic Identity in the Americas: An Interdisciplinary Approach*." *Sephardic Horizons* 4:2 (Spring 2014), *https://www.sephardichorizons.org/Volume4/Issue2/Igel.html*.

Israel-Pelletier, Aimée. "Edmond Jabès, Jacques Hassoun, and Melancholy: The Second Exodus in the Shadow of the Holocaust." *MLN: Modern Language Notes* 123:4 (2008): 797–818.

Israel-Pelletier, Aimée. *On the Mediterranean and the Nile: The Jews of Egypt*. Bloomington: Indiana University Press, 2018.

Jabes, Edmond. *Le Livre des questions*, Vol. 3, *Le Retour au livre*. Paris: Gallimard, 1965.

Jabès, Edmond. *The Book of Questions*. Vol. 3, *Return to the book*. Middletown, CT: Wesleyan Univ. Press, 1976.

Judaken, Jonathan and Michael Lejman. *An Albert Memmi Reader*. Lincoln: University of Nebraska Press, 2021.

Kalechofsky, Roberta, ed. *Echad: An Anthology of Latin American Jewish Writings*. Trans. David Pritchard and Marilyn Rae. Marblehead, Mass: Micah Publications, 1984.

Kamen, Henry. *The Disinherited: Exile and the Making of Spanish Culture 1492–1975*. New York: Harper Collins, 2007.

Kandiyoti, Dalia. *Migrant Sites: America, Place and Diaspora Literatures.* Lebanon NH: Dartmouth College Press, 2009.

Kandiyoti, Dalia. *The Converso's Return: Conversion and Sephardi History in Contemporary Literature and Culture.* Stanford: Stanford University Press, 2020.

Kaplan, Edward. "Jabès, Edmond." *The Blackwell Companion to Jewish Culture: From the Eighteenth Century to the Present.* By Glenda Abramson and Dovid Katz. Oxford, UK: Blackwell Reference, 1989.

Kattan, Naïm. *Adieu, Babylone* (1975). *Farewell Babylon: Coming of Age in Jewish Baghdad.* Trans. Sheila Fischman. London: Souvenir, 2007.

Kattan, Naïm. "Le Séfaradisme." *L'écrivain migrant: Essais sur des cités et des hommes.* Montréal: Hurtubise, 2001. 93–100.

Kattan, Naïm. "Jewish of Arab Origin and Culture." *Covenant Global Jewish Magazine* 1:1 (2006): n. pag.

Kattan, Naïm. *Écrire le réel.* Montreal: Hurtubise, 2008.

Kayat, Claude. *Mohammed Cohen.* Paris: Éditions du Seuil, 1981.

Kayat, Claude. *Mohammed Cohen: The Adventures of an Arabian Jew.* Trans. Patricia Wolf. New York, NY: Bergh Pub., 1989.

Kayat, Claude. *La Synagogue de Sfax.* Paris: Punctum, 2006.

Kazdaghli, Habib. "*La Justice* (Tunis)." *Encyclopedia of Jews in the Islamic World.* Ed. Norman Stillman. 2010. *Brill Online.*

Khatibi, Abdelkébir. Trans. Whitney Sandford. "Diglossia: In Memory of Kateb Yacine." Ed. Anne-Emmanuelle Berger. *Algeria in Others' Languages.* Ithaca: Cornell Univ. Press, 2002. 157–60.

Khazoom, J. Daniel. *No Way Back: The Journey of a Jew from Baghdad.* Sacramento: KOH Library, 2010.

Khemiri, Moncef. "Mohammed Cohen ou la fraternité à l'épreuve de l'Histoire." *La Tunisie dans la littérature tunisienne de langue arabe et de langue française: Actes du colloque organisé les 17 et 18 Avril 1998 à la Faculté des Lettres de Manouba.* Ed. Habib Salha. Tunis: L'Or du Temps, 2001. 189–204.

Koen-Sarano, Matilda. *Por el plaser de kontar: Kuentos de mi vida.* Jerusalem: Nur Akafot, 2006.

König, Yaël. "Rencontre avec Nine Moati." n.d., https://harissa.com/D_Arts/rencontreavecninemoatty.htm

Koskas, Marco. *Balace Bounel.* Paris: Ramsay, 1979.

Koskas, Marco. *Avoue d'abord: Roman.* Paris: Table Ronde, 2007.

Koskas, Marco. *Bande de Français.* San Bernardino: Createspace, 2018.

Krupnick, Mark, ed. *Displacement: Derrida and after.* Bloomington: Indiana Univ. Press, 1983.

Larlee, Louise. *Représentations littéraires de l'histoire sépharade dans Le Chemin de l'exil de Didier Nebot:* M.A. Thesis. McGill University, 2009.

Laskier, Michael M., et al., eds. *The Jews of the Middle East and North Africa in Modern Times.* New York: Columbia Univ. Press, 2003.

Lazar, Moshe. *The Sephardic Tradition.* New York: Norton, 1972.

Lazar, Moshe. "*Me'am Lo'ez*: The Crown-Jewel of Sephardic Culture in the Ottoman Empire." *Echoes of Sepharad* 2.2 (1991).

Lazar, Moshe, ed. *Sefarad in My Heart: A Ladino Reader*. Lancaster, CA: Labyrinthos, 1999.

Lazar, Philippe. "Richard Marienstras, inoubliable pionnier du 'diasporisme.'" *Diasporiques* ns. 14 (2011): n. pag.

Lehmann, Mattias. *Ladino Rabbinic Literature and Ottoman Sephardic Culture*. Bloomington: Indiana Univ. Press, 2005.

Leibman, Laura. "What is Sephardic Culture?" *Vida Sefaradí: A Century of Jewish Life in Portland [Exhibit Catalogue]*. Portland, OR: Congregation Ahavath Achim and Oregon Jewish Museum, 2014. 11–16.

Levi, Carlo. *Cristo si è fermato a Eboli*. Turin: Einaudi, 1945.

Lévy Clara. "L'identité sépharade d'Albert Cohen." *Les Sépharades en littérature: Un parcours millénaire*. Ed. Esther Benbassa. Paris: Presses de l'Université Paris-Sorbonne, 2005, pp. 139–157.

Lévy, Isaac Jack, Rosemary Lévy Zumwalt. *The Sephardim in the Holocaust: A Forgotten People* (Tuscaloosa: University of Alabama Press, 2020).

Lévy, Raphaël (Ryvel). *Les Lumières de la Hara (nouvelles)*. Tunis: La Kahéna, 1935.

Lévy, Raphaël (Ryvel). *Le Nebel du Galouth*. Tunis: La Cité des Livres, 1946.

Lévy, Raphaël (Ryvel). *L'Enfant de l'Oukala et autres contes de la Hara*. Ed. and pref. Serge Moscovici. Paris: J.C. Lattès, 1980.

Lewental, D. Gershon. "*La Nation* (Salonica)." *Encyclopedia of Jews in the Islamic World*. Ed. Norman Stillman. 2010. Brill Online.

Lewis, Bernard. *The Jews of Islam*. Princeton, NJ: Princeton Univ. Press, 1984.

Lewis, Bernard. "Muslims, Christians and Jews: The Dream of Coexistence." *New York Review of Books* 34.6 (1992): 48–52.

Lichtenstadter, Ilse. *Introduction to Classical Arabic Literature: With Selections from Representative Works in English Translation*. New York: Twayne, 1974.

Lichtenstein, Nina. "Silent Exodus and Forgotten Voices: Sephardic Women Writers in Postcolonial Discourse." *Sephardic Horizons* 2.1 (Winter 2012). www.sephardichorizons.org/Volume2/Issue1/Lichtenstein.html.

Lichtenstein, Nina B. "North Africa, France, and Israel: Sephardic Identities in the Work of Chochana Boukhobza." *Sephardic Horizons* 3.2 (Summer 2013). https://www.sephardichorizons.org/Volume3/Issue2/Identities.html.

Lichtenstein, Nina B. *Sephardic Women's Voices: Out of North Africa*. Santa Fe, NM: Gaon Books, 2017.

Lionnet, Françoise and Ronnie Scharfman, eds. *Post/Colonial Conditions: Exiles, Migrations, and Nomadisms*. *Yale French Studies* 82 (1993). Also New Haven: Yale Univ. Press, 1993.

Lyons, Malcolm C., and Robert Irwin, eds. *Tales from 1,001 Nights*. New York: Penguin Classics, 2012.

McCormick, John. *Fiction as Knowledge: The Modern Post-Romantic Novel* (1975). New Brunswick, NJ: Transaction, 1999.

Madelain, Jacques. *L'errance et l'itinéraire: Lecture du roman maghrébin de langue française*. Paris: Sindbad, 1983.

Maiser, Véronique. "Sépharades et Ashkenazes dans l'oeuvre romanesque d'Albert Cohen." *LittéRealité* 16.1 (2004): 23–30.

Malabou, Catherine, and Jacques Derrida. *Jacques Derrida: La Contre-allée*. Paris: Quinzaine Littéraire-Louis Vuitton, 1999.

Malka, Victor and Albert Memmi. *La Terre intérieure: Entretiens avec Victor Malka* (Paris: Gallimard, 1976).

Malule, Chen. "The Story of Daniel Hagège: Judeo-Arabic Author and Documenter of Tunisian Jewry." *The Librarians Newsletter* (National Library of Israel). 7/9/2020. Blog.nli.org.il/en/lbh_hagege.

Marienstras, Richard. *Être un peuple en Diaspora: Essais*. Paris: Maspero, 1975.

Marzouki, Afifa, and Samir Marzuqi. *Individu et communautés dans l'oeuvre littéraire d'Albert Memmi*. Paris: Harmattan, 2010.

Matza, Diane. "Introduction." *Sephardic-American Voices: Two Hundred Years of a Literary Legacy*. Hanover, NH: Univ. Press of New England [for] Brandeis Univ. Press, 1997. 1–13.

Mays, Devi. *Forging Ties, Forging Passports: Migration and the Modern Sephardi Diaspora*. (Stanford: Stanford Univ. Press, 2020).

Melammed, Renée L. *An Ode to Salonika: The Ladino Verses of Bouena Sarfatty*. Bloomington: Indiana Univ. Press, 2013.

Memmi, Albert. *La Statue de sel* (1953); *The Pillar of Salt* (1955). Trans. Edouard Roditi. Boston: Beacon, 1992.

Memmi, Albert. *The Colonizer and the Colonized* (1965). Trans. Howard Greenfield. Boston: Beacon, 1967.

Memmi, Albert. *L'Homme Dominé* (1968). Paris: Payot, 1973. Trans. Eleanor Levieux. *Dominated Man: Notes Towards a Portrait*. New York: Orion, 1968.

Memmi, Albert. *The Scorpion, Or, The Imaginary Confession* (1969). Trans. Eleanor Levieux (1971). Chicago: O'Hara, 1975.

Memmi, Albert. "La Vie impossible de Frantz Fanon." *Esprit* 39: 406 (1971): 248–73.

Memmi, Albert. *Portrait du colonisé précédé du Portrait du colonisateur*. Paris: Payot, 1973.

Memmi, Albert. "Le Personnage de Jeha dans la littérature orale des Arabes et des Juifs." Lecture. Jerusalem: Ben Zvi Institute, 1973.

Memmi, Albert. *Juifs et Arabes*, (1974); *Jews and Arabs*. Trans. Eleanor Levieux. Chicago: O'Hara, 1975.

Memmi, Albert. *La Terre intérieure: Entretiens avec Victor Malka*. Paris: Gallimard, 1976.

Memmi, Albert. *Le Désert ou, La Vie et les aventures de Jubaïr Ouali El-Mammi*. Paris: Gallimard, 1977. Trans. Judith Roumani, *The Desert*. Syracuse: Syracuse Univ. Press, 2015.

Memmi, Albert. *À Contre-courants: Dictionnaire pour s'éviter des errements,complaisances et complicités*. Paris: Nouvel Objet, 1993.

Memmi, Albert. "Naïm Kattan, mon semblable, mon frère." *Naïm Kattan: L'écrivain du passage*. Ed. Jacques Allard, Naïm Kattan, and Simone Douek. Moëlan-sur-Mer [France]: Blanc Silex, 2002. 91–94.

Memmi, Albert. "Growing Up as a Minority Child." Trans. Ralph Tarica. *Sephardic Horizons* 1: 3 (Spring 2011): n. pag. https://www.sephardichorizons.org/Volume1/Issue3/AlbertMemmi.html.

Memmi, Max. "Dans l'intimité d'Albert Memmi." Presentation. International Colloquium in Homage to Albert Memmi. Ben Zvi Institute, Jerusalem, May 23, 2021.
Mendelson, David, ed. *Emergences des Francophonies: Israël, la Méditerranée, le monde*. Limoges: Presses Universitaires de Limoges (PULIM), 2001.
Menocal, María Rosa. *The Ornament of the World: How Muslims, Jews, and Christians Created a Culture of Tolerance in Medieval Spain*. Boston: Back Bay / Little, Brown, 2002.
Miccoli, Dario. "Sephardic Jewish Heritage across the Mediterranean: Migration, Memory and New Diasporas." In Simona Pinton and Lauso Zagato, eds., *Cultural Heritage Scenarios 2015–2017*. Venice: Edizioni Ca'Foscari, 2018. Pp. 485–505.
Mickelson, David. "Types of Spatial Structure in Narrative." Jeffrey Smitten et al., *Spatial Form in Narrative* (Ithaca: Cornell Univ. Press, 1981), pp. 74–76.
Miron, Dan. *From Continuity to Contiguity: Toward a New Jewish Literary Thinking*. Stanford: Stanford Univ. Press, 2010.
Mizrahi, Maurice M. "Growing up under Pharaoh." Historical Society of Jews from Egypt, 15 Oct. 2004. http://www.hsje.org/growing_up_under_pharaoh.htm#. UopJuuDB604.
Moati, Nine. *La Passagère sans étoile*. Paris: Seuil, 1989.
Moati, Nine. *Les Belles de Tunis* (1983). Tunis: Cérès, 1999; 2004, 2010.
Modern Language Association of America. "Practices of the Ethnic Archive." *PMLA*, 127:2 (March 2012).
Mole, Gary. "The Representation of the Holocaust in French-Language Jewish Poetry." *Covenant* 2.1 (2008): n. pag. https://*www.covenant.idc.ac.il*.
Montaigne, Michel de. *Des Cannibales*. Paris: Mille et Une Nuits, 2000.
Montaigne, Michel de. *Les Essais de Michel de Montaigne* (1580). Ed. Pierre Villey. Paris: Presses Universitaires de France, 1965.
Muñiz-Huberman, Angelina. *Huerto Ferraro* (1985). *Enclosed Garden*. Trans. Lois Parkinson Zamora. Pittsburgh: Latin American Literary Review, 1988.
Muñiz-Huberman, Angelina. *Tierra Adentro*. México: J. Mortiz, 1977.
Muñoz Molina, Antonio. *Sefarad* (2001); *Sepharad* trans. Margaret Sayers Peden. New York: Harcourt, 2003.
Nadeau, Jean-Benoît, and Julie Barlow. *The Story of French*. New York: St. Martin's, 2006.
Nahon, Gérard. "La Transition de l'histoire sépharade vers la modernité." *Le Monde sépharade Histoire: Tome 1*. Ed. Shmuel Trigano. Paris: Éditions du Seuil, 2006. 723–44.
Nebot, Didier. *Le Chemin de l'exil*. Paris: Presses de la Renaissance, 1992.
Nebot, Didier. *La Kahéna: Reine D'Ifrikia*. Paris: Editions Carrière, 1998.
Nebot, Didier. *Les Tribus oubliées d'Israël: L'Afrique Judéo-berbère, des origines aux Almohades*. Paris: Romillat, 1999.
Nicoïdski, Clarisse and Haim Vidal Sephiha. *Lus ojus, las manus, la boca*. Louvain: Peeters, 1979.
Nicoïdski, Clarisse. *Couvre-feux*. Paris: Ramsay, 1981.
Nissán, Rosa. *Novia que te vea*. México: Planeta, 1992.

Nissán, Rosa. *Like a Bride/Like a Mother*. Trans. Dick Gerdes. Albuquerque: Univ. of New Mexico Press, 2002.

Nolden, Thomas. "A la Recherche du Judaïsme perdu: Contemporary Jewish Writing in France." Ed. Vivian Liska and Thomas Nolden. *Contemporary Jewish Writing in Europe: A Guide*. Bloomington: Indiana Univ. Press, 2008. 118–38.

Oliel, Jacob. *Les Juifs au Sahara: Le Touat au Moyen Age*. Paris: CNRS, 1994.

Oliel, Jacob. *Les Juifs au Sahara: Une Présence millénaire*. Montreal: Éditions Élysée, 2007.

Ong, Walter J. *Rhetoric, Romance and Technology: Studies in the Interaction of Expression and Culture*. Cornell: Cornell Univ., 1971.

Oppenheimer, Yohai. "Representations of Space in Mizrahi Fiction." *Hebrew Studies* 53 (2012): 335–64.

Ostle, R. C. "Mahmud Al-Mas'adi and Tunisia's 'Lost Generation.'" *Journal of Arabic Literature* 8 (1977): 153–54.

Podselver, Laurence. "Le Pèlerinage du Maarabi à Sarcelles: Un Pèlerinage transposé du Judaïsme tunisien." *La Mémoire sépharade: Entre l'oubli et l'avenir*. Hélène and Shmuel Trigano, eds. Paris: In Press Editions, 2000. 205–15.

Poirot-Delpech, Bertrand. "Parias." *Le Monde Des Livres* 21 Sept. 1979: 22.

Pressman, Hannah. "Ladino as Sephardi Cultural Bedrock." *Hadassah Magazine*. (Nov.-Dec. 2021): 14–16.

Pressman, Milena. "L'Émancipation de la femme juive nord-africaine dans les romans d'Élissa Rhaïs et de Blanche Bendahan." *Archives Juives* 48:2 (2015): 67–83.

Ray, Jonathan. *The Sephardic Frontier: The Reconquista and the Jewish Community in Medieval Iberia*. Ithaca: Cornell UP, 2006.

Ray, Jonathan. "New Approaches to the Jewish Diaspora: The Sephardim as a Sub-Ethnic Group." *Jewish Social Studies* 15.1 (2008): 10–30.

Redouane, Najib. "Editorial." *International Journal of Francophone Studies* 7:1–2 (2004): 3–4.

Redouane, Najib and Yvette Bénayoun-Szmidt, eds. *Ami Bouganim: Voix marocaine en Israël*. Paris: L'Harmattan, 2021.

Redouane, Najib. "Histoire et écriture chez Albert Memmi." In Najib Redouane and Yvette Bénayoun-Szmidt, eds. *Albert Memmi: Voix tunisienne universelle*. Forthcoming.

Rodrigue, Aron. *Images of Sephardi and Eastern Jewries in Transition: The Teachers of the Alliance Israélite Universelle, 1860–1939*. Seattle: Univ. of Washington Press, 1993.

Roniger, Luis. "The Western Sephardic Diaspora: Ancestral Birthplaces and Displacement, Diaspora Formation and Multiple Homelands," *Latin American Research Review*, 54:4 (Dec. 2019), 1031–1038. https://doi.org/10.25222/larr600.

Rosello, Mireille. *France and the Maghreb: Performative Encounters*. Gainsville: Univ. Press of Florida, 2005.

Rosen, Alan, ed. *Holocaust Literature: A Critical Introduction*. Cambridge: Cambridge Univ. Press, 2013.

Rosenman, Anny D. "Les Représentations de l'histoire dans l'oeuvre romanesque d'Albert Memmi." *Lire Albert Memmi: Déracinement, exil, identité.* David Ohana, Claude Sitbon, and David Mendelson, eds. Paris: Editions Factuel, 2002. 57–66.

Roskies, David G. "The Story's the Thing: Afterword." *Prooftexts* 5.1 (1985): 67–74.

Roumani, Jacques. "Interview with Albert Memmi." 4 Dec. 1977. Audiotape.

Roumani, Judith. *The Role of Organic Nationalism in Some Recent Novels of Spanish America and French-Speaking North Africa.* Ph.D. diss., Rutgers University, 1977.

Roumani, Judith. "Elissa Rhaïs: Enslaved Imagination in Colonial Algeria." *CELFAN Review: Review of the Center for the Studies of the Literatures and Arts of North Africa Special Issue Jews of Tunisia* 2.1 (1982): 8–11.

Roumani, Judith. "Memmi's Introduction to History: *Le Désert* as Folktale, Chronicle and Biography." *Philological Quarterly* 61.2 (1982): 193–207.

Roumani, Judith. "The Portable Homeland of North African Jewish Fiction: Ryvel and Koskas." *Prooftexts* 4 (1984): 253–67.

Roumani, Judith. "Storytelling in Tunisian Jewish Literature." *CELFAN Review* 4.2 (1985): 17–19.

Roumani, Judith. *Albert Memmi.* Philadelphia: CELFAN Editions Monographs, 1987.

Roumani, Judith. "Hagira Be Romanim Me'et Sofrim Yehudim Me-Tzfon Africa: Bensoussan, Bouganim, Kayat [Heb.]." *Peamim* 35 (1988): 130–40.

Roumani, Judith. "Responses to North African Independence in the Novels of Dib, Memmi and Koskas: The End of Muslim-Jewish Symbiosis?" *Middle East Review* 20.2 (1988): 33–40.

Roumani, Judith. "Review of Isidro Bango, *Remembering Sepharad: Jewish Culture in Medieval Spain.*" *La Lettre Sépharade English Edition.* 17 (2004): 8–10.

Roumani, Judith. "Un Juif Espagnol: Sephardism and the Idea of Sepharad in Jewish Francophone Writers of Colonial and Post-Colonial Times." *International Sephardic Journal* 2.1 (2005): 108–31.

Roumani, Judith. "In Search of the Garden of the Finzi-Continis, Finding the Courtyard of the Finzi-Magrinis." *Sephardic Horizons* 1:2 (Winter 2011). https://www.sephardichorizons.org/Volume1/Issue2/Articles_V1I2/TravelogueZ.html.

Roumani, Judith. "Two Tunisian Jewish Novelists: Claude Kayat and Marco Koskas: Interviews" Https://sephardichorizons.org/Volume1/Issue3/TunisianJewishNovelists. *Sephardic Horizons* 1.3 (2011): n. pag.

Roumani, Judith. "Le Juif Espagnol: The Idea of Sepharad among Colonial and Postcolonial Francophone Jewish Writers." Yael Halevi-Wise, ed. *Sephardism: Spanish Jewish History and the Modern Literary Imagination.* Stanford, CA: Stanford UP, 2012. 213–34.

Roumani, Judith. "Sephardic Literary Responses to the Holocaust," in Alan Rosen, *Critical Interpretations of Literature of the Holocaust.* Cambridge: Cambridge University Press, 2013, 225–237.

Roumani, Judith. "Interview with Israeli Novelist A. B. Yehoshua on his New Novel, *The Retrospective [Hesed Sefaradi]. Sephardic Horizons* 3.1 (2013): n. pag. http://sephardichorizons.org/Volume3/Issue1/YehoshuaReprint.html#sthash.wfZPXRwj.dpuf.

Roumani, Judith. "A Plurality of Bridges: The Sephardic Scholar as Literary Archeologist." *Sephardic Horizons* 3:2 (2013): n. pag. https://www.sephardichorizons.org/Volume3/Issue2/plurality.html.

Roumani, Judith. "The Holocaust in Sephardi-Mizrahi Literature: A Review of Some Responses in Prose." *Sephardic Horizons* 4:2 (Spring 2014). https://www.sephardichorizons.org/Volume4/Issue2/Roumani.html

Roumani, Judith. "Review of Vitalis Danon, trans. Jane Kuntz, *Ninette of Sin Street*. Ed. Lia Brozgal and Sarah Abrevaya Stein." *Sephardic Horizons* 10:2 (Spring 2020). https://www.sephardichorizons.org/Volume10/Issue2/Roumani.html.

Roumani, Judith. "Review of Devi Mays, *Forging Ties, Forging Passports: Migration and the Modern Sephardi Diaspora.*" *Sephardic Horizons* 11:2 (Summer 2021). https://www.sephardichorizons.org/Volume11/Issue2-3/Roumani.html.

Roumani-Denn, Vivienne. "Review of the film *Sefarad*, dir. Luis Ismael, 2019." *Sephardic Horizons*, 20:1, Spring 2020, https://www.sephardichorizons.org/Volume10/Issue1/Roumani-Denn.html).

Roskies, David G. "The Story's the Thing: Afterword." *Prooftexts* 5:1 (Jan. 1985), 67–74.

Rozen, Minna, ed., *Homelands and Diasporas: Greeks, Jews and Their Migrations*. London: I. B. Tauris, 2008.

Saadon, Haim. "Tunisia." *The Jews of the Middle East and North Africa in Modern Times*. Reeva S. Simon, Michael M. Laskier, and Sara Reguer, eds. New York: Columbia Univ. Press, 2003. 444–57.

Sabato, Haim. *Sipure Aleppo* (2007). *Aleppo Tales*. Trans. Philip Simpson. New Milford: Toby Press, 2009.

Sabato, Haim. *Bo'i ha-ruach*. *From the Four Winds*. Trans. Yaacob Dweck. New Milford: Toby, 2010.

Sadock, Johann. "Anti-Arab and Anti-French Tendencies in Post-1948 Oriental Jewish Literature Written in French." *Transnational Spaces and Identities in the Francophone World*. Ed. Hafid Gafaïti, Patricia M. E. Lorcin, and David G. Troyansky. Lincoln: University of Nebraska, 2009. 243–63.

Sadun, Joseph. "L'Orient pittoresque et Aladin retrouvé." *Emergences des francophonies: Israël, La Méditerranée, Le Monde*. Ed. David Mendelson. Limoges: PULIM, 2001. 169–84.

Said, Edward W. *Beginnings: Intention and Method*. New York: Basic, 1975.

Sartre, Jean-Paul. *Situations V* (Paris: Gallimard, 1964).

Satloff, Robert B. *Among the Righteous: Lost Stories from the Holocaust's Long Reach into Arab Lands*. New York: Public Affairs, 2006.

Satloff, Robert B., dir. *Among the Righteous: Lost Stories from the Holocaust's Long Reach into Arab Lands*. MacNeil/Lehrer Productions, 2010. DVD.

Scharfman, Ronnie. "The Other's Other: The Moroccan-Jewish Trajectory of Edmond Amran El Maleh." *Yale French Studies* 82.1 (1993): 135–45.

Schorsh, Jonathan. "Disappearing Origins: Sephardic Autobiography Today." *Prooftexts* 27.1 (2007): 82–150.

Schousboë, Elisabeth. *Albert Bensoussan*. Paris: L'Harmattan, 1991.

Sciaky, Leon. *Farewell to Salonica*. 1946; Philadelphia: Paul Dry Books, 2003.

Schwartz, Howard, ed. *Elijah's Violin and Other Jewish Folktales Selected and Retold,* (1983). Harmondsworth: Penguin, 1987.
Sebag, Paul. *La Hara de Tunis: L'Évolution d'un ghetto nord-africain.* Paris: Presses Universitaires de France, 1959.
Sebbar, Leïla. "Rien sur l'enfance." *Une Enfance juive en Méditerranée musulmane.* Saint-Pourçain-sur-Sioule: Bleu Autour, 2012. 81–87.
Sephardic Horizons. Special Issue devoted to the Jews of Tunisia and Libya. 11:2–3, (Spring-Summer 2021). https://www.sephardichorizons.org.
Septimus, Bernard. "Hispano-Jewish Views of Christendom and Islam." In Bernard Cooperman et al., eds. *In Iberia and Beyond: Hispanic Jews Between Two Cultures.* College Park, Md.: University of Maryland, 1991.
Serels, Mitchell, et al., eds. *Del Fuego: Sephardim and the Holocaust.* New York: Sepher-Hermon, 1995.
Shah, Idries. *Tales of the Dervishes: Teaching-Stories of the Sufi Masters over the Past Thousand Years: Selected from the Sufi Classics, from Oral Tradition, from Unpublished Manuscripts and Schools of Sufi Teaching in Many Countries.* New York: Arkana, 1993.
Shanks, Hershel. "Saddam's Jewish Archives." *Moment* 28.5 (2003): 44–49.
Shillony, Helena. "'La Langue est ma patrie': Edmond Jabès et le français." *Emergence des Francophonies: Israël, La Méditerranée, Le Monde.* Ed. David Mendelson. Limoges: PULIM, 2001, 87–92.
Sibony, Daniel. *Psychopathologie de l'actuel.* Part of a trilogy entitled *Événements.* Paris: Seuil, 1999.
Sibony, Daniel. *Marrakech, le départ.* Paris: Jacob, 2009.
Sigal, Raphaël. "Edmond Jabès et l'Egypte." Netanya Academic College Conference on Francophonie. Netanya, Israel. Apr. 2008. Lecture.
Sitbon, Claude. "La Littérature juive tunisienne d'expression française." *Regards sur les Juifs de Tunisie.* Ed. Robert Attal and Claude Sitbon. Paris: A. Michel, 1979. 211–17.
Slouschz, Nahum. *Travels in North Africa.* Philadelphia: Jewish Publication Society of America, 1927.
Smitten, Jeffrey, et al. *Spatial Form in Narrative.* Ithaca: Cornell Univ. Press, 1981.
Somekh, Sasson. *Baghdad Yesterday: The Making of an Arab Jew.* Jerusalem: Ibis, 2008.
Somekh, Sasson. *Life after Baghdad: Memoirs of an Arab-Jew in Israel, 1950–2000.* Eastbourne: Sussex Academic Press, 2012.
Stein, Sarah Abrevaya. "Sephardi and Middle Eastern Jewries since 1492." *Oxford Handbook of Jewish Studies.* Oxford: Oxford Univ. Press, 2002. 327–362.
Stein, Sarah Abrevaya. *Making Jews Modern: The Yiddish and Ladino Press in the Russian and Ottoman Empires.* Bloomington: Indiana Univ. Press, 2004.
Stein, Sarah Abrevaya. "Extraterritorial Dreams: European Citizenship, Sephardi Jews, and the Ottoman Twentieth Century." *Jewish History.* 31:3–4 (2018): 391–393.
Stern, Bezalel. "Beyond Agnon," http://www.jbooks.com/fiction/index/FI_Stern_Sabato.htm

Stevens, Christa. "Judéités, à lire dans l'oeuvre d'Hélène Cixous." *International Journal of Francophone Studies* 7.1–2 (2004): 81–93.
Stewart, Susan. Review of M. M. Bahktin, *Speech Genres and Other Late Essays*. *New York Times Book Review* 22 Mar. 1987.
Stora, Benjamin. *Les Trois exils: Juifs d'Algérie*. Paris: Pluriel, 2012.
Stroumsa, Sarah. *Maimonides in his World*. Princeton: Princeton University Press, 2009.
Sussman, Sarah. "Jews from Algeria and French Jewish Identity." *Transnational Spaces and Identities in the Francophone World*. Hafid Gafaïti, Patricia M. E. Lorcin, and David G. Troyansky, eds. Lincoln: University of Nebraska, 2009. 217–42.
Taos Amrouche, Marguerite. *Le Grain magique: Contes, poèmes et proverbes berbères de Kabylie*. Paris: Maspero, 1966.
Taranto, Leon. "The Taranto-Capouya-Crespin-Family History." *Sephardic Horizons* 2.2 (2012): n. pag. https://www.sephardichorizons.org/Volume1/Issue4/familyhistory.html.
Tartakowsky, Ewa. *Les Juifs et le Maghreb: Fonctions sociales d'une littérature d'exil*. Paris: Presses universitaires François-Rabelais, 2016.
Tessler, Mark, and Linda Hawkins. "The Political Culture of Jews in Tunisia and Morocco." *International Journal of Middle East Studies* 11.1 (1980): 59–86. *JSTOR*. 17 Nov. 2013.
Toumi, Alek Baylee. *Maghreb divers: Langue française, langues parlées, littératures et représentations des Maghrébins à partir d'Albert Memmi et de Kateb Yacine*. New York: Peter Lang, 2002.
Trela, Bailey. "The Jewish Half-Lives of Patrick Modiano: The Nobel Laureate on the Paper Trail of Evanescent French Jews, in *Family Record*." *Tablet Magazine* Sept. 6, 2019. https://www.tabletmag.com/sections/arts-letters/articles/patrick-modiano-family-record.
Trevisan Semi, Emanuela. *Diaspore: Esempi storici e modelli interpretative*. Bologna: Casa Editrice il Ponte, 2008.
Trigano, Hélène, and Shmuel Trigano, eds. *La Mémoire sépharade: Entre l'oubli et l'avenir*. Paris: In Press Editions, 2000.
Trigano, Shmuel, ed. *L'Identité des Juifs d'Algérie: Une Expérience originale de la modernité*. Paris: Editions du Nadir, 2003.
Trigano, Shmuel. "Histoire." *Le Monde sépharade: Vol. 1: Histoire*. Paris: Éditions du Seuil, 2006. 243–78.
Trigano, Shmuel. "L'Invention sépharade du sionisme moderne." *Le Monde sépharade Histoire:* Vol. 1. Ed. Shmuel Trigano. Paris: Éditions Du Seuil, 2006. 861–78.
Trigano, Shmuel, ed. *La Fin du judaïsme en terres d'islam*. Paris; Denoël, 2009.
Trivellato, Francesca. *The Familiarity of Strangers: The Sephardic Diaspora, Livorno, and Cross-Cultural Trade in the Early Modern Period*. New Haven: Yale Univ. Press, 2009.
Turki, Zoubeir. *Tunis, naguère et aujourd'hui*. Tunis: Maison Tunisienne de l'Édition, 1967.

Tye, Larry. *Homelands: Portraits of the New Jewish Diaspora.* New York: Henry Holt, 2001, pp. 218–240.
Udovitch, Abraham and Lucette Valensi. *The Last Arab Jews: The Communities of Jerba, Tunisia.* London, Paris, New York: Harwood Academic Publishers, 1984.
Valensi, Lucette. "From Sacred History to Historical Memory and Back: The Jewish Past." *History and Anthropology* 2 (1986): 283–305.
Varol, Marie-Christine. *Manual of Judeo-Spanish.* Trans. Ralph Tarica. Bethesda: University Press of Maryland, 2008.
Vassel, Eusèbe. "La Littérature populaire des Israélites tunisiens." *Revue Tunisienne* 11 (1904).
Wacks, David. *Double Diaspora in Sephardic Literature.* Bloomington: Indiana University Press, 2015.
Wacks, David. "Sefarad." *Humanities Commons. LLC Medieval Iberian.* Oct. 18, 2021. http://dx.doi.org/1017613/zene-w672.
Waldrop, Rosmarie. *Lavish Absence: Recalling and Rereading Edmond Jabès.* Middletown, CT: Wesleyan Univ. Press, 2002.
Watson, Robert. "Memories (out) of Place: Franco-Judeo-Algerian Autobiographical Writing, 1995–2010." *The Journal of North African Studies* 17.1 (2012).
Werblowsky, R.I. Zwi and Geoffrey Wigoder, eds., *The Oxford Dictionary of the Jewish Religion* (New York, Oxford: Oxford University Press, 1997), entries "Babylonia," "Responsa."
Williams, Laurence. "Reframing the Oriental Tale." *Cambridge Quarterly* 38.2 (2009): 183–87.
Wolosky, Shira. "Derrida, Jabès, Lévinas: Sign-Theory as Ethical Discourse." *Prooftexts* 2.3 (1982): 283–302.
Yehoshua, A. B. *Mar Mani* (1990). Trans. Hillel Halkin. New York: Doubleday, 1992.
Yehoshua, A. B. *Hesed sefaradi..* Bnai Brak: Ha-Kibbutz Hameuhad, 2011.
Yehoshua, A. B., trans. Stuart Schoffman. *The Retrospective.* Boston: Houghton Mifflin Harcourt, 2013.
Yeroushalmy, Ovadia. "*La Revue sioniste* (Cairo)." *Encyclopedia of Jews in the Islamic World.* Ed. Norman Stillman, 2010. Brill Online.
Yeroushalmy, Ovadia. "*La Tribune juive* (Cairo)." *Encyclopedia of Jews in the Islamic World.* Ed. Norman Stillman. 2010. Brill Online.
Yeroushalmy, Ovadia. "*La Voix juive* (Alexandria)." *Encyclopedia of Jews in the Islamic World.* Ed. Norman Stillman. 2010. Brill Online.
Yetiv, Isaac. *Le Thème de l'aliénation dans le roman maghrébin d'expression française: De 1952 à 1956.* Québec: Univ. of Sherbrook, 1972.
Yetiv, Isaac. "L'Aliénation dans le roman maghrébin contemporain," in *Colloque sur les littératures d'expression française: Écrivains du Maghreb.* 2nd Ed. Paris: Éditions de la Francité, 1973.
Yetiv, Isaac. "Du *Scorpion* au *Désert*: Albert Memmi Revisited." *STCL.* 7.1 (1982), 77–87.
Yetiv, Isaac. "From Ethnocentrism to Humanism: Albert Memmi's *Le Désert.*" *International Fiction Review* 16.2 (1989): 128–31.

Zafrani, Haim. "Edmond El Maleh, *Parcours Immobile*." *Revue des études juives* 141.1–2 (1982): 278.

Zaid, Afaf. "*Le Cri de l'arbre* de Ami Bouganim." Pp. 51–60 in Najib Redouane, Yvette Bénayoun-Szmidt, eds. *Ami Bouganim: Voix marocaine en Israël*. Paris: L'Harmattan, 2021.

Zohar, Zion, ed. *Sephardic and Mizrachi Jewry from the Golden Age of Spain to Modern Times*. New York: New York Univ. Press, 2005.

Zonana, Joyce. "On Translating from the French *A Land Like You* by Tobie Nathan." *Lilith* (Fall 2020).

Index

Abécassis, Eliette, 14, 113, 126, 131n41; *Sépharade*, 14, 113, 126
Abravanel, Don Isaac, 68
Aciman, Andre, 6, 13–14, 67, 74–75, 108, 136, 140; *Out of Egypt*, 6, 67, 74
Adieu Babylone, 67, 69, 78, 100
Agnon, Shai, 31, 43n19
Aizenberg, Edna, 10
Alcalay, Ammiel, 6, 110n9
Aleichem, Sholom, 28
Alliance Israélite Universelle, 7, 9, 16–17, 25n62, 32, 48, 50, 52, 70, 133–134, 140
American Sephardi Federation, 5, 21n25
Améry, Jean, 11, 14
L'Andalouse, 107
Les Anges de Sodome, 35
Ascher, Gloria, 35n62
Avenue de France, 113, 124

Les Bagnoulis, 34
Balace Bounel, 48, 54, 56–59, 63n20, 64n28, 67, 73
Balbuena, Monique, 10; *Homeless Tongues*, 10
Bar-Itzhak, Haya, 39
Bar Yohai, Shimon, 13

Bassani, Giorgio, 66, 68, 75, 76nn7–8, 136; *Il Giardino dei Finzi-Contini*, 66, 76n66
Bejarano, Margalit, 10
Belle du seigneur, 32, 101
Les Belles de Tunis, 113, 122–123, 130n26
Benarroch, Mois, 13, 15, 142n11; *Bufanda Blues*, 15; *La trilogía tetuaní*, 15
Benbassa, Esther, 17
Bendahan, Blanche, 136
Bendahan, Esther, 102
Ben Labrat, Dunash, 4, 6, 69
Ben-Rubi, Isaac, 134; *El Sekreto del mudo*, 134
Bensoussan, Albert, 29, 34–35, 40, 43n24, 81, 85–88, 90, 92, 95n13, 108, 136–137, 140; *Frimaldjézar*, 85, 87–88, 97n25; *Isbilia*, 34; *L'Echelle de Mesrod ou parcours algérien de mémoire juive*, 88; *L'Echelle sépharade*, 34; *Le Cri de l'arbre*, 88; *Le Marrane Ou la confession d'un traitre*, 34; *Les Anges de Sodome*, 35; *Les Bagnoulis*, 34; *Mémoire et fidelité séfarades*, 34

Ben-Ur, Aviva, 5, 10, 31n25; *Sephardic Jews in America: A Diasporic History*, 10
Berque, Jacques, 57
Bouganim, Ami, 81, 85, 88–90, 95n14, 96n22, 137
Bourguiba, Habib, 135
El Boxeador polaco, 31
Brozgal, Lia, 117
Bufanda Blues, 15
Bunis, David, 2, 5, 20n6, 24n51

Canetti, Elias, 13, 28–30, 35, 38, 45n43, 105–106, 136; *Earwitness*, 29; *The Tongue Set Free*, 29; *Voices of Marrakesh*, 29
Canetti, Veza, 29–30; *The Tortoises*, 30
Le Chemin de l'exil, 66, 113, 123
Cheyette, Bryan, 11
Chocrón, Isaac, 30, 42n15
Cixous, Hélène, 103–105, 137; *Portrait of Jacques Derrida as a Young Jewish Saint*, 104
Cohen, Albert, 13, 29, 32–35, 37, 40, 101–102, 108, 110nn7–8, 136–137, 140; *Belle du seigneur*, 32, 101; *Solal*, 32, 35
Cohen, Jacob, 113, 125; *Du danger de monter sur la terrasse*, 113, 125
Cohen, Mark R., 21n2
The Colonizer and the Colonized, 73, 79n23
Contemporary Sephardic Identity in the Americas: A Collection of Interdisciplinary Studies, 10
converso, 30, 68, 88, 122–123
The Converso's Return, 16
convivencia, 65, 75, 75n2, 123, 139–140
Couvre-feu, 113, 121
Crémieux Decree, 18, 134
Le Cri de l'arbre, 88

Danon, Vitalis, 17, 48; *Ninette de la rue du péché*, 18
Dans le café de la jeunesse perdue, 120

Daudet, Alphonse, 50
Derrida, Jacques, 16, 85, 93n2, 94n10, 95, 103–105, 108, 111nn21–22, 137
Le Désert, 39, 41n5, 108, 113, 115–117, 123, 137
The Desert: Or, The Life and Adventures of Jubair Wali al-Mammi, 40, 46n51, 115
Dhimma, 19n3
Dhimmi, 70
Dhimmitude, 71, 125
Díaz-Mas, Paloma, 1, 19n3; *Los Sefardíes ante los retos del mundo contemporáneo: identidad y mentalidades*, 10
Dib, Mohammed, 63n22, 73–74; *Qui se souvient de la mer*, 63n22, 73
diglossia, 12–13, 32, 105–107, 121–122, 137, 139
Djoha festival, 108, 134
Dominated Man, 73
Double Diaspora, 12
Du danger de monter sur la terrasse, 113, 125

Earwitness, 29
Eberhardt, Isabelle, 23n44
L'Echelle de Mesrod ou parcours algérien de mémoire juive, 88
L'Echelle sépharade, 34
Elazar, Daniel, 3, 5, 21n22, 23n39, 69; *The Other Jews: The Sephardim Today*, 3
Elbaz, André, 27
Elbaz, Robert, 35, 44n32
El Maleh, Edmond Amran, 37–38, 45n40, 45n44, 94n7, 103, 105–106, 136–137; *Mille ans, un jour*, 37, 45n40, 103
Emeq Habaka, 65, 76n3
Une Enfance juive en Meditérranée musulmane, 137
L'Enfant de l'Oukala, 48, 50, 53–54, 58, 60n3, 94n8

*Los Esperandos: Piratas
  judeoportugueses . . . y yo*, 113–114
Un été à la Goulette, 134
Etre un peuple en diaspora, 11, 23n43
Expulsion, 1–4, 9–10, 14, 21n24, 24n51,
  29, 65–67, 75, 102, 109, 114–115,
  123, 127, 136–137, 139

Fanon, Frantz, 73, 84, 95n12
Farhud, 67, 69–70, 100
Fellous, Colette, 113, 124, 131n35;
  Avenue de France, 113, 124
Fitoussi, Annie, 22n31, 36, 39–40, 60n6,
  136–137, 139; *La Mémoire folle de
  Mouchi Rabbinou*, 36, 44n36, 60n6
*Folktales of the Canadian
  Sephardim*, 27
Francophone, 7–8, 11, 18–19, 29, 48,
  58, 66, 74, 81–82, 99, 101, 105, 127,
  134, 139, 141; Francophonie, 18, 133
Fresco, David, 139
Fresco, Mauricio, 118
Frimaldjézar, 85, 87–88, 97n25

Galante, Avraham, 17–18, 134; *Histoire
  des Juifs de Turquie*, 134
Gerber, Jane, 65
Il Giardino dei Finzi-Contini, 66, 76n66
Golden Age, 4, 6, 13, 21n24, 24n51,
  65, 69, 99
Guattari, Felix, 12

Hagège, Daniel, 48
haketia, 15, 90, 105
Ha-Kohen, Yosef, 65–67, 76n3; *Emeq
  Habaka*, 65, 76n3
Halevi-Wise, Yael, 8, 15, 41n2, 43n21,
  99, 112n30, 114, 127n2, 128n3
Halfon, Eduardo, 31; *El Boxeador
  polaco*, 31
Halimi, Gisèle, 113, 125; *La
  Kahina*, 113, 125
Halkin, Hillel, 6
hara, 47–53, 56, 58–59, 101, 136, 139
Heschel, Abraham, 2–3

Histoire des Juifs de Turquie, 134
Holocaust, 1, 8–9, 14, 16, 18, 31,
  65–66, 68–69, 77n8, 82–83, 86,
  102–103, 110, 115, 118, 120–122,
  130n31, 134–135, 137–140
Homeless Tongues, 10
Huerto cerrado, huerto sellado, 30

Ibn Khaldun, 116–117
Isbilia, 34
Israel-Pelletier, Aimé, 102, 110, 111n12

Jabès, Edmond, 18, 102–104, 110nn9–
  11, 111n12, 137, 139–140; *Le Livre
  des questions*, 102–103; *Le Livre des
  Ressemblances*, 102
Jews and Arabs, 72–73
Joha, 9, 27, 34–35, 40, 41n2, 41n4,
  46n51, 108, 134, 136
*A Journey to the End of the
  Millennium*, 113
Judeo-Arabic, 7, 39, 41n5, 48, 52,
  54, 58, 60–61n6, 64n28, 100, 124,
  135, 139–140

La Kahina, 113, 125
Kandiyoti, Dalia, 13, 16; *Migrant
  Sites: America, Place and Diaspora
  Literatures*, 13; *The Converso's
  Return*, 16
Karmona, Elia, 13
Kattan, Naim, 13, 67, 69, 75, 77n11,
  78n16, 79n22, 100–102, 109n3, 136;
  Adieu Babylone, 67, 69, 78, 100
Kayat, Claude, 39, 61n6, 81, 85, 90, 92,
  108, 136–137; *Mohammed Cohen*,
  90–91, 97n24, 108; *La Synagogue de
  Sfax*, 61, 108
Khatibi, Abdelkebir, 105
khurafa, 39, 46n49, 49, 53, 58, 61n9
Koskas, Marco, 29, 35, 39, 47–49,
  54–55, 58, 63n20, 67, 71, 73, 75,
  80n26, 108, 136–137; *Balace
  Bounel*, 48, 54, 56–59, 63n20,
  64n28, 67, 73

Ladino, 2–3, 9, 13, 16–18, 106–107, 118, 121, 134
Ladino/Judeo-Spanish, 2, 5, 7, 17, 31–32, 42n8, 46n50, 89, 105–106, 118, 121, 133–134, 139–140
Larlee, Louise, 123
Lazar, Moshe, 2–3, 27, 40n1
Lehmann, Matthias, 16
Levi, Primo, 11, 14, 118
Le Livre des questions, 102–103
Le Livre des ressemblances, 102

Maghreb, 4, 7–9, 19, 22n34, 30, 40, 81, 93n4, 117, 123, 125
Maghrebian, 34, 49, 51, 58–59, 61n19, 63n22, 65, 82–87, 89, 99, 105, 107, 117, 122, 135, 142n14
Maimonides, 2–4, 13
Marienstras, Richard, 11; *Etre un peuple en diaspora*, 11, 23n43
Mar Mani, 31, 41n2, 43n21, 106, 115, 137; *Mr. Mani*, 113
Marrane ou la confession d'un traître, 44, 88
Mays, Devi, 22, 129, 160
Memmi, Albert, 10, 28–29, 35–36, 39–40, 41n5, 46n49, 46n51, 47–48, 59, 60n1, 60n10, 67, 71–73, 75, 78n19, 79nn21–23, 82–85, 96–97n24, 99–102, 107–108, 109n3, 113, 115–117, 123, 125, 127, 129n11, 135–137, 139, 142n14; *Dominated Man*, 73; *Jews and Arabs*, 72–73; *La Statue de sel*, 67, 78, 82, 96–96n24, 99, 109; *Le Désert*, 39, 41n5, 108, 113, 115–117, 123, 137; *Le Scorpion, ou la confession imaginaire*, 28, 115, 117; *The Colonizer and the Colonized*, 73, 79n23; *The Pillar of Salt*, 82
Memmi, Georges, 73; *Qui se souvient du Café Rubens*, 73
Mémoire et fidelité séfarades, 34
La Mémoire folle de Mouchi Rabbinou, 36, 44n36, 60n6

La Mémoire sépharade, 10
Migrant Sites: America, Place and Diaspora Literatures, 13
Mille ans, un jour, 37, 45n40, 103
Mille et une nuits, 37, 42n6
Miron, Dan, 12–13
Moati, Nine, 113, 122–123, 127, 130n31, 137; *Les Belles de Tunis*, 113, 122–123; *L'Orientale*, 122; *La Passagère sans étoile*, 113, 123, 130n31
Modiano, Patrick, 113, 117–120, 127, 129n17, 129–130n20, 130n23, 137; *Dans le café de la jeunesse perdue*, 120; *La Rue des boutiques obscures*, 118; *Missing Person*, 118; *Un Pedigrée*, 120
Mohammed Cohen, 90–91, 97n24, 108
Le Monde sépharade, 99
Le muet de Auschwitz, 134
Muñiz-Huberman, Angelina, 30, 113–114, 128n4, 137; *Huerto cerrado, huerto sellado*, 30; *Los Esperandos: Piratas judeoportugueses . . . y yo*, 113–114; *Tierra adentro*, 113–114, 128n4, 137
Muñoz Molina, Antonio, 14, 115; *Sefarad* [*Sepharad*, English title], 14, 115, 201

Naturalist aesthetic viewpoint, 47, 51, 53, 58
Nebot, Didier, 66, 75, 113, 123, 125, 127, 136–137, 139; *Le Chemin de l'exil*, 66, 113, 123
Nehama, Isaac, 134
Nehama, Joseph, 18
Nicoïdski, Clarisse, 113, 121, 127; *Couvre-feux*, 113, 121
Ninette de la rue du péché, 18
Nissan, Rosa, 6, 106, 112n30; *Novia que te vea*, 6, 106
Novia que te vea, 6, 106
Noy, Dov, 27, 41n1

L'Orientale, 122
The Other Jews: The Sephardim Today, 3
Ottoman Empire, 2, 4, 7, 11, 16–17, 21n24, 27, 29, 68
Out of Egypt, 6, 67, 74

La Passagère sans étoile, 113, 123, 130n31
Un Pedigrée, 120
Perera, Victor, 13
Portrait of Jacques Derrida as a Young Jewish Saint, 104

Qui se souvient de la mer, 63n22, 73
Qui se souvient du Café Rubens, 73

Ray, Jonathan, 11, 138; *The Sephardic Frontier*, 11
The Retrospective, 114
Rhaïs, Elissa, 13, 107, 122–123, 130n28, 136–137; *L'Andalouse*, 107
Rodrigue, Aron, 8, 17
Roskies, David G., 28
La Rue des boutiques obscures, 118; *Missing Person*, 118
Ryvel (Raphaël Lévy), 29, 35, 47–56, 58–59, 60n3, 60n5, 62n14, 62n19, 107, 136; *L'Enfant de l'Oukala*, 48, 50, 53–54, 58, 60n3, 94n8

Sabato, Haim, 6, 28, 31
Sadock, Johann, 7
Sánchez Pérez, María, 10
Sarfati, Hai, 48
Sarfatty, Bouena, 31
Sartre, Jean-Paul, 84, 95n12
Scharfman, Ronnie, 11, 45n40
Le Scorpion, ou la confession imaginaire, 28, 115, 117
Sebbar, Leïla, 96, 137; *Une Enfance juive en Meditérranée musulmane*, 137
Sefarad [*Sepharad*, English title], 14, 115, 201

Los Sefardíes ante los retos del mundo contemporáneo: identidad y mentalidades, 10
El Sekreto del mudo, 134
Sépharade, 14, 113, 126
The Sephardic Frontier, 11
Sephardic Jews in America: A Diasporic History, 10
Sephardism: Spanish Jewish History and Modern Literary Imagination, 8, 15
Sephiha, Haim-Vidal, 17, 134
Shenhar, Aliza, 39
Sibony, Daniel, 11 23n42
Sitbon, Claude, 48
Solal, 32, 35
Spinoza, Baruch, 99
La Statue de sel, 67, 78, 82, 96–96n24, 99, 109; *The Pillar of Salt*, 82
Stein, Sarah Abrevaya, 2, 16, 22n31
Stora, Benjamin, 107
Sussman, Sarah, 18
La Synagogue de Sfax, 61, 108

Thousand and One Nights, 9, 41n5, 50
Tierra adentro, 113–114, 128n4, 137
The Tongue Set Free, 29
The Tortoises, 30
Trevisan Semi, Emanuela, 138
Trigano, Hélène, 10, 134; *La Mémoire sépharade*, 10; *Un été à la Goulette*, 134; *Villa Jasmin*, 134
Trigano, Shmuel, 10, 99; *La Mémoire sépharade*, 10; *Le Monde sépharade*, 99
La trilogía tetuaní, 15
Turki, Zoubeir, 41n5

Uzan, Rafael, 35–36

Vargas Llosa, Mario, 88
Varol, Marie Christine, 17
Vehel, Jean, 48
Villa Jasmin, 134
Voices of Marrakesh, 29, 105–106

Wacks, David, 3, 12; *Double Diaspora*, 12
World Sephardi Federation, 5

Yacine, Kateb, 105
Yehoshua, A. B., 31–32, 106–107, 112n29, 113–115, 127, 127–8n3; *A Journey to the End of the Millennium*, 113; *Mar Mani*, 31, 41n2, 43n21, 106, 115, 137; *Mr. Mani*, 113; *The Retrospective*, 114

Zohar, 13
Zohar, Zion, 5
Zola, Émile, 51

About the Author

Judith Roumani has a PhD in comparative literature from Rutgers University. She is the translator of Renzo De Felice's *Jews in an Arab Land: Libya* (Texas University Press) and of Albert Memmi's novel *The Desert* (Syracuse University Press), co-editor of *Jewish Libya* (Syracuse), author of a *Albert Memmi* and of Lexington's *Jews in Southern Tuscany during the Holocaust: Ambiguous Refuge*, plus numerous articles on Sephardic literature. She is also the founder and editor of the online journal, *Sephardic Horizons*, and founder and director of the Jewish Institute of Pitigliano. She previously taught at the University of Maryland, College Park, and is a translator and lecturer. She has won fellowships from the National Endowment for the Humanities, the Fulbright Senior Research Program, and the United States Holocaust Memorial Museum.

www.ingramcontent.com/pod-product-compliance
Lightning Source LLC
Chambersburg PA
CBHW020123010526
44115CB00008B/949